IN SEARCH OF WALES

Books by H. V. Morton
published as Methuen Paperbacks

A Traveller in Italy
A Traveller in Southern Italy
A Stranger in Spain
A Traveller in Rome
In Search of Ireland
In Search of Scotland
In Search of England
In the Steps of the Master

In Search of Wales

H. V. MORTON

Yet in whose fiery love for their own land,
No hatred of another finds a place.
William Watson

METHUEN . LONDON

A METHUEN PAPERBACK

First published in Great Britain 1932
Reprinted twenty-one times
This edition first published 1986
by Methuen London Ltd
11 New Fetter Lane, London EC4P 4EE

Printed in Great Britain

British Library Cataloguing in Publication Data

Morton, H.V.
In search of Wales.
1. Wales——Description and travel——1801–1950
I. Title
914.29′0483 DA730

ISBN 0–413–40740–3

British Library Cataloguing in Publication Data

ISBN 0 413 40740 3

I
MAIR
sy'n caru
Cymru

CONTENTS

LIST OF ILLUSTRATIONS

Acknowledgement and thanks for permission to reproduce photographs are due to the British Tourist Authority for plates 1a, 2b, 3a, 3b, 5, 6a, 6b, 7a and 7b; the Welsh Tourist Board for plates 1b, 2a, 4a, 4b, 8, 9a, 9b and 10a; Frith for plate 11; and Odhams Press for plates 10b, 12a and 12b. The map is from a drawing by A. E. Taylor.

Holyhead
Beaumaris
Llansair
Gaerwen
Bangor
Conway
Caernarvon
Pass of Llanberis
Capel Curig
Snowdon
Clynnog-fawr
Beddgelert
Nevin
Ffestiniog
Criccieth
Pwllheli
Bala
Bala L.
Aberdaron
Harlech
Barmouth
Dolgelly
R. Dovey
THE IRISH SEA
Cardigan Bay
Aberystwyth
R. Keidol
Aberayron
Cardigan
R. Teifi
Fishguard
St Davids
R. Towy
Haverfordwest
Narberth
Carmarthen
Milford Haven
Kidwelly
R. Neath
Llanelly
Pembroke
Tenby
Morriston
Neath
Llannadog
Swansea
Bristol Channel

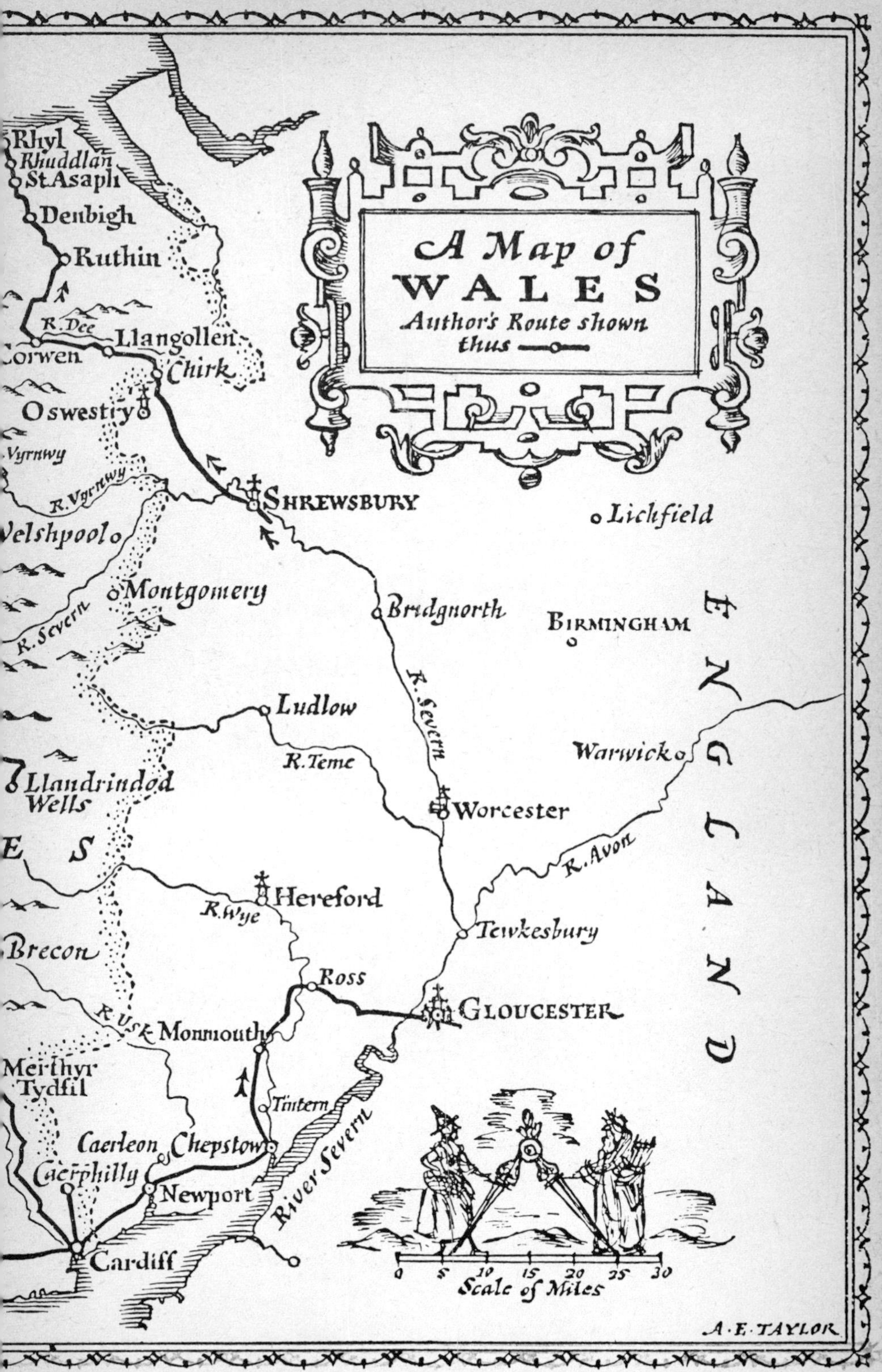

A Map of
WALES
Author's Route shown
thus
Rhyl
Rhuddlan
St. Asaph
Denbigh
Ruthin
R. Dee
Llangollen
Corwen
Chirk
Oswestry
Vyrnwy
R. Vyrnwy
SHREWSBURY
Lichfield
Welshpool
Montgomery
R. Severn
Bridgnorth
BIRMINGHAM
ENGLAND
R. Severn
Ludlow
R. Teme
Warwick
Llandrindod
Wells
Worcester
R. Avon
Hereford
R. Wye
Tewkesbury
Brecon
Ross
GLOUCESTER
R. Usk
Monmouth
Merthyr
Tydfil
Tintern
Caerleon
Chepstow
Caerphilly
Newport
River Severn
Cardiff
0
5
10
15
20
25
30
Scale of Miles
A. E. TAYLOR

INTRODUCTION

THIS book was written during a long tour through Wales. It reflects the impression made by Wales and the Welsh upon the mind of a stranger. I cannot pretend that it was an easy book to write, because the Welsh people possess that surest of all retreats from the outsider, their own language.

Wales, unlike Ireland, is not separated from her more powerful neighbour by the sea, and, unlike Scotland, her Border Marches are not Cheviot Hills; but, in spite of this, the Welsh have managed to retain their language and their individuality. The stranger who admires such things must pay tribute to the vitality and strength of the smallest of the four nations which compose the British Isles.

Most books about Wales treat the country as if it is something to look at and not to understand. They deal at great length with North Wales and its beauties, but they fight shy of the black country in the South, where the mass of the Welsh people earn their living in once beautiful valleys now deformed by a hundred and fifty years of coal mining. I have not done this. I have explored the black valleys of the South as I have explored the green valleys of the North. I went down a coal mine with as much interest as I climbed Snowdon. And if I have written anything in this book which will encourage travellers in Wales to carry on from the well-worn roads of North Wales into the mining valleys of the South, I shall feel justified.

Part of the last two chapters, which deals with the miner and his life, appeared serially in the pages of the *Daily Herald*, and my thanks are due to the editor for permission to reprint several pictures taken by James Jarché. The photograph of miners at work on the coal face is a particularly fine one. It is the only flashlight photograph ever taken in a mine which contains explosive gas. In order to secure this picture Mr. Jarché used a new safe-light apparatus. Even so, the perfectly safe flash of light made us very nervous!

The Eisteddfod was held in Bangor during my tour in

Wales. I was in Bangor in May but returned in August for the Eisteddfod, and I have thought it better to give an impression of it in Chapter Five rather than to include it in an appendix.

I must thank the friendly Welshmen and Welshwomen in the North and the South who gave me help and offered me the hospitality of their homes. I shall always remember their kindliness, their quick wit, their ready humour and their beautiful voices.

H. V. M.

LONDON
May 1932

IN SEARCH OF WALES

CHAPTER ONE

I GO IN SEARCH OF WALES, FIND MY WAY TO THE BORDER MARCHES, STAND ON THE BATTLEMENTS OF LUDLOW CASTLE, ENCOUNTER A HORRIBLE BEDROOM IN SHREWSBURY, AND, ON A FINE MORNING, GO INTO WALES OVER THE BRIDGE AT CHIRK.

§ I

TWENTY years ago I set out for Wales with a copy of *Aucassin and Nicolette* in my pocket. I was in love with a girl who was spending a holiday with her family in Pwllheli. The family was not in love with me. It said that I was too young, too poor and too uncertain. So I decided to go secretly into Wales by a cheap week-end night train. It was in the summer and hot, as those summers always seemed to be. I sat in my corner reading:

Who would list a pleasant lay
Pastime of the old and grey?
Of two lovers, children yet,
Aucassin and Nicolette;
Of the sorrows he went through,
Of the great things he did do,
All for his bright-favoured may
Sweet the song is, fair the say,
Full of art and full of grace . . .

The man opposite to me—I remember him more vividly than I now remember the girl I was going to see—was a big red lout from Birmingham. He took off his boots and placed them on the rack overhead. He then pulled out a flask of whiskey from a hip-pocket and asked me if I would like a drink. I was nineteen years of age and a notorious prig. I looked him right in his red eyes and said 'No'. He then took a long swig at his flask, placed a dirty handkerchief over his face and went to sleep. I sat there hating him as only a boy who is reading *Aucassin and Nicolette* can hate a man who drinks neat whiskey, so to speak, in his socks.

The train rushed through the hot night, and I remember getting out at cool wayside stations, conscious that I was in a strange, new land, a land of mountains and mad streams. I could hear water falling and running over stones, and I could see the shadow of great hills, like arcs of black velvet blotting out the summer stars.

I suppose I must have fallen asleep, because I recollect walking along the platform at Pwllheli, mazed and light-headed in more senses than one, as the stars were fading from the sky. And she was there alone in a big hat and a red coat. . . .

Some few miles from Pwllheli is a place called Llanbedrog, where I had lodgings in a cottage. I seem to remember a small bedroom at the top of the cottage and a small sitting-room full of pictures of bearded men in bowler hats leaning against chairs occupied by stiff and unnatural young women. I caused a minor scandal in Llanbedrog by pulling up the blind in the sitting-room because a passing funeral interested me. But I was flung out not because of this irreverence but because, when the week-end was over, another visitor arrived to take possession of my rooms. I remember travelling to Pwllheli in a carrier's cart with two arms full of books in the hope that the family might ask me to stay with them. But they did not. The girl thought I was wonderful, but her father, who had more experience of the world, considered me to be one of the greatest fools he had ever seen. I forget the end of this story. . . .

So, twenty years after, on a fresh May morning I think of that—my only slender contact with Wales—as I steer my way out of London. It is a heavenly morning, the sun shining; Hyde Park shivering in the sharp freshness of new leaves. The milkmen—mostly Welshmen—deliver white bottles on doorsteps. And I am going again to Wales for the first time since my sentimental journey so long ago. It is, I suppose, strange to feel no older. But how can a man feel old when he is starting out alone on a Spring morning to see a country that is new to him?

If the day ever comes when I am too old to sing to myself

when I am alone on the road, or to feel slightly cold down the back when I meet an apple-tree, pink and white in a green field, I hope I shall have enough sense to stay at home; at least it would serve me right to be packed off to the south of France (from which Heaven save me!) like an old bloodhound in a plaid rug.

It is a fine thing to be going through the freshness of a May morning to a country you do not know. As I pass through the Park a man is mowing a lawn. I can smell the good scent of cut grass. It goes to my head and I feel sorry for every one who is not off and away, as I am, with plenty of time to waste on roads that run over hills and into valleys.

Wales, I feel, is going to be interesting. She is, of the three sister nations which, with England, compose the British Isles, the smallest and the most mysterious. I wonder, as I find my way out of London, what any man in the street would reply if I asked him:

'What does the word "Wales" convey to you?'

He might possibly reply:

'The Prince of Wales, Lloyd George, the Eisteddfod, Snowdon, Welsh Rarebit. . . .'

There he might stick. Perhaps a more literate member of the public might add:

'St. David, Fluellen, Parson Evans in *The Merry Wives of Windsor*, leeks, pictures of Caernarvon Castle in railway carriages, mine disasters, and Cardiff.'

Some one might even recite the old libel that has stuck so hard to Wales and the Welsh:

Taffy was a Welshman,
Taffy was a thief.

But I fear one would get no more except from a student of history. We in England do not hear so much of the glory of being Welsh as we do of the glory of being Scottish or Irish. I cannot remember one occasion on which a Welshman when drunk has hit his chest and announced to the company:

'I'm Welsh and—proud of it!'

The nearest thing to this were some of Mr. Lloyd George's early speeches about mountains and sunrise. And the Englishman, although he never boasts about being English, loves to hear a Scotsman bragging about Scotland and an Irishman crying about Ireland. Jock and Paddy are clear and definite characters, but Taffy is more elusive. His silence is strange. No comic papers have made him lovable, as they made Paddy lovable during centuries of Home Rule argument. No music-hall has developed him as a type which common people can recognize at sight, as they have, with pardonable fantasy, done to the Scot. Every one laughs in a friendly way at the parsimony of the Scot and the belligerency of the Irish, but no joke has been made up about the Welsh. This is significant. The impression that the Welsh are untruthful is definitely unkind. It must be admitted that a touch of the sinister is imparted to the thousands of apparently English Joneses and Williamses when they suddenly speak in a strange and difficult tongue. The Englishman, who hates the unfamiliar and the unexpected, begins to feel that there is something queer and uncomfortable about Taffy. There is something unnecessary, and—yes—sly, about this second language, almost as if Taffy belonged to a secret society!

This reputation of slyness and untruthfulness is one which was attributed to the Greeks in ancient times, and a foreign writer, Paul Cohen-Portheim, has pointed out not only that these qualities are the reverse side of the gift of imagination but that it is not such a far cry from the many-wiled Ulysses to Lloyd George!

The Welsh are our oldest allies. Five thousand Welsh archers and spearmen fought with us at Crecy. They drew their bows at Agincourt. The Welsh long-bow, which became the national weapon of England, gave us victories in France and Scotland. No small nation has ever stood up to the might of England as Wales resisted conquest until, her honour satisfied, she saw a Welshman, the first Tudor, on the throne.

Thoughts of this kind took me out of London, and very soon I was running between green hedges on my way to Wales.

§ 2

One of the joys of travelling alone is that you can suddenly change your mind without being called a fool. Why, I thought, should I not go to Wales through Stratford-on-Avon and Droitwich? I could then sit for a moment on my favourite gravestone in the church of Holy Trinity and I could also, if I did not loiter, take a bath in the comic brine of Droitwich Spa.

It is, I admit, a slightly eccentric way of getting to Wales, but none the worse for that. The more I looked at the map, however, the more I convinced myself that it is the only sensible way of entering the Principality, because I would go on through the Border Marches to Ludlow, which was once the most significant place from Dee to Usk. . . .

Hours afterwards I was lost in a tangle of confusing side-roads about thirty miles from Stratford-on-Avon. I was in a maze. It began to rain, first with a smile and then in grim earnest. As I was splashing through those Warwickshire lanes, I saw a tent in a field not far from the road. I climbed the gate and walked to it. When I hit the canvas, a cheerful voice said:

'Hallo; who's that?'

I put my head inside where four men were sitting round a dixie of tea. They wore khaki shorts and khaki shirts. The tent was full of tobacco smoke and that fug of warm air and crushed grass that you get only in a closed tent.

'Will you come in out of the rain?' asked one of the men.

I went in and sat down on an oil sheet.

I explained myself and they explained themselves. They were on a week-end walk, camping on the farmer's land and returning to their tent at night. They regarded all motorists with hatred and, up to a point, I agreed with them.

'Have a cup of tea?' said one of them.

'I will.'

He dipped a tin mug in the dixie and handed it to me. I tasted the hot tin and the strong tea. I smelt the warm air: the hempen canvas like musty carpet, the smell of bodies, the reek of tobacco, and, as a background to it, the sweetness of the crushed grass. All the time the rain was drumming on the tent. A bead of water would form along a seam and drop like ice on some one's neck. A hand would go up to the leak.

'Don't touch it—for God's sake!' a voice would shout.

I began to feel happy and amused. Years had fallen from this weary world.

'Isn't this like old times?' I said in a sudden rush of memories.

The four men looked at me rather stupidly.

'What old times?' asked one of them.

I laughed.

'The War, of course . . . the same old tent fug, the same old dixie, the same old red tea and even the same old tin mug with a chip on the lip.'

The men pulled at their pipes.

'We don't remember the War,' they said.

I looked at their great shoulders and their huge, hairy knees. It was inconceivable. I began to feel suddenly old and out of place, out of my generation, a stranger from a far country.

'I was five years old when the War ended,' said a young giant.

'I was at school,' said a lad who looked like the lance-corporal of the party.

'I was three years old,' said another.

I lit a pipe gloomily. Age, I suppose, is an imperceptible progress. I remembered a girl at a cocktail party whom I regarded as a contemporary until she replied to some remark of mine:

'How I *loathe* the pre-War man!'

I suppose we have all experienced these distressing contacts with the next generation. And here I was, having set out from London in the early morning feeling about twenty, now sitting in a damp tent bowed down with years! The boys had no idea how typical they were of any tent full of lads from 1914 to 1918. They had no idea that the smell of their tent presupposed at any moment the stick of a company sergeant-major on the canvas; that the taste of their strong tea suggested the imminence of 'Lights Out'.

I got up sadly, feeling rather like a Crimean veteran, said good-bye and squelched back over the wet field.

Stratford-on-Avon in maiden meditation was clean and lovely after the rain. The Avon, rather high, came moving swiftly under Hugh Clopton's fine bridge and straying over the opposite meadows. I walked down the tall elm avenue to Holy Trinity, where, behind the east window, a few yards from the place where Shakespeare's bones rest, I found the gravestone on which I have, at intervals, sat all my life. It is near the high wall above the Avon, and I could hear the water rushing through the mill-race a little lower down.

I have always felt that Shakespeare was thinking of this spot when he described Ophelia's death:

There is a willow grows ascaunt the brook,
That shows his hoar leaves in the glassy stream. . . .

It must have been of this place he was thinking also when he wrote the scene with Bottom in the enchanted wood; for that 'wood near Athens' is too obviously the brake that lifts itself above the Avon beyond the mill. And any day you like you can walk through that 'wood near Athens' and meet Snout, the tinker; and Flute, the bellows-mender and Snug, the joiner. They still live round Stratford and Shottery, but they listen now, I suppose, to Broadcasting House instead of to Titania's small elves.

I waited until the bell of Holy Trinity struck the hour and then reluctantly went away. . . .

Droitwich was pervaded by an elderly calm. I went to St. Andrew's Baths and entered the most amusing water in the kingdom. This brine is from ten to twelve times as salt as the sea. It shoots up out of the earth in prodigious quantities, and its buoyancy is so great that the human body cannot sink in it. When you wade gently into it you find that your feet try to rise up so that you have some difficulty in walking. If you wade out until the water reaches your arm-pits, it is impossible to stand: up come your feet and you are either lying on your back or sitting in an invisible arm-chair. You can then paddle yourself about, taking care not to give yourself a blinding eye-full of salt brine.

Aged and rheumaticky colonels and their sciatic wives were ridiculously paddling themselves through this green water, while young men and women in the pink of health were roaring with laughter as they enjoyed the only comic experience a spa can afford.

I dressed, rubbed the caked salt from my hair and ears, and was soon on my way to Ludlow.

§ 3

As I went through that lovely land of half-timbered houses, orchards, gentle hills, green meadows and gracious rivers, I turned my disorderly mind again to Wales.

I suppose the first thing to realize about the Welsh is that they are not really Welsh at all. They are the real Britons. I believe it is a general rule that in any country which has known invasion you will find the older races in the mountains and the younger and more vigorous races on the good, flat farmlands which they have stolen from the original owners. This happened in England when, after five centuries of enervating Roman rule the Britons were forced to face wave after wave of Teutonic invasion.

The withdrawal of the Roman legions left the Britons in possession of civilized towns which they could not defend: and so gradually the aggressive Saxon drove the Britons westward into the mountains, northward to Strathclyde and southward into the Cornish peninsula.

These Saxons had a valuable superiority complex in which some observers might claim to see the germ of the English public school. This took the form of calling every person whose language they could not understand a 'foreigner'. Much the same intolerance is shown to-day by old maids and retired officials of the State who believe, when they travel abroad, that if only the English language is spoken in a sufficiently loud and domineering tone of voice it will be universally understood.

The word 'Welsh', which the invading Saxon gave to the Britons whose lands they took, is simply the Saxon word for 'foreigner'. The real meaning of the word is seen in the German verb 'Wälschen', which means to jabber or talk nonsense. Wherever the self-sufficient Teuton settled he stigmatized the real owners of the land as Welshmen, or strangers! They called Italy 'Walschland'; they called the Bulgarians 'Wlochi' and Bulgaria 'Wallachia'; they called the Celts of Flanders 'Walloons'. All these words are derived from the same root and are explained by the conviction that the Saxon conquerors believed themselves to be the only true speakers.

The Britons did not for a long time accept the word 'Welsh', because they knew that they were not 'strangers' or 'foreigners'. (If anybody had called King Arthur a 'stranger' he would have been very annoyed.) As they gathered together in the hills they called themselves 'Cymry', which means 'comrades'. They called their mountains 'Cymru', which means 'for their land'.

So in two words you can read the arrogance of the conqueror and the patriotism of those who dreamt of regaining their heritage.

§ 4

Towards the end of a sunny afternoon the town of Ludlow looks like a man-at-arms asleep at his post. You want to cry an alarm in the streets to awaken the spirit of the place. It is, like Berwick-on-Tweed, a frontier town that dozes with one eye on the old front line.

A drover comes with his slow grey wave of sheep down the main street, a Shropshire lad mounted on a shire gelding jingles heavily from the fields, and men in breeches and leggings, who are living in what little is left of eighteenth-century England, discuss the growing corn, the lambs and the weight and price of beasts. There is something sane and solid about towns like Ludlow, so that a man, in this transitional and uncertain age when old faiths are dying and the new ones are unborn, feels that here is something strong and old and worth loving. In such towns are the very roots of England. And you walk the quiet, dignified little streets with the feeling that, no matter what catastrophe overtook these islands, such market towns would survive unchanged. The vulgarity and the superficiality which rot our cities are unknown to the Ludlows of England. Great cities die, vanish and become mounds in which men dig curiously for coins and potsherds, but the villages and the small places live for ever.

I left the main street and went to the Castle, which stands on a green hill where the Teme joins the Corve. I walked over a dry moat into a grassy courtyard and round me rose the towers and battlements of the greatest stronghold in the March. Small flowers were growing in the Round Chapel, ferns were high in the armoury, and I climbed to a sentry walk and, gazing through an arrow-slit, saw far off to the westward the blue hills of Wales.

The windows of Ludlow Castle still look out to Wales as if they expected to see a movement from the hills. The courtyards of Ludlow and the huge roofless halls wear even in their decay an air of expectancy. When England was growing easy and comfortable, and when men were building manor-houses instead of castles, the fierceness of the Middle Ages lingered and at last died along the great chain of castles that divided England from Wales. The Lords of the Marches—those wild, self-seeking men—each of whom in his castle was an independent monarch with his own army, dined with swords beside them on the Welsh Border when men in England dined in silk gowns. In days when England was growing corn and breeding sheep, the lances were thick on the Welsh Border. Sentries paced the walls of castles like Ludlow, gazing in the night towards the hills of Wales for a stealthy movement in the dark or the gleam of light on a sword.

What a gallant but hopeless fight was the long struggle of the tribes of Wales against the Anglo-Norman. Their enemies were not cut off by sea from reinforcements, as were the Barons of Ireland. From Chester and Bristol their fleets watched the Welsh river mouths. Like men playing chess, the 'Marcher Lords' advanced their castles into Wales; and the Welsh fled higher in the hills. What an incredible place the Border March must have been! The distant hills were filled with fugitive princes of Wales, who gazed with the hatred of the dispossessed at the fortresses of the invader. They dreamt only of regaining their land, of assembling their tribes and leading them towards the land of their fathers.

And wherever the 'Marcher Lords' built their castles little towns grew up round them. Saxon and Norman and Celt huddled together in the strong shadow of the keep. How many a Welsh spy, I wonder, worked as a serf in these Border fastnesses and crept out at night to send a message to his chieftain in the distant heather? It was the old struggle between Celt and Anglo-Norman, between feudalism and centralized government on one hand and romantic tribalism on the other, the same struggle that in Scotland ended on the field of Culloden and in Ireland ended, technically, at any rate, with the establishment of the Irish Free State.

There were said to be at one time one hundred and forty-three 'Marcher Lords' encamped in their castles among the hills and valleys of the Welsh Border. It was as if time stood still. England in the Plantagenet Age was learning the arts of peace and developing agriculture and industry; Wales was still Norman in spirit. One can imagine that many a young man, wearied by the placid life of an English manor-house, would regard the Welsh Border as the world's last romance and, mounting his horse and taking his grandfather's sword, would ride over the Border into a vanished age in search of knightly adventure. This must have been the one period in our history when a man could sample the life of past centuries and find out if the 'good old days' were really good!

And as I lay in a patch of sun in the Outer Ward of Ludlow Castle I remembered the *Geste of Fulk Fitzwarine*, which tells us what those days were like. Ludlow is the only castle in England which possesses in the *Geste* its own mediaeval romance.

When Josse de Dinant, who was a favourite of Henry I, was struggling to hold Ludlow against the Welsh and against his own private enemies, Warine de Metz, Lord of Abberbury, sent his son, Fulk, to learn to be a gentleman at Ludlow Castle. The lad became a page in the household of Josse de Dinant. He was to see and learn much.

His master was at war with two powerful enemies, Hugh Mortimer and Walter de Lacy. One day the young page stood in a tower and saw Mortimer, who had been captured in an ambush, brought to the castle and locked in the turret that still bears his name. Some years later he stood again in a tower with the wife and the two daughters of Josse de Dinant, who were most beautifully called Sybil and Hawise. A terrific fight between Josse and the de Lacys was taking place almost under the castle walls. Fulk and the ladies saw with horror that Josse, ahead of his men, was just demanding the surrender of de Lacy when three enemy knights thundered up to the rescue. The girls began to moan and shriek at the sight of their poor father in such danger. One girl, Hawise, turned towards young Fulk and said that it was a pity he was such a useless child. This stung Fulk to action. He ran from the turret, placed on his head a rusty helmet and seizing an old curio, a Danish battle-axe, entered the fray mounted on a cart-horse.

He arrived when Josse, dismounted, was beaten to his knees. He lifted the Danish axe and clove two knights to the chine. He then captured de Lacy and the third knight, Arnold de Lisle.

This gallant deed, although it saved the life of Josse and made Fulk the hero of the hour and Hawise the proudest girl in the March, was destined to lead to disaster. Arnold, the captured knight, was a handsome young man, and within the castle was a maiden of dangerous beauty called Marion de la Bruyère. It has been proved again and again in history that when women take a hand in affairs life becomes far more dangerous than it is when men are left to hack themselves to bits with axes.

Marion was dark, forceful and passionate. She is the first recorded Norman 'vamp'. Arnold is one of the first Norman cads. She fell violently in love with him, and he used her shamefully. He persuaded her to give him a rope of knotted linen and, with the help of this, he and de Lacy one dark night escaped from Ludlow.

Now young Fulk, no longer regarded as a beardless lad, was married to Hawise in the chapel, and after the wedding feast, which lasted for two weeks, he and his bride and Josse de Dinant left the castle on a journey to a place called 'Hartland'.

Ludlow was now left without a lord. Marion sat at her window thinking of Arnold de Lisle. She brooded dangerously, and at last, unable any longer to do without him, sent him a message telling him that she was almost alone in the castle and that if he came quietly at night she would open a window and fling down a rope.

Arnold, who had, of course, not received a public school education, told his friend de Lacy about it, and they decided that this was a perfect opportunity for a piece of exceedingly dirty work. Arnold would keep the assignation and in due time would admit de Lacy with a force of armed men to the sleeping castle.

And so it turned out. Arnold climbed to the window. He and Marion went to her bower. Meanwhile, in the darkness outside, a hundred of de Lacy's men climbed the ladder and padded softly through the castle. They slew the watchman and opened the gates to the main body. De Lacy and his men slaughtered the garrison to a man. The screams of the dying awakened Marion. She sprang from her lover's arms and ran to the window. One glance told her what had happened. Arnold's sword was lying in the bed-chamber. She seized it and ran her lover through the body; then, with a wild cry, she leapt from the window and died on the rocks below.

The sequel was this. Josse and Fulk returned and laid

siege to Ludlow. De Lacy was so hard pressed that he, dead to all decency, performed a breach of Border etiquette that must have made his name a byword in every castle from Dee to Usk: he called in the Welsh! This was not playing the game! The 'Marcher Lords' might quarrel among themselves, but no decent baron would dream of appealing to the enemy!

However, the Welsh, led by the Prince of Gwynedd and the Prince of Powys, came swarming to the fight. They drove off the besiegers and captured Josse, who was locked up in his own castle. Young Fulk, thanks to his horse, escaped. He went to Henry I and told the story. The King ordered de Lacy to release Josse and send the Welsh home. The first command was easily fulfilled; the second took four years to accomplish! The Welsh, like a river that has burst its dam, over-ran the Shropshire Marches, and only after years of fighting, negotiation and barefaced bribery, were persuaded to retire westward.

I sit in the shadow of Mortimer's Tower and remember that from Ludlow the Tudors ruled Wales. Henry VII, proud of his Welsh blood, christened his eldest son, Arthur, Prince of Wales. He sent him to hold court at Ludlow, and this castle became the centre of Welsh political life.

It was to Ludlow in the year 1502 that a young Spanish Princess of Wales, Katherine of Aragon, came riding on a pillion behind her master of horse. Eleven Spanish ladies followed her on palfreys. She came as the bride of Prince Arthur, the King's regent in Wales. They lived at Ludlow for a short time, playing at kingship, holding a court modelled on that of Westminster. Then after a few months, Arthur, Prince of Wales, became ill and died. The suite of rooms in which he died are roofless and the ferns grow on the high walls. In these rooms the Spanish princess, whose name was to roll round Europe like a thunder-storm, wept beside the body of the boy to whom she had been married scarcely six months.

So Ludlow is the scene of one of the most provoking deaths in British history. It is impossible to contemplate Arthur's death without wondering how history might have been changed had he lived and had Katherine borne him sons.

His mighty brother, Henry VIII, would never have ascended the throne. He would never have married Katherine of Aragon. What a speculation!

In later years Ludlow knew many famous men. Philip, son of Sir Henry Sidney, spent his childhood there. On Michaelmas night in 1634, John, Earl of Bridgewater, Lord President of Wales, was bidden by his children to attend the banqueting hall where they acted a masque called *Comus*, written for them by John Milton.

The shadows began to lengthen on the grass of the Outer Ward, and I took the road north through the March, leaving the old town of Ludlow like a drowsy sentinel with his head towards the blue hills of the west.

§ 5

I entered Shrewsbury in the dusk and was shown into a horrid little bedroom by a neat-waisted chambermaid who would have delighted Laurence Sterne. It seems to me so easy to make a room companionable. This room was designed with evil intelligence to make the unfortunate creature condemned to sleep in it feel abandoned and unloved. I would rather sleep on the floor of a barn, as I have done many a time, than in the pale, cold rooms that the traveller strikes now and then, where a hateful dressing-table mirror reflects the disillusion of a weary double-bed. It was impossible to impart to this room a welcoming smile of any kind, because what had once been the fire-place was occupied by a vile gas fire, placed there also, I imagine, by the same evil intelligence to encourage suicide.

I looked at the charming country girl and was glad that her neatness and freshness saved me from losing my manners.

'Squalid and revolting,' I said, smiling at her in order to disguise my meaning.

'I beg your pardon,' she said stupidly.

'Revolting and squalid,' I said, smiling again.

'Sez you?' she replied.

This was terrible.

'Do you talk like that in Shrewsbury?' I asked.

'I come from London,' she said.

'Well then, you may, or may not, recognize this disgraceful patch of horror as the sort of room in a small verminous hotel near Paddington or Euston in which critical men are found dead with their throats cut.'

'Don't you like it?' she said.

'I adore it,' I said. 'Every corner of it is sheer joy to me. I feel that all the long, weary miles that separate me from civilization are justified now that I shall sink into unconsciousness surrounded by this beauty. I shall probably die of happiness in the night.'

There was, of course, no bedside light, and I hated the room so much that I would not even ask for string in order to yank out the light from the bed.

'Bring me twelve candles,' I said.

She went away, and when I opened the wardrobe door I was not surprised to see that the previous occupant had left his shirt there.

'I can only find eight,' said the girl, returning with eight half-consumed candles.

I gave her the relic of the last body which had occupied this patch of purgatory and went out into the streets of Shrewsbury, thinking that one loses one's temper not when things are really bad but when they are half good. I know hotels in Ireland whose very badness is a joy and a delight: lovely hotels in which nothing works, in which nothing is ever right, and nothing ever to time, so that life in them is an enchanted dream. If a mattress crashes to the floor when you are in bed you would never think of trying to put it right: you would just lie there, go to sleep and wait for the boots to roar with laughter when he brings the tea in the morning. I don't mind that sort of thing; in fact I rather enjoy it. It has the heady charm of the unexpected. . . .

Shrewsbury is a glorious town. I always seem to find myself there at night, with the church bells striking ten or eleven and the streets full of people whose speech is just a trifle quicker and a tone higher than the speech of southerners. It is the Welsh strain that comes out in the voice of Shrewsbury.

I stood on a bridge and looked at the Severn in flood. The river makes a perfect loop round Shrewsbury, save for that narrow neck of land to the north where in the old days they planted a castle. At night-time the old streets of Shrewsbury are as romantic as anything in England. The houses nod together so that you could shake hands from the upper windows with an opposite neighbour, just as the black and white houses lean towards each other in the Shambles at York.

Shrewsbury runs York very close with its street names, although York wins easily with Whipmawhopmagate. But Shoplatch Street is good, so is Dogpole and Wyle Cop and Murivance and Mardol. A hint of the old wild days when Shrewsbury was a frontier town are the names of the bridges over the Severn ; that on the west is ' Welsh Bridge ', and that to the south-east, ' English Bridge '.

In Wyle Cop is a half timbered house where the Welshman, Harry Richmond, who became Henry VII, lodged on his way to Bosworth Field. In Dogpole is the Olde House where his grand-daughter, Mary Tudor, lodged for a time in those days before she became ' Bloody '. Probably the happiest years of her miserable life were spent on the Welsh Border.

When I had tired myself out, I returned to my hotel. The bed was extremely comfortable and I slept like a child of four.

§ 6

It was a morning of sheer enchantment, cold, sunny with high gold clouds, when I took the road that runs north-west from Shrewsbury into Wales.

I could feel something new in the air. It was the same thing you feel when you cross into Scotland over Carter Bar : the wildness of a No Man's Land between two countries.

Beside the road in Whittington stands a castle that might have come straight from a ballad. Its round towers flank a drawbridge that lies above a moat. On the green water of the moat swim two swans. I knocked at the castle gate and saw a pretty girl bending over a wash-tub. The castle is now a laundry !

I went along the road for a few miles until it ran steeply downhill towards the bridge at Chirk. I was now on the boundary of Wales.

' Tell me,' I asked a man who was sweeping the road, ' where Wales begins.'

He looked at my car.

' Your front wheels are in Wales,' he replied, ' and your back wheels in England.'

'There is nothing to indicate that.'

'No.'

'You are Welsh,' I said, because of his quick sing-song voice.

'No—English!' he said quickly.

I had touched his Border pride.

He continued to sweep the dust of Wales into England over Telford's Bridge at Chirk. I suppose his ancestors had been raiders. I suppose they had gone to Taffy's house to steal a leg of mutton and the Welsh had come to his house to steal a rib of beef. It was rather like being in Northumberland or Cumberland.

I wonder why there is no sign-post on the Welsh boundary, as there is on the line between England and Scotland. Wales should see to this. Two million people, many of whom speak their own language, and all of whom are proud of their country and its traditions, should tell the traveller where it begins.

I ran over the bridge into Wales.

CHAPTER TWO

IN WHICH I GO TO LLANGOLLEN, HEAR ABOUT THE OLD LADIES, VISIT THE HUNTING-LODGE OF A WELSH PRINCE AND COME AT EVENING TO THE VALLEY OF THE CROSS, ENDING WITH SOME REMARKS ON WELSH RAREBIT

§ 1

I CAME to Llangollen, which is a small town, or a large village, lying in the shadow of mountains. A salmon river sings to it day and night. It is the sacred Dee. I now had the feeling that I had crossed a frontier. I was in a foreign country. To come straight out of England into Llangollen is as surprising as if you were suddenly projected in a flash from England to Ballater in the Balmoral Highlands. And Llangollen, although it is softer, is the Welsh sister of Ballater: they are both little stone-built towns among mountains with a salmon river running straight through them. Each of these rivers is called the Dee.

I went into a shop. The shopman was talking to a customer in Welsh. He broke off and said in that precise English which you hear also in the Hebrides:

'And what can I get for you, please?'

He then resumed his Welsh in a pretty sing-song voice, talking as swiftly as an excited Frenchman.

'How have you managed to keep your language on the very borders of England?' I asked him.

'We had to fight to keep it,' he said. 'The chapels saved Welsh for us years ago.'

'You prefer to speak in Welsh?'

'I can say more in my own language. The words come quickly and are better.'

'How many people speak Welsh?'

'I do not know. It varies in districts. Every one speaks it in Caernarvonshire. . . .'

I went out into the streets of Llangollen, which seemed

more than ever foreign streets lying in the shadow of their mountains. It was even strange to realize that letters collected by the postman that night in Llangollen would be in London the next day.

I walked beside the Dee all the afternoon, reading what John Rhys and David Brynmor Jones say about the Welsh language. The survival of this language—the ancient speech of the Britons—is a remarkable thing. It is the most marvellous survival in Great Britain. When the Romans conquered Britain under Claudius Caesar in A.D. 43, Latin became the official language for nearly four hundred years. Wales, unlike Ireland and Scotland, was Romanized. Roman castles were dotted about the country ; the legions drove their roads through Wales ; they based their legions at Deva on the north and Caerleon on the south. Still the speech of the Britons endured.

Many words in Welsh are Latin words. 'Ceffyl' is horse, 'cwlltwr' is ploughshare, 'ffos' is ditch, 'mur' is wall, 'ffenestr' is window, 'sebon' is soap, 'cyllell' is knife, 'tarw' is bull, 'pont' is bridge.

It is surprising that the British, or Welsh, tongue should have lived on for four centuries with the Latin language that conquered Gaul and Spain, but it is something of a miracle that in after years it should have stubbornly refused to be vanquished by French and, later, by English. No doubt a continuous struggle against invaders, bent on breaking down the barriers of nationalism, causes a people to cling with greater strength to the speech of their fathers. It is still surely a great romance that thousands of men, women and children use to-day words that would probably be understood by Boadicea and King Arthur.

'For five centuries,' writes W. Llewelyn Williams in *The Making of Modern Wales*, 'Welsh has lived as the close neighbour of this all-powerful, all-pervading language. (English.) It has been divided from it by no range of Cheviot Hills, still less by a St. George's Channel. For centuries English has crossed Offa's Dyke, and even in the poems of Dafydd ap Gwilym there are to be found many words taken from the English. Yet to-day Welsh not only survives as a spoken tongue ; its literature is more versatile and its students and readers more numerous than ever before.'

In the morning I looked out at a pocket paradise. Llangollen in one stride takes you right into Wales. There is nothing of the Border Marches about it. It is definitely a foreign country.

The broad Dee flows through meadowland with the majestic leisure of a salmon river. It cascades over rocks and, beneath the lovely old bridge which Bishop Trevor built five centuries ago, it rushes madly, foaming at the arches.

The mountains lift themselves all round, some long and gentle, some sharp and rugged, some dark with trees, some green with grass, and others bare and brown, lit up with patches of bright gorse.

To any one with an eye for landscape its charm is in compression. Here is a little masterpiece in mountains; an exercise in the blending of hill against hill, woodland against moorland. The Vale of Llangollen looks as though Nature had made a scale model for a section of the milder Scottish Highlands, and, liking it very well, had also gained a few ideas for Switzerland and the German Rhine. It is a country that is neat and well-groomed. Every meadow, it seems, has its valet and every tree its lady's maid.

Beauty, of course, is one of the basic industries of North Wales. The fame of places like the Vale of Llangollen brings every year a steady river of money from the Midlands and the North. It has suffered, like many another beauty-spot in these islands, from over-praise by writers such as Ruskin, who employed superlatives in days when travel was not easy and a man could not be expected to know every valley in the kingdom. While I prefer the beauty of Glen Shiel and Glen Moriston in the Highlands of Scotland, I admit that the Vale of Llangollen has a gentle, gracious beauty of its own which puts it high up in the list of valleys, but not, as Ruskin and Browning believed, first on that list.

One of the glories of Llangollen that could never grow stale, though a man spent all his days there, is the early fifteenth-century bridge over the Dee. Its four pointed arches are set at a part of the river designed, so it seems, to give them full battle with the swift current. I have a passion for looking from bridges into swift mountain streams, especially when, as with this bridge, it spans a river scooped out of a rocky bed. I could lean for hours over Bishop Trevor's bridge admiring the dark pools, the sudden eddies, the quick shallow channels of the nut-brown Dee. It is a great thing for a town to have a salmon river whispering at its walls day and night, just as the other Dee whispers to Ballater. In past ages this bridge was one of the Seven Wonders of Wales and the old rhyme goes:

Pistyll Rhaiadr and Wrexham steeple,
Snowdon's mountain without its people,
Overton yew-trees, St. Winefride's Wells,
Llangollen Bridge and Gresford bells.

I suppose the Seven Wonders to-day would include the Birmingham Water Works and the Menai Bridge! Still Llangollen Bridge, although no 'wonder' in the sense that it causes astonishment, is one of those bridges that a man never forgets. There are still some of us who would rather lean over it than admire the greatest engineering feat in the world.

I feel about Llangollen that it must have been—possibly still is—a great place for honeymoons. It suggests to me Victorian honeymoons: men with side-whiskers and check trousers; brides with little waists and puffed sleeves. The stiles round Llangollen and the shady reaches of the Dee seem sacred to the rather formal love-affairs of our fathers and our grandfathers, who, I feel sure, sat sententiously on rustic seats, reading *Sesame and the Lilies* to their obedient and reverent brides.

§ 2

On a bright morning I set off to climb the conical hill on whose summit stands the ruined castle of Dinas Bran. A path led up the slope and zigzagged over the open moor. George Borrow climbed this hill at least twice, but did not seem impressed with the view, although he appeared to have had clear weather on both occasions.

I mounted steadily, with the butterflies flickering over the gorse, larks in the sky and the wind coming cool from the hill. A labourer passed me on his way down. He carried a spade and a sack. He was a sallow, good-looking fellow with a dark rim round his face where his beard would have been before the invention of the safety razor. He was a pure-blooded Iberian, the very man who occupied England and Wales when the Romans came. I suppose the dark

Welshman is the purest-bred individual in Great Britain. In Wales as in Ireland the uncouth bumpkin is unknown. The yokel is a Saxon creation. The Celt, no matter how humble he may be, is always quick-brained, easy-mannered and fluent in his speech. I spoke to this man and discovered that he came from the south.

'And what does Dinas Bran mean in Welsh ? ' I asked him.

'Dinas Bran means the City of Bran,' he replied.

'Some books call it the City of Crows,' I said.

'Bran is the Welsh word for crow,' he said, 'but it is wrong to call Dinas Bran the City of Crows, for Bran was the name of the King who lived long ago in the castle on the hill-top.

'And what did he do ? '

He smiled a slow, mischievous smile :

'I think you may know better than I do,' he said.

I felt utterly rebuked. The man knew that I was pumping him. I covered my confusion with a bad joke and went on up the hill.

All that is left of the castle of Dinas Bran is like an old tooth sticking out of the earth. But what a spot for a castle ! Nowhere, except perhaps on the Rhine or on the eastern slopes of the Apennines, have I seen a castle so impregnably planted on a hill. How harsh and difficult life must have been up there in the clouds. Water, they had, of course, and their cattle would have been herded on the hill-side, but even so life in the City of Bran must at its best have seemed like a siege.

Bran, from whom the castle takes its name, was a Welsh king who reigned over the district of Powys in the sixth century. It was not, however, until Norman times that the castle became famous. The man who fortified Dinas Bran held the key to the Dee Valley. But, strangely enough, it is not of war that these ruins speak, but of a fair lady, Myfanwy Fechan, a daughter of the house of Trevor, the family which occupied Bran towards the end of the Middle Ages.

Welsh poetry from early times down to that of John Ceiriog Hughes, the great lyric poet of Wales, is full of tributes to her beauty.

'Would that I were a gust of wind blowing through the garden of Dinas Bran,' cries Ceiriog, 'whispering mine secret in thine ear, making ringlets of thine hair.'

The story goes that a young Welsh troubadour named Howell ap Eynion Llygliw believed himself to be dying of love for Myfanwy. This is the very best delusion from which any poet can suffer. It brings out any talent that may lie hidden in him, especially if the girl, like Myfanwy, gives him the cold shoulder, turns up her nose at him and says in the rudest manner that almost any other man of her acquaintance could make rings round him with a harp. It is to Myfanwy's coldness and to Howell's ardour that we are indebted for the only intimate glimpse of the people who inhabited this queer eyrie in the old times. Myfanwy walked abroad, we learn, 'in scarlet robes with queenly gait, all bowing before her'. Her face was 'fair as the snow new fallen on Aran's crest'. Even Howell's horse, says the poet, shared his master's enthusiasm and pawed the ground, eager to climb the great hill where this scornful paragon of beauty lived. Howell's last words to his beautiful iceberg were:

O bid me sing, as well I may,
Nor scorn my melody in vain,
Or 'neath the walls of Dinas Bran
Behold me perish in my pain.

Of course he did nothing of the sort. He behaved like an eminently sensible poet. After immortalizing his lady, he forgot her at the festive board of the Abbey of Valle Crucis. . . .

What a view is that from the hill-top! I looked west where the Dee twisted its silver course to Corwen; to the north were the queer, pink limestone terraces of the Eglwyseg Rocks; to the south-west the massive Berwyn Hills; but, best of all, was the wide vista of the magnificent green plain of Shropshire. I cannot imagine why Borrow, normally so ready to appreciate good things, failed to be inspired by this view. It is to my mind a magnificent hill-top view. Perhaps it is the influence of those dead Welshmen who manned this height for centuries which causes one to turn east and gaze with a certain expectancy towards the distant Marches.

§ 3

There is one place in Llangollen visited by every stranger. It is a queer black and white house called Plâs Newydd. I was rather amused to find it described in an excellent book on Wales as a 'perfect example of black and white architecture'. It is nothing of the sort. It is a perfect example of the ease with which an ordinary building can, with the aid of whitewash, half-inch timber and pitch, be converted into an impressive Elizabethan manor-house!

In this house there lived 150 years ago those two strange women—'the most celebrated virgins in Europe'—Lady Eleanor Butler and Miss Sarah Ponsonby, the famous 'Ladies of Llangollen'.

The girls were born into the hectic Ireland of the eighteenth century.

'Lady Eleanor's family, though degraded from their ancient rank for political reasons, lived in the unrefined splendour of those days in the castle of Kilkenny,' states Caroline Hamilton in her *Journal*. 'Mr. Butler—her father—one day entertaining his neighbours with lavish hospitality, a servant in gaudy livery standing behind every chair, spent the next day drinking in an ale house. One of his contemporaries told me that he was completely governed by his wife, who went by the name of old Madam Butler. She was a bigoted Roman Catholic, ashamed of her family, for whom she would never go into mourning. She was proud and overbearing, always surrounded by priests, and prevailed upon her husband to send his daughter to be educated in a convent in France. Madam Butler's funeral it is said was magnificent, but the drivers of the Hearse, getting drunk along with the rest of the Company, carried the corpse in a gallop to the family burying-place, and a looker-on, knowing the lady's furious temper, exclaimed: "O if Madam Butler could see you what a passion she would be in!"'

The daughter, Eleanor, was tall, handsome and masculine. Sarah Ponsonby, with whom she had enjoyed a friendship that dated from their schooldays, was feminine and attractive, with eyes like speedwells, a mischievous face, arched brows and a jolly little nose. They lived apparently in a state of nervous irritation with their homes and relatives, and discovered in each other a passion for solitude and retirement.

When Eleanor was thirty and Sarah was slightly younger, they decided to shake the dust of fashionable Ireland from their feet and escape together, pledged to resist matrimony and to devote their lives to friendship and celibacy.

'Sarah Ponsonby and Eleanor Butler were without any visible means of support—dependent creatures and unable to earn a penny,' writes Mrs. G. H. Bell in *The Hamwood Papers*. 'Nevertheless they ventured forth into a world which holds strict conventions as to payment for daily bread. Society could make neither head nor tail of such a proceeding. It was a rebellion in which all that is sensitive braved all that is harsh, for the sake of a terribly sought peace of mind. Two fiery young hearts had no notion of a quiet and unromantic flight. They were nothing if not romantic. Despising doors they jumped out of windows, carried firearms, bribed servants. Everything was extremely secret. They had a secret correspondence, and hid, stuffily, in cupboards or, freezingly, in barns. Sarah, very becomingly, nearly died of it. But, through all the domestic drama which they so simply and so ardently contrived, they remained resolute. They knew their own minds.'

On an April night in the year 1778 Sarah climbed out of the parlour window carrying a pistol under her arm. She went to a barn, where she met Eleanor. The runaways were soon afterwards captured on their way to Waterford, where they hoped to take ship. Eleanor was dressed as a man and Sarah was suffering from an appalling cold. They were taken home.

'There were no gentlemen concerned,' wrote a friend, 'nor does it appear to be anything more than a scheme of Romantic Friendship.'

Their second attempt was successful. They took boat from Waterford to Milford Haven. They journeyed across Wales until they came to Llangollen, where they lodged with the postmaster until they settled in the little cottage which, with additions and alterations, is now Plâs Newydd. Their first act was to send to Ireland for their faithful servant, Mary Caryll, who was something of an Amazon, having been discharged for flinging a candlestick at a fellow-servant. She was known as Molly the Bruiser.

The strange establishment then took on the form which it was to keep for half a century.

In flying from the world, however, they had planted themselves on one of its main roads! The Holyhead coach road —the main road from London to Ireland—passed through Llangollen. Quite naturally the strange *ménage* became the talk of dinner-tables in London and Dublin. The 'Ladies of Llangollen' were poor as church mice, but their personalities were so powerful that their retreat in an obscure Welsh village became a kind of court at which all the great ones of their time presented themselves. The Duke of Wellington, De Quincey as a boy, Wordsworth, Madame de Genlis and Walter Scott stayed with the Platonists. Every coach that passed through Llangollen brought the exiles some gossip from London or Dublin. They were extraordinarily well-informed. Although their main recreations were mutual admiration, literature and gardening and an appreciation of Nature, they enjoyed the news of the world which they had renounced.

Eleanor Butler, who was, of course, the dominant character, began a diary in 1788 which gives a fairly clear impression of life in New Place. This is the sort of thing:

'Thin blue transparent smoke curling and spiring up the mountain side through the trees from the village. Writing. The Joiner came to fasten the back board of the book case by Lady Anne Wesley's picture. . . . Artichokes coming up for the winter. Evan's of Oswestry's man came previous to this most hated Chester Fair. We had nothing to give him. Lord help us. . . . Reading, working. My Beloved and I walked to the white gate, delicious calm warm dark evening. Met a little Boy coming down the field with a Basket of Potatoes on his head. We asked him his name. "Peter Jones, son of Thomas the Lime Burner." "Where do you get those potatoes?" "On the Bank beyond yonder wood, they are my Father's." "Shall we take one or two?" "Yes and welcome; I am very much obliged to you." "For what, my good boy?—It is we who should thank you for your generosity." "Indeed you are kindly welcome to the whole basket." "Will you come to our house, and we will give you Something?" "No, indeed, I will not take anything, but you are welcome to the Basket and I am greatly obliged to you." We made him come with us, took 3 potatoes and gave him a huge piece of Bread and Butter. We shall always reflect with pleasure on this instance of the kindness and generosity of this poor child.'

They could, while lavishing praise on the beauties of Nature and feeling compassion for all animals and humble folk, be exceedingly cruel.

'Peggy, our undermaid' (wrote Eleanor in 1789), 'who has lived with us three years, was this day discharged our service. Unfortunate girl. Her Pregnancy she could no longer conceal, nor could she plead in her excuse that she had been seduced by promises of marriage. Nine till Twelve in the Dressing Room concerning that Poor Peggy Jones. Her father would not admit her to return to his House. We prevailed on the Weaver and his wife to receive her. What is to become of her ?'

Murmurs of the great world whispered about the queer little house in Llangollen and came to rest in brief sentences in Eleanor's diary. The 'ladies' were much concerned about the 'illness' of the King and the fractiousness of the Prince of Wales. The trials of their own uneasy country worried them, and they received first-hand accounts of everything from the distinguished ones who stepped out of the London coach. As time went on they became eccentric in appearance. They dressed in riding-habits and wore tall hats. Mathews, the actor, who performed locally, left an account of them in which he confessed that he nearly choked with laughter when he caught sight of them in the audience.

'Oh, such curiosities !' he wrote. 'I was nearly convulsed. I could scarcely get on for the first ten minutes after my eye caught them. As they are seated there is not one point to distinguish them from men ; the dressing and powdering of the hair ; their well-starched neck-cloths ; the upper part of their habits, which they always wear, even at a dinner-party, made precisely like men's coats ; and regular black beaver hats. They looked exactly like two respectable, superannuated clergymen.'

But they maintained their hold on the imagination, and even the affection, of Society until the end. The two queer old women were one of life's side-shows. Eleanor died in 1829 and her 'better half'—as she sometimes called Sarah—two years afterwards. They lie in Llangollen churchyard.

When you explore Plâs Newydd to-day you find yourself among a hushed crowd of varied tourists who have no idea why they are there beyond the fact that it is the thing to do.

The gardener, who is also the guide, will leave his lawn-mower and take you round the house, explaining, as he does so, the placid life of the two friends. There is nothing in the house worth seeing except the incredible assortment of old oak—bits of chests, rood-screens, choir-stalls and so forth—which have been so skilfully fitted together that the whole place is panelled with them. They had an insatiable passion for oddments, and it was the recognized custom for their many friends to contribute to the collection.

The vague tourists regard all that is visible of this spectacular friendship with dull eyes. They are faintly interested to be told that towards the end of her life Mary Caryll—'Molly the Bruiser'—saved enough money to present the freehold of New Place to her mistress.

§ 4

I wonder if the 'Ladies of Llangollen' ever visited the neighbouring mansion of Plâs Eglwyseg and reflected with a shocked expression how very untidy and difficult life can be when a man takes control of things. The memories of Plâs Newydd and Plâs Eglwyseg could not be more sharply different.

Seven miles by lovely narrow lanes bring you to a green fairyland at the foot of the Eglwyseg Rocks, and here, well hidden, is an attractive Tudor manor-house that is built on haunted earth. Over the door is an inscription which states that 'This Manor of Eglwyseg was inherited by the Princess of Powys from Bleddyn ap Cynvyn, King of North Wales, who fell in Battle 1073.' Beneath a shield are the words 'Ovna na ovno angau,' which mean 'Fear him who fears not death'.

Centuries ago there stood on this spot a hunting-lodge of young Prince Owen of Powys, who ruled these parts in the time of Henry I. In the year 1108 his father Cadwgan made a great feast in honour of God at Christmas-time in Ceredigion. To this feast came his turbulent son, Prince Owen. This young man was typical of his time and class. He was a violent, headstrong man, a type that goes down to posterity in ballads. After dinner the conversation turned on the beauty of Nesta, the wife of Gerald of Windsor, the Norman baron who held Pembroke Castle for King Henry.

Nesta has been called the 'Helen of Wales'. She was a daughter of Rhys ap Tudor, Prince of South Wales, and had been a ward, and mistress, of Henry I. The King had married her to his favourite, Gerald.

As the Christmas drink circulated, the young Prince of Powys decided to pay a visit to the beautiful Nesta. He went into Pembrokeshire, entered the newly-built castle which Gerald had just built at Cenarth in the Valley of the Teivy, and became so infatuated by the charms of Nesta that he decided to carry her off under the eyes of her husband. Owen must have been either blind with love or mad with youth. A more sober head might have seen that to abduct a woman who had borne a son to the King of England, and was now the wife of the royal Constable in Pembrokeshire, would plunge Wales into war and deny those still independent regions in the north the peace they so desperately needed. Nothing like this seems to have occurred to him.

He gathered together a band of young Welshmen as crazy as himself. They crept by night to the castle, dug their way under the gate, set fire to it and in the confusion seized Nesta and her two children and were soon galloping like madmen for Powys. Gerald, the unfortunate Menelaus, suffered the indignity of escaping down a drain-pipe.

While Owen and Nesta lived in the hunting-lodge in the shadow of the Eglwyseg cliffs, the whole of Wales and the Border Marches were on fire. King Henry was furious. Cadwgan trembled for his safety. He attempted to persuade his son to return Nesta to her husband. Owen refused. But he returned the children! Cadwgan's lands were seized. Owen was forced to fly to Ireland. Nesta after some time returned, so it seems, to Pembroke.

She retained her sway over the hearts of men even when she was a grandmother. Her children and her grandchildren were among those stormy knights who conquered Ireland under Strongbow. So Nesta, the Beautiful, passes across a page of Welsh history like a figure in a mist. . . .

I wandered in the green lanes listening to the song of birds and watching the sunlight play over the pink limestone cliffs. Any place in which men and women have felt deeply retains a pathetic significance. It seems almost as if some part of their passion has scorched the earth. We shall never know whether Nesta loved her stormy prince; and there is no answer to our thought but the swaying of the trees and the brightness of the primroses that have grown in her footsteps.

§ 5

In the evening, if you would like to enjoy one of the most beautiful short walks in Great Britain, take the right bank of the Dee and follow the canal to the ruins of the Abbey of Valle Crucis.

You will see all that is left of a small Cistercian abbey nestling in the shelter of hills and set in that peaceful beauty which the monks loved so well. On the hills at the back the Cistercians, who were great sheep farmers, kept their flocks. The languishing flannel industry of Llangollen is an inheritance from the monks of Valle Crucis.

The evening sun pours through the ruined arches and lies in gold bars over grass. A thrush sings his evensong from the top of a larch-tree. The Lord of Powys, Madoc ap Gryffydd, built this church in the Valley of the Cross in 1201; and for centuries while the wrath of man raged in the hill-top castles, this little acre in the glen basked in the peace of the Church. They say that Myfanwy Fychan, the scornful beauty of Dinas Bran, lies buried there; but no stone marks her resting-place. Lost also is the grave of Iolo Goch, the bard of Owen Glendower.

You can think of this story as you stand in the peaceful shell of this abbey. Early one morning when the Abbot of Valle Crucis was praying on the hill at the back, the figure of a man appeared silently before him. It was Owen Glendower.

'Sir Abbot,' said Glendower, 'you have risen too early.'

'No,' replied the Abbot, 'it is you who have risen too early by a hundred years.'

The Welsh patriot gazed at the man of God and disappeared as silently as he had come.

§ 6

There is a delicious cream-coloured cheese named after the town of Caerphilly in South Wales, but, alas, so I am told by grocers, no longer made there. This is a delightful cheese, and I would rather eat it in a field with bread and butter than endure the pretentious luncheons of most wayside hotels.

On one of these occasions it occurred to me that cheese is the only food to which Wales has given her name. Welsh rabbit, or possibly Welsh 'rarebit', to give it the earlier title, belongs to a fairly large group of slang terms which describe humorously the special dish or product of a district. We have an 'Essex lion' which is a calf; a 'Glasgow magistrate' which is a red herring; a 'Norfolk capon' which is also a red herring; 'Gravesend sweetmeats' which are shrimps; 'Irish apricots' and 'Munster plums' which are potatoes. And Welsh rarebit or toasted cheese, is a dish which, rightly or wrongly, is supposed to delight the Welsh.

I have not been able to discover among the Welsh any abnormal passion for Welsh rarebit; in fact, I think you would find it more frequently on the menu in London than in Wales. There is, however, abundant evidence that in past times Welshmen adored toasted cheese.

Shakespeare has a lot of good-humoured fun about Welshmen and cheese in *The Merry Wives of Windsor*.

Most of these jests centre round Hugh Evans, the Welsh parson and schoolmaster. On one occasion Evans returns to the dinner-table because 'there's pippins and cheese to come'. Nym, the Englishman, on the other hand, loves not 'the humour of bread and cheese'. Ford says that he would rather trust 'Parson Hugh, the Welshman with my cheese . . . than my wife with herself'. Falstaff bellows: 'Heavens defend me from that Welsh fairy, lest he transform me to a piece of cheese.'

There are other authorities which prove the Welsh fondness for cheese. 'The naturall disposicians of Welshmen,' says a writer in 1542, are towards 'good rosted chese'. Another writer in 1607 states that 'the Welshman loves leeks and cheese'.

A Welshman describing the characteristics of his nation in Andrew Boorde's *First Boke of the Introduction of Knowledge*, published in 1547, says: 'I am a Welshman. I do love *cause boby*, good roasted cheese.'

An even earlier work has a funny story about the Welsh and cheese. It is a collection of stories, *Mery Talys*, published in 1525.

'I fynde wrytten amonge old gestes,' says the writer, 'howe God mayde Saynt Peter porter of heuen, and that God of hys goodnes, sone after hys passyon, suffered many men to come to the Kyngdome of Heuen with small deseruynge; at which tyme there was in heuen a great company of Welchmen, whyche with their crackynge and babelynge troubled all the other. Wherefore God sayde to Saynte Peter, that He was weary of them, and that he wolde fayne have them out of heuen. To whom Saynte Peter sayd:

'"Good Lorde, I warrente you, that shal be done."

'Wherefore Saynte Peter wente out of heuen gates and cryed with a loud voyce, "*Cause bobe*", that is as moche to saye as rosted chese, whiche thynge the Welchemen herynge, ranne out of Heuen a great pace. Saynt Peter sawe them all out, he sodenly wente into Heuen and locked the dore and so spaned all the Welchemen out. . . .'

In the year 1613 the following was written in *Springes for Woodcockes*:

A Welshman and an Englishman disputed
Which of their lands maintained the greatest state,
The Englishman the Welshman quite confuted
Yet would the Welshman naught his brags abate:
'Ten cookes in Wales,' quoth he, 'one wedding sees.'
'True,' quoth the other—'each man toasts his cheese.'

What, I wonder, is the explanation of all these jokes about Welsh rarebit? In Shakespeare's day the cheese-producing counties were Essex, Suffolk and Cheshire. Wales apparently did not produce cheese. It is probably safe to assume that cheese was to the Welsh of those days 'a rarebit', and that their fondness for what was a commonplace on an English table led to a lot of good-humoured laughter.

The actual toasting of cheese may be, of course, a Welsh custom which amused the English of the sixteenth century. The Elizabethans took their cheese seriously. Tussar makes frequent references to the importance of cheese-making.

'Now what cheese is well made or otherwise,' says Cogan, 'may partly be perceived by this old Latine verse:

Non nix, non Argos, Methusalem, Magdaleneve,
Esaus, non Lazarus, caseus ille bonus.

'That is to say, Cheese should not be white as Snowe is, nor full of eyes as Argos was, nor old as Methusalem was, nor full of whey or weeping as Mary Magdalen was, nor rough as Esau was, nor full of spots as Lazarus.'

Entertaining old Gervase Markham, who knew how to do everything from the curing of apoplexy in hawks to the making of a cherry pie, has a lot of say about cheese and cheese-making, but there is not one word about the toasting of cheese. Possibly Welsh rarebit came to England with the Tudors and was regarded as a peculiar passion, as amusing to those not addicted to it as the consuming love of an Italian for macaroni, which, even now, can raise a laugh in an English music-hall.

CHAPTER THREE

HOW I LEAVE LLANGOLLEN, COME TO OWEN GLENDOWER'S LAND, TRAVEL UP THE LOVELY VALE OF CLWYD, EXPLORE THE DARK TOWN OF CORWEN, REMEMBER BATTLES IN RUTHIN, CLIMB THE WINDY RAMPARTS OF DENBIGH AND ENTER FLINTSHIRE

§ I

BIRDS singing, the meadows full of buttercups, the Dee high to the brim rushing through Llangollen, the cloud shadows moving over green hills and the sun shining—on such a morning I set off along the pretty road to Corwen.

There are few things in life so satisfying as the feeling of well-being which comes over a man early on a spring morning. I have noticed that as we grow older we become less willing to face the day. In cities we writhe at the thought of morning cheerfulness. We hate as a social pest the man who is hearty at breakfast. What a ghastly reflection is this on our general state of health.

On this morning I threw open the window with a shout of joy when I saw the freckled fields wet with dew, an early sun stealing through the woods and the quiet morning shadows lying over the ground. It was good to be alive. It was good to be setting out over a long road into Wales.

'When you get to Corwen,' said the hotel man, 'you must take the road to the left and go to Bala.'

People are always trying to make me change my plans.

'Why?' I asked.

'Because Bala is one of the most beautiful lakes in the world.'

'But I want to see Ruthin and Denbigh.'

'There is nothing there.'

I looked at the man and realized that he was an Englishman; so I lied to him and told him that I would go to Bala. He appeared gratified. . . .

The road now ran, with the delicious Dee to the right, bending and twisting through one of the most peaceful and gentle valleys I have ever seen. The river suddenly lost itself in a great loop, but I met it again in a mile or so, cool, brown and, I am sure, full of trout ; and then I came to a little place which calls itself Glyn Dyfrdwy. I met a postman on a bicycle :

'How do you pronounce this name ?' I asked.

'Glynduvrdooe,' he said quickly with the accent on the penultimate syllable and an upward kick to his voice.

'Say it slowly.'

Eventually I got it. Like so many Welsh words it looks terrible in print but when spoken is exquisite.

Glyn-duvr-doo-e. . . .

It is like the cooing of doves in a wood.

§ 2

This village of Glyn-duvr-dooe, known now only to men with trout and salmon rods, was part of the patrimony of one of the greatest characters in Welsh history—Owen Glendower, or Owain Glyn Dwr as the modern historians spell him. (I will stick to Shakespeare's spelling.)

Glendower, had he been an Englishman, would perhaps not have become a national hero, because he was a material failure. The Saxon mind will endure any amount of idealism as long as it ends in a practical success. The Celtic mind, on the other hand, adores a sad ending to a story and is often liable to idealize failure. Bonnie Prince Charlie, for instance, in failure and in flight is a more appealing figure to the Celtic imagination than Bonnie Prince Charlie in victory. So it is with Owen Glendower, a great Welshman who has something in common with Wallace, Charles Edward and Michael Collins.

At Glyn-duvr-dooe stood one of his two mansions. His name was Owen of Glyndyfrdwy, or Owen of the Glen of Dee. His other mansion was at Sycharth in Denbighshire. He was born about 1359, a fortunate young man who owned land which his forefathers had ruled as Welsh princes. He was therefore supplied with that blue blood without which no Welsh nationalist could be successful in the old days.

We see him first of all moving through the colourful London

of Edward III's time, a young law student. This does not mean that he was a professional law student. In those days the Inns of Court were a more fashionable and expensive University than Oxford. Only the very rich could afford to send their sons to London to be socially educated in the shadow of the Law.

His next appearance is on the field of battle. He is a squire to that unhappy king, Richard II. He serves in France, Scotland and Ireland. We have one glimpse of him in battle at Berwick-on-Tweed. The plume of a flamingo rises from his helmet. He gallops up to a Scottish knight and unhorses him. In the struggle his lance is shivered, but, grasping the splintered haft, he fights as with a sword and drives the Scots like wild goats before him.

We see him later settled on his Welsh estates, a happy married man with a family growing up round him. The surroundings of a Welsh man of property in those days were vastly superior to those of an Irish or a Scottish chieftain of the same period. They are minutely described by his bard, Iolo Goch:

'Encircled with a moat filled with water, the entrance to this Baron's Place, this mansion of generosity the magnificent habitation of the chief Lord of Powys, is a costly gate. . . . A Neapolitan building of eighteen apartments, a fair timber structure on the summit of a green hill, reared towards heaven on four admirable pilasters. . . .'

Orchards and vineyards surround the mansion, while herds of deer graze in the park. There is a tall stone pigeon-house, a fish-pond and a heronry. Most eloquent of all, as the bard notes, is the absence of door latch or porter, so that nothing bars the way to Glendower's abundance. This is the inheritance which the patriot was to lose because he dreamed of a Welsh Wales. . . .

It is the year A.D. 1400. The wretched Richard II, the last of the Plantagenets, has been deposed and murdered by Henry Bolingbroke, who ascends the throne as the first Lancastrian—Henry IV. The sympathy of Wales is with the murdered Richard. He has inherited the love and sympathy shown by this nation to his father, the Black Prince. And now the new king, Henry IV, earns the hatred of the Welsh people by a series of harsh statutes. It is clear to the Welsh that their language and their traditions are to be stamped out.

The three old Kingdoms of Wales are now just a name. Ninety years have passed since Edward I planted his great chain of castles in the north and shired that country into Anglesey, Caernarvon, Merioneth, Cardigan, and Carmarthen after the Norman pattern.

Race prejudice has died down. Towns have sprung up. In the south the Marcher Barons fight and raid in the old way; but it is, outwardly, a new Wales: an almost conquered Wales. The energy which had been pent up within Wales during the time of Llewelyn has burst free. Thousands of Welsh bowmen are fighting in all the armies of Europe. But no country is conquered while there lives a man who can speak its language. In the calm that precedes the storm, the bards of Wales tune their harps and sing a dangerous old song about a prince who would one day rise up with a sword in his hand. . . .

The fight begins with a private quarrel between Owen Glendower and his neighbour Lord Grey of Ruthin. The King of England summons Glendower to attend him in the Scottish War. The message, entrusted to Lord Grey, is not delivered. The king is angry with Glendower, and Glendower with the man who has attempted to show him as a traitor.

In mid-September of the year 1400 Glendower plans revenge. His friends gather in the village of Glyn Dyfrdwy and marching on Lord Grey's town of Ruthin burn it to the ground on the eve of the fair of St. Matthew. For three days they ravage the neighbouring English settlements. Their action fans into flame the smouldering revolt of the Welsh people. Ninety years fall from the country and men talk as they did in the time of Llewelyn. All rebellions require a signal; and the red glare of burning Ruthin is the sign that a Welshman is in the field again.

Messengers ride over the Border with despatches to the king, who is marching south from Scotland. The chamberlain of Caernarvon states that he sees men selling their cattle to buy horses and weapons. Welsh labourers hear of the revolt as they stand in English harvest fields. They drop their sickles and tramp west. Welsh students at Oxford cross the border. The news flies over the channel. Welsh mercenaries desert their armies and crowd to the seaports.

In Wales a great banner flies out on the wind. It bears a golden dragon on a white ground. Beneath it stands Owen Glendower. Men call him 'Prince of Wales'. Old Iolo of the Red Mantle sweeps his hands over the harp-strings and puts the heart of Wales into two lines:

Many a time have I desired
To see a lord of our own kin.

The wind blows cold from the wildness of Snowdon as King Henry IV comes with a great army to seek out Owen Glendower. But the Man of Wales has vanished! He has wisely disbanded his armies, knowing that they cannot fight an English army in the field. Henry declares all Glendower's lands forfeit and re-crosses the Border.

In the following year, on the morning of Good Friday, forty Welshmen climb the ramparts of Conway Castle and take it while the garrison is at church. This is the second signal, as the burning of Ruthin was the first. Once again men all over Wales are thinking not of sheep but of horses, not of ploughs but of bows. But where is Glendower? No man knows. Only the loneliest ravines of Snowdon have seen the thin trail of his camp fire as the Welsh Prince of Wales hides in caves and woods, an outlaw biding his time. In north and south men speak of him as they might have spoken of Arthur. They wait for him to appear as if for some supernatural deliverer. They have not long to wait.

He appears out of a blue summer sky in the wilds of Plynlimmon and smites a great host gathered there to destroy him. The news travels. His prestige leaps sky-high. Men flock to the dragon standard in the marches of Carmarthen. It is whispered that the Prince of Wales will lead his armies into England and exterminate the English tongue.

Meanwhile an English horseman rides to Westminster to place before King Henry a letter written by Owen Glendower but captured before it could reach the hands for whom it was intended. In this letter, written in Latin, Glendower drops the title of 'Prince of Wales': he claims only to be the deliverer appointed by God to liberate the Welsh people from the bondage of their English enemies. This is the mood in which the poet and visionary, turned soldier, came down from the Welsh hills to carry on the fight.

In the autumn King Henry comes again to Wales in search of his enemy. He ravages Cardiganshire. Frightened children see the English horses stabled near the high altar of Strata Florida. But Glendower is never where the English expect him to be—the first qualification of a guerilla leader. He pursues, as all Celtic leaders have pursued from Caractacus to Michael Collins, a nerve-wracking, fly-by-night, warfare, hanging on the flanks and rearguard of the English forces, delivering a blow and disappearing. One day the Welsh Prince of Wales captures the arms, tents and horses of the English Prince of Wales!

In the following year Glendower advances to greater success. He shows superb qualities of organization and statesmanship. He uses pen as well as sword. He tries to win over the English barons. He plans alliances with Ireland and Scotland and France. At the same time his forces are in the field. He captures his old enemy, Lord Grey, and carries him in fetters to the mountains. In June the Welsh and the English meet at Bryn Glas, a hill to the west of the village of Pilleth in Radnorshire. The Welsh archers in the English army, suddenly becoming nationalist, turn their bows on their masters. So terrible is the slaughter that for days no English dare approach the battle-field where the corpses of their comrades lie by the thousand. And to Owen Glendower is led prisoner Edmund Mortimer, uncle to the boy Earl of March, the Yorkist heir to the Throne—a trump card.

The king is at Berkhampstead when this news is brought to him. He marches in three divisions into Wales. Rain, cold and snow meet him. In the Vigil of the Nativity of our Lady he pitches his tent in a fair plain. A sudden wind blows so violently that the tent is cast down. Out of the night comes a spear flung by an unknown hand. Only a coat of mail saves him from death. And men in the English army whisper that Glendower is a necromancer who can control the elements.

Month by month his power grows. Lord Grey improves Glendower's finances by paying to him a ransom that leaves him a poor man for the rest of his life. Mortimer marries Glendower's daughter and allies himself with the Welsh cause. The king views this alliance with fear. Will this incredible Welshman come thundering into England to claim the throne for the rightful heir, the young Earl of March? He is not long in doubt. Mortimer rides to the Border and tells his tenants that he is pledged with his father-in-law, Owen Glendower, to restore King Richard to the throne—for a tradition still persisted that Richard II is alive—or, that if the king is dead, his honoured nephew, the Earl of March, shall be king.

So Wales, a century too soon, dreamt of placing a king on the throne of England.

By the end of the year 1404 'Owen, by the Grace of God Prince of Wales', was recognized as ruler of the country. He summoned parliaments on the English pattern at Dolgelly, Harlech and Machynlleth. He received help from France. The French king agreed to assist in the patriot's dream: Wales to be purged of Saxon elements, the Welsh Church to be ruled by Welshmen and two universities to be established, one for the north, the other for the south.

But his dream came to nothing. In the following year his fortunes began to crumble and fall. There is something mysterious and inexplicable about his end. Here was a man who might have been one of the most powerful figures of the Middle Ages, a man who sacrificed everything for a dream, a man who had the magnetism and the ability to lead a small nation against a larger nation, only to be left at the end deserted and alone.

'Slowly but surely the pressure of Henry's armies and those of the Lords Marchers, was beginning to tell,' writes Mr. W. Watkin Davies in *Wales*. 'Most of the grievances of the peasants had been redressed, and they longed for the time when they could till their fields in peace, unmolested by either friend or foe. Owen's high ideals were beyond the comprehension of the selfish and illiterate labouring classes upon whom he had depended for his strength; and they now deserted in hundreds from his camp. The general *débâcle* was assisted by the young Henry's policy of studied clemency. He was no foreigner but a rival Prince of Wales; and he strove to prove that he cared just as much as did Owen for the welfare of his Welsh subjects. The Abbot of Valle Crucis was quite right when he told Owen that he had risen a century too soon.'

Owen Glendower's end is one of the mysteries of history.

There is a tradition that he wandered in solitude with a few supporters, hiding in the mountains of the north, assuming disguises and living from hand to mouth. Sometimes he would appear in the dress of a common labourer, only to disappear again for months.

When Henry V came to the throne he proved how Glendower's cause had fallen by offering the old patriot a free pardon. This is the greatest insult a patriot can suffer!

This was in 1415. But the pardon was refused. It was offered in the following year. Henry sent Owen's only surviving son to Wales to offer peace and safety to the broken warrior. Glendower was as silent as his native mountains.

No man knows where his bones lie. Some say that at the end he came like an old dog to die in Glyn Dyfrdwy among the scenes of his youth. There is a legend that he lies buried in Corwen. There is another tradition which says that, after wandering in many disguises, he found a home at last with one of his daughters, all of whom married well. There is a slab in a churchyard on the Wye which is pointed out as his grave. But no one knows.

'His courage and high spirit have never been impugned,' writes Mr. J. E. Lloyd in *Owen Glendower*, 'and it is clear testimony to the loyalty and affection which he inspired that not even in his darkest hour was any one found to betray him to his foes. He stands alone among the great figures of Welsh history in that no bard attempted to sing his elegy; this we must attribute, not merely to the mystery which shrouded his end, but also to the belief that he had but disappeared, and would rise again in his wrath in the hour of his country's sorest need. From that day to this, his name has been one of power in Wales; attempts to reduce him to the stature of a robber chief and lawless brigand have been ineffectual to quench the national devotion to his memory. For the Welshmen of all subsequent ages, Glyn Dwr has been a national hero, the first, indeed, in the country's history to command the willing support alike of north and south, east and west, Gwynedd and Powys, Deheubarth and Morgannwg. He may with propriety be called the father of modern Welsh nationalism.'

And near the river bank at Glyn Dyfrdwy—which men call Glyn-duvr-doo-e—is a grassy mound with trees growing on it: all that is left of the dwelling from which the golden dragon was let loose on Wales.

§ 3

I received, not for the first time, the impression that I was in a foreign country when I entered the little market town of Corwen. The streets were full of men. There was some kind of weekly market in progress. The men stood about in dark groups on the pavement and in the road. They were talking in Welsh. I understood them less than I would have understood a crowd in Greece or Turkey.

Many of the men were obviously mountaineers. They carried switches. Others were farmers from the valley. They carried sticks. They were dressed much as any rural crowd is dressed in England: bowler hats or caps, dark coats, breeches and leggings; yet by no stretch of the imagination could it have been an English crowd.

I walked about among them full of despair. How idiotic to attempt to write a book about Wales with no knowledge of the Welsh language. Even George Borrow's Welsh, which I have an idea was extremely bad, carried him a little way behind the scenes. I realized that the Welsh language is the most important thing in Wales; or at least in those parts of Wales, like Corwen, in which it is spoken. And any one like myself would be for ever an outsider. I went into a newsagent's shop. All the London morning papers were spread out on the counter. English books were on the shelves. I met again, as I met at Llangollen, the polite bilingual shopkeeper. He spoke to a woman in Welsh and addressed me in English. I bought some newspapers.

'What are they talking about?' I asked with a nod towards the crowd:

'The price of sheep and vegetables,' he said.

I went out and listened to them. It seemed to me that they were hatching another Glendower rebellion. A very excited old man, who was probably talking about mutton, appeared to me to be exhorting the tribes to rise and march on Shrewsbury. It is not strange to hear the Gaelic far out in the Western Isles of Scotland; but it is strange to hear Welsh within a stone's throw of the English Border. The men, too, were a distinct type. They were better dressed than a similar fair-day crowd in an Irish town. They were neater and more prosperous looking. Yet there was something akin to an Irish crowd in their concentration; in their appearance of sharing a secret.

Corwen seemed to me rather a hard little town which might have been built by a firm of solicitors. It hugged the flank of a great mountain that rose so steeply behind it that the streets were darkened by its shadow.

I went to the church and saw the mark on the stone which is supposed to be that of Glendower's Dagger. They say that one day in a rage he hurled the weapon at Corwen from the top of Pen-pigin, a distance of nearly a mile!

On my way through the crowd again I heard a great burst of laughter. Two or three Welshmen were making fun of something. The laughter passed through the crowd in the jolliest manner. I felt too much of an alien to ask what it was about. A Roman might have felt like this in a British village. So I left Corwen and went on by the road that goes north to Ruthin.

§ 4

I turned to the right about a mile out of Corwen and was soon in the village of Bryn-Eglwys. This is, I suppose, one of the places in Wales which every American visits. The name means the Hill of the Church. All round about is property which once belonged to the Yale family.

'The Yale family owned it till the other day,' writes A. G. Bradley in his delightful book, *In Praise of North Wales*, 'and it was from one of them, who did so much towards founding the famous university in New England two hundred years ago, that it derived its name. He lies buried not in the Yale chapel attached to this church of Bryn-Eglwys, but at Wrexham, ten miles away, under an inscribed monument on which his career is briefly but quaintly epitomized:

Born in America: in Europe bred,
In Africa travelled and in India wed,
Where long he lived and strived: at London dead.

'Many Americans, I believe, do pay their respects to Elihu Yale's dust in the beautiful church at Wrexham. But I never heard of one coming up to Yale and Bryn-Eglwys, though about here myself a good deal in old days. The Yale chapel where Elihu should by rights have been buried, like the rest of his family, forms the south transept of the little church of Bryn-Eglwys. The name itself has some interest as being one of the very few territorial surnames surviving in Wales. Indeed I can only recall three or four more, outside English Pembrokeshire, at any period, though the Border counties had many. . . .

' I venture to think that should any alumnus of that famous university find his way up here some Sunday and take his seat in the Yale chapel of the old church of Bryn-Eglwys, among a few hill farmers and shepherds, and hear the old Church of England service read and sung through in the ancient Cymric tongue, he will feel that the cradle, or at least the god-parent, of his Alma Mater is a strange and primitive and romantic spot.'

About two miles from the church is Plâs-yn-Yale, the family seat, from which the father of Elihu Yale left for America, in the days of the Pilgrim Fathers.

' Do many Americans visit this place ? ' I asked a man who was working in a field.

' Yes, indeed,' he replied. ' We had two young men from America who were going round Wales on bicycles. Their grandfathers came from these parts, and they could speak the Welsh too ; but not very well. And they could drink beer. They were fine young men. . . .'

I gathered that these ambassadors had paved the way for other pilgrims in the pretty village beneath the mountain of Llantysilio.

§ 5

I do not care how often I see the town of Ruthin, which is pronounced ' Rithin '. I arrived there in a midday hush. The sun spilt itself into the square of St. Peter, the most distinguished town square I have seen in Wales. Ruthin is as balanced and distinctive as Corwen is incoherent and ugly. Even the modern Welsh builder has not been able to take away from Ruthin the grave and mellow beauty of age.

On the south side of the square is a picturesque fifteenth-century building which was once used as prison and court-house. In the old days public hangings used to take place from a gallows that protruded from this building, and I believe that the last execution was that of a Jesuit in the reign of Elizabeth.

This building must have been erected after the burning of Ruthin in Owen Glendower's insurrection. The only building that escaped destruction at that time is said to be No. 2 Well Street.

I spent an hour wandering round this delightful town admiring the old timbered houses, the small shops, notably the grocers' with their windows piled high with various cheeses, the Old Grammar School which was founded in 1589, the almshouses of Christ Hospital and twelve cottages near the church. The almshouses were founded by Gabriel Goodman, Dean of Westminster, a native of Ruthin, and one of the translators of the New Testament.

The Church of St. Peter, though it has suffered severely from the centuries, contains a magnificent roof to the north aisle—the original nave. It is a tradition in Ruthin that this roof was the gift of the first Welsh King of England, Henry VII. It is divided into about five hundred carved panels, no two of which are alike. . . .

I went to the hotel. Two maids presided over a heavy and desolate dining-room. I retreated and entered a satisfactory bar parlour which contained about six men, five of whom were drinking beer and the sixth whiskey. Several of the men were obviously farmers from the valley, and one or two were, I judged, either prosperous shopkeepers or professional men. I ordered beer and cheese in an English voice, and I could tell that they wondered whether I was some kind of commercial traveller or the first swallow of the tourist season. When I entered they were talking rapidly in Welsh. First one and then another spoke in English until I could understand the conversation, which I thought very good manners. It was about root crops and the extremely bad price which sheep were fetching at the weekly markets. Two of the men finished their beer and went out. In the conversational lull, one of the shopkeepers or professional men said to me :

'Are you motoring for pleasure ?'

I said 'Yes'. He then, actuated purely by a desire to be polite to a stranger, talked trivially about the show places of Wales. I must go to see the waterfall at Bettws-y-Coed. I must not miss a fairy glen somewhere. Would I be going to Caernarvon ?

I told him that, while I wanted to see all these places, I was seriously interested in Wales and the Welsh people. I wanted to find out how and why they were different from Englishmen, Irishmen and Scotsmen. His manner changed at once. He was delighted. What could he tell me ?

'These towns,' I said. 'Do the young people find life dull in them ? A town of this size in England would have at least one huge cinema.'

'No, indeed,' he said. 'There is plenty for them to do. There are night classes and we practise for the Eisteddfod.'

The passion for education in Wales is like that of Scotland.

'The Eisteddfod is in August. Do you mean to say that you are practising for it now ? '

'Yes, the whole country is practising for it ; schools, choirs, singers, instrumentalists. We are a naturally musical nation. A Welshman will sing till his heart breaks. Song and music are the ways in which we express ourselves most easily. One of the finest things that has happened to us—for we have instinct but require a lot of education—is the wireless. It is improving our taste in music. . . .'

The other men, who listened to all this and nodded, went out, leaving me alone with my expansive friend.

'I have lived in England years ago,' he said suddenly. 'Do you know many Welshmen there ? '

'Not one. I believe my milkman is Welsh—Williams.'

'Yes : he would be. Carmarthenshire. The Welsh are not popular in England.'

I made a polite denial.

'No ; it is so,' said this man. 'It is a very interesting subject. We are the least-liked branch of the Celtic race. The average Englishman likes an Irishman and loves a Scotsman. Ask any Scotsman. A Scottish accent is a kind of passport in England. When I first went to England I suppose I spoke with a Welsh accent, but it only made people laugh. Paddy and Jock are good fellows, but "Taffy is a Welshman, Taffy is a thief. . . ." '

I was rather taken aback, but so dispassionate was my friend that I lost any sense of embarrassment I might have felt had he been bitter.

'Every English school-child knows that rhyme,' I said.

'Yes ; the way that rhyme has lived has done a lot of harm to Wales. It would be a good thing if it could be forgotten.

I suppose it goes back to the days of the Border raids when the Welsh stole the English cattle and the English stole the Welsh sheep. . . . Then the Welshman is supposed to be a liar.'

'So is the Irishman.'

'Yes; but to the English the Irishman's lies are always amusing,' he replied.

'Well, do you think the Welsh have the gift of lying?'

'No, it is not lying. The Welsh, like the Irish, have vivid imaginations. They can't resist the temptation to improve a story. I have found myself doing it. The matter-of-fact English mind does not understand, or like, this. And you'll find as you get to know Wales better that we are a very sensitive crowd. We can expand in the right atmosphere, but put us in the wrong and we close up like oysters. My own objection to my countrymen is that they do not trust one another. We are very suspicious. It may be a relic of tribal days. I can't say. We are an emotional people, with all the drawbacks it implies. For instance, a movement will start with tremendous enthusiasm. We will all be talking about it. Then—suddenly—it will die. We lose interest in it. We do not carry it through. Now, you in England are more enterprising, more thorough, more consistent. . . .'

I made polite negative noises.

'Oh, yes, indeed, it is so. You will also find that we Welsh as a nation have what is called an inferiority complex.'

'But why?'

I was never to know why. The door opened. A troop of men came in, shouted greetings in Welsh to my friend and drove him into silence. He finished his drink, leant over to me and said in a low voice:

'I'm proud to be Welsh. I lost money when I left England to come back to Wales. You'll find, as you go on, that we're as warm-hearted, as trustful, and as truthful as . . .'

He got up and said mischievously:

'Well, the English or the Irish or the Scots.'

I saw him vanish with regret, because I had the feeling that he had a lot more to say.

§ 6

The day was so fine and the sky so clear that I could not resist a great green mountain which I saw to the right.

It was Moel Fammau, the highest point in the Clwydian Hills.

'Which is the best way to climb Moel Fammau?' I asked a man outside Ruthin.

'Moel Vamma?' he said. 'Go to Llanbedr and turn to the right past the church. . . .'

But I found at Llanbedr that it would be easier and quicker to go on to Tafarn Gelyn, which is only a little over two miles from the summit. Here I left the car and struck off over a narrow road to the left.

It was the perfect day for an uphill walk: the wind like iced champagne, the sun shining in a blue sky, the gorse in bloom and the air full of the exciting scent of spring. Bwlch-pen-Barras is the col of the Clwydian range between Ruthin and Mold, and there I sat down to rest beside a young man in tweed clothes, who, like myself, was going up to 'the Mother of Mountains'. He came from Birmingham and was spending some time in Wales after an illness. We went on together.

'I like Wales,' he said, 'but I don't like the people, do you?'

'Do you know many of them?'

'Well, seaside landladies and people. We come to Wales in the summer every year.'

'Do you think any one would love the English if we were judged by, say, the landladies of Margate?'

'Perhaps not; but the Welsh are so close: you never get to know them.'

'Have you tried?'

'Good Lord! I've got a Welsh aunt. We know her all right. She'll talk your head off . . .'

I told this young man of the conversation in the inn at Ruthin with the Welshman.

'It's quite true,' he said. 'There is a prejudice against the Welsh.'

'I wonder,' I said, 'if it may not be the ancient hate between Celt and Saxon.'

'What do you mean?'

'Well, the Welsh once inhabited England. They are the real Britons. When the Angles and the Jutes and, later, the Saxons came in war-bands and fought them, driving them slowly west into the mountains and capturing their country, they hated them too much even to Christianize them.'

'I never knew that,' said the young man. 'Do you mean to say the Welsh were Christians before the English ?'

'Of course. They took with them on their westward flight whatever was left of Roman Christianity.'

At the end of a grassy climb we reached the summit of Moel Fammau.

What a view ! The Clwydian Hills are the highest between the Snowdon range and the Derbyshire Peak. Below us lay the green Vale of Clwyd, with its little river winding to the north ; northward lay the green summits of the hills and southward they ran also to Llangollen. We saw the sea and the town of Rhyl, Rhuddlan Castle, the white spire of Bodelwyddan, the tower of St. Asaph Cathedral and a little to the south the spire of Ruthin Church.

We looked backward over the Dee to the Berwyns and westward, right across Wales, where in every shade of grey and blue rose up a great chain of mountains. Snowdon.

What a gorgeous sight ! Snowdon is the most magnificent looking mountain in Britain. It is not as high as Ben Nevis but its shape is sharper and more regal. We saw it far off, lifting its head above its fellows while gold clouds sailed landwards from the sea to hang over it for a moment and pass on.

As we raced down to Tafarn Gelyn at a good pace I thought that in the autumn, when the heather is purple, this view from Moel Fammau must be one of the glories of Wales.

§ 7

I was soon going with the sun before me through the lovely Vale of Clwyd. This is a part of Wales that I adored at first sight. I love the rich look of well-farmed land. The Valley of the Clwyd may not possess the picture post-card beauty of Llangollen, but to any eye that enjoys fat land it is a more splendid sight.

The neat, well-ordered farms lie on the hills or nestle cosily in the valleys. They are as pretty as anything you will see in Somerset or Devon, where farms and cottages look as though they have grown naturally out of the soil like trees. These Welsh farms have the same splendid rightness. They are built of the local stone. They are rooted like their own crops in the rich Welsh earth that supports them.

It is a land of small farmers. I suppose the average holding is from fifty to eighty acres. The men who own them have no need to advertise. Their acres speak for them. Even a Norfolk farmer—one from the wheat-lands at Fakenham who believes that nothing good exists out of Norfolk—would, I feel sure, pay a slow and reluctant tribute to the excellence of the farm-lands of Clwyd. Along the valley at equal distances are market towns. They are small, neat, quiet and distinctive. There is something that I am beginning to recognize as Welsh about them: something that is discreet and solid and dignified.

Their individualism is pronounced. They seem to be living a healthy, self-contained life. In English towns of the same size you are astounded and annoyed by the size of the cinemas, the frequency of dance-halls and other amusements which make a community dependent on outside and alien influences. These Welsh market towns have—how I do not know—resisted the cinema and the multiple store. They are towns which serve very effectively and very simply a small agricultural population which is bound together by the same local interests. The wireless aerial alone indicates that they have any interest in the outside world.

The strength of a nation is ultimately not in its cities but in its villages and its small towns; places where the national spirit can thrive in peace. I feel that quite a number of the best things in Wales exist beneath what to the English-speaking stranger seems to be the discreet placidity of such towns as those in the Vale of Clwyd.

§ 8

In the evening I stood on the windy height where the castle of Denbigh gazes over the wild hills. This is one of the finest sights in the Vale of the Clwyd.

The castle rises 500 feet above the plain on a crag as harsh and definite as Edinburgh Rock. Its high grey walls are lifted to every wind that blows. This was the castle which Queen Elizabeth gave to the Earl of Leicester, who drained the surrounding country of its resources and lined his pockets so well that the Queen had to interfere.

1a. LUDLOW CASTLE.

1b. LLANGOLLEN BRIDGE OVER THE RIVER DEE.

2a. THE RUINS OF DINAS BRAN CASTLE.

2b. CONWAY CASTLE.

Into this grim keep rode Charles I after the battle of Rowton Moor, and it was Denbigh Castle that defied the Parliamentarians for eleven months before it surrendered.

'And if you look down there, please,' said the guide, 'you'll see a little cottage. It stands on the site of a much older cottage where Stanley, the explorer who found Livingstone, was born. He was a poor boy, and his real name was John Rowlands. . . . It's a pity they pulled down the old place, for he was a great man.'

In a few miles I had entered the county of Flintshire.

CHAPTER FOUR

I VISIT THE CATHEDRAL OF ST. ASAPH AND THE CASTLE OF RHUDDLAN, REMEMBER THE LOVE STORY OF LLEWELYN AND ELEANOR, EXPLORE THE WELSH CORNICHE ROAD FROM RHYL TO LLANDUDNO, VISIT A CURSING-WELL, WALK THE RAMPARTS OF CONWAY, AND HEAR THE VOICE OF WALES

§ 1

WHEN the saintly Kentigern, or St. Mungo, was driven from his cell where the City of Glasgow now stands, he crossed the mountains into Wales to seek the protection of the Prince of North Wales.

The founder of Glasgow is always described as a Scotsman : he was a Welshman and his Welsh name was Cynderyn Garthwys. St. Patrick, by the way, was also a Strathclyde Welshman.

St. Mungo was given as a residence Llan Elwy, now St. Asaph, where about the year A.D. 560 he founded an episcopal seat and a monastery. Before he was recalled to Scotland, he nominated as his successor a devout monk called Asa or Asaph, one of his followers. So for over 1,370 years a Christian church has stood where St. Asaph's Cathedral stands to-day. It was burnt down time and again in the Anglo-Welsh wars, but no sooner were the ruins cold than the monks crept back to rebuild their church—except for a period during which it remained a ruin for nearly a hundred years. . . .

I was surprised and amused by the city of St. Asaph. When any one from England thinks of a cathedral city, Canterbury or Winchester rise to the mind's eye : large country places dominated by the immense bulk of a Gothic building, so vast that it is an embarrassment to those who have to restore it, so Catholic in design that the few who huddle near the choir for a Protestant service have the air of refugees. But St. Asaph is unlike any other city in Great Britain : it is really a village ! Giraldus Cambrensis, who sang Mass here in 1128, called the cathedral 'the poor little church of Llan Elwy'. Though I could not call St. Asaph's Cathedral 'poor' there is an endearing smallness about it that brings the phrase of Giraldus to mind. It is, I think, the smallest cathedral in England and Wales, and it has endowed a village of 2,000 souls with the title of ' city '.

I thought the interior dignified but undistinguished. Men were restoring the tower, and the huge canvas sheets which they had hung up prevented an uninterrupted view from the west end to the east window.

' Would you like to see the museum in our Chapter House ? ' asked a polite verger.

He took me into a portion of the south transept, called the Chapter House, where something that looked remarkably like a school museum was displayed in glass cases.

There are several interesting early Welsh books and also copies of the ' Breeches ' and the ' Vinegar ' Bibles. I was surprised recently to discover that a man who was perfectly familiar with these editions could not explain how they got their nicknames. The ' Breeches Bible ', which was published in 1579, gets its title from the passage in Genesis where Adam and Eve discover their nakedness :

' The eyes of them both were opened . . . and they sewed figge-tree leaves together, and made themselves breeches.'

The ' Vinegar Bible ' is much later. It was printed in 1717 and gets its name from the misprint at the head of Chapter 20, St. Luke, where the Parable of the Vineyard is given as the Parable of the Vinegar.

Cathedrals exert a hypnotic influence over those condemned to ' verge ' in them. My friend was intensely interested in everything connected with St. Asaph's, though he was forced to admit that he had seen finer cathedrals in England. But as a Welsh churchman he was justly proud of that day in June, 1920, when Dr. Edwards was enthroned as the first archbishop of the reconstructed Church of Wales.

In front of the cathedral I stopped to examine an ' Eleanor ' Cross about thirty feet high. It has eight figures on it, the principal being that of Bishop Morgan who became Bishop of St. Asaph in 1601, the translator of the Bible into Welsh.

The English traveller in Wales should realize that this monument commemorates one of the outstanding events in Welsh history. When the Reformation took place the Welsh people were given nothing to take the place of Catholicism. They sank into a spiritual coma. In 1585 a writer stated that 'many places in Wales, yea, whole counties, have not a single Christian within them, but live like animals, most of them knowing nothing of righteousness, but merely keeping the name of Christ in memory'.

In 1563 Parliament passed an Act commanding the Welsh bishops to have a complete Welsh Bible ready by 1566. It was not, however, until Bishop Morgan published his version of the Scriptures in Welsh that the Bible took hold of the Welsh imagination. It did for Wales what Luther's Bible did for Germany. It is still regarded as a masterpiece of Welsh prose.

'Bishop Morgan not only gave the Welsh people their Bible,' wrote a Welsh divine, 'but also resuscitated and reformed the ancient language of the Cymry. Under his magic hand what had been a dying patois became a living and literary speech. The Welsh language was by him recreated and standardized. He took it up rough-hewn and crude and out of it fashioned the majestic and sonorous speech which now conveys the Word of God to the Welsh people.'

This great Welshman was the son of a small farmer in one of the glens of Conway.

§ 2

It began to rain with a grim enthusiasm as I left St. Asaph. The road runs through the broadening Vale of Clwyd with the river to the right hand and the green hills of Flintshire receding to the east, the wilder uplands of Denbighshire to the west. Great clouds blown inland from the sea stole slowly over the hills, so that I went on through a landscape that, lacking its highland frame, might have been a slice of easy, comfortable Herefordshire.

Rhuddlan, which I came to in a few miles, is now a village that was once an important seaport. There is nothing to be seen there but the ivy-covered shell of the castle and a house in the High Street, called Old Parliament House, on which is written the following inscription:

> 'This fragment is the remains of the building where King Edward the First held his Parliament, A.D. 1283, in which was passed the Statute of Rhuddlan, securing to the Principality of Wales its judicial rights and independence. The Statute was really a code of laws assimilating the Welsh laws with the laws of England.'

What a bare, bald statement! I wonder if it conveys anything to the thousands of people who see it every year.

When King Edward I returned from the Holy Land in 1274 he was crowned at Westminster in August. It was usual to summon the King of Scotland and the Prince of Wales to do homage at a coronation. King Alexander of Scotland obeyed; Llewelyn of Wales refused.

Edward and Llewelyn were old enemies. Both men were valiant soldiers, clever statesmen, strong-minded and sincere. They might have been admirable friends. But Edward considered Llewelyn to be untrustworthy and Llewelyn considered Edward to be crafty and full of guile.

The King of England again summoned the Prince of Wales to do homage; and a second time the Prince refused, excusing himself on the plea that it would not be safe to visit London. At this moment one of the few women in Welsh history came sailing into the drama.

Llewelyn, when at Kenilworth, had fallen in love with Eleanor, daughter of Simon de Montfort. She was then a child of twelve. After de Montfort's fall, his widow retired with her daughter to a Dominican nunnery in France, but it was arranged that Llewelyn's bride should be sent to him in Wales in the year 1275.

She set sail with her brother, two French knights and two friars. When their vessel was passing the Scilly Isles a Bristol merchantman captured it and took the prize to London. Eleanor found herself in the hands of her cousin, Edward I. The King at once saw her value. He sent a message to Wales that the bride would be allowed to enter that country on one condition—that Llewelyn should come to England for her and perform homage at the same time!

Llewelyn might have been a great figure in romance had he agreed to do this, but he would not perhaps have been so great a statesman. He refused to permit his heart to rule his head. He refused for a third time to bend the knee to the King of England; and Wales and England prepared for war.

In the autumn of 1277 Edward's great army began to close on Wales. Edward in command of one division marched on Rhuddlan from Chester. The Earl of Lincoln marched through Montgomery. The Earl of Hereford moved on

Brecon. A fourth army under Edmund of Lancaster based itself on Carmarthen. Wales was beset on every side and Llewelyn, like so many Welsh patriots, soon discovered that his only safety lay in the fastnesses of Snowdon. As he looked down from the mountains towards the sea he saw that an English fleet cut off his retreat to Ireland. The sailors had landed in Mona, or Anglesey, and had destroyed the standing corn. The islanders had retreated to the mainland. The lowlanders had rushed to Snowdon for safety. As winter was approaching with its threat of famine, there was nothing for the Welsh leader but to capitulate. On November 10th, 1277, he signed a treaty which, after his death six years later, was replaced by the harsh Statute of Rhuddlan.

Edward's policy from the earliest times was to establish the Norman shire system in Wales. This meant the substitution of English law for Welsh law, English administrative systems, English customs, English language.

This was the principle which William the Conqueror employed in England. He found the country divided into great Saxon earldoms. He split them up into 'shires'—a word which means a portion of land 'shorn off' or separated by boundaries from a larger division of land. These smaller and scattered portions of land became the counties of England.

Edward found Wales much as William had found England: the country was divided into enormous tracts of land known as Cantrevs and Commotes. The Statute of Rhuddlan created from the ancient divisions of North Wales the six counties of Flintshire, Caernarvonshire, Anglesey, Merionethshire, Cardiganshire and Carmarthenshire.

So the map of Wales, as we know it to-day, began to form in that distant time. But for two and a half centuries the rest of the country lay under the iron hands of the Lords Marchers, an unhappy territory ruled from about a hundred and forty castles by men who recognized only might and the sword. It was Henry VIII who swept these legalized brigands out of existence and gave to Wales its remaining shires by the Act of Union of 1536.

But what of Llewelyn and his Eleanor?

The Prince of Wales and his chieftains followed the King to London, where they spent a possibly unhappy Christmas. Llewelyn was made to perform homage in a Parliament held at Westminster. The London crowds followed the Welsh chiefs, interested in their strange dress, much as they do to-day when a foreign potentate and his court come to England. The chiefs detested London and were glad to go home.

In the following autumn Llewelyn was married to Eleanor at the door of Worcester Cathedral. Edward of England and Alexander of Scotland were present at the ceremony. It was a magnificent but miserable marriage. Edward sent the Welsh leader home doubly bound, tied in the bonds of matrimony and in those of complete dependence on England. But trouble was not yet over.

'It is well known by all historians and statesmen,' says W. Watkin Davies in *Wales*, 'that a too severe treaty is always the parent of new wars, and the Treaty of Rhuddlan was undoubtedly too severe. The latent discontent which was felt throughout Wales, and especially in the North, was greatly exacerbated by the oppressive administration of the king's Welsh lands by his officials. Justice was denied. Englishmen might murder and steal with impunity so long as their victims were only Welsh. Offices were sold: and extortionate fines were exacted. The old Welsh laws were disregarded, the excuse being that they conflicted with the king's superior sense of justice. So terrible was the oppression, and so impossible was it to obtain redress by constitutional means, that in 1282 revolts broke out in many parts of the country. Llewelyn had scrupulously abstained from giving the least encouragement to any of these revolts; but once they had broken out of their own accord, he perceived how essential it was that they should be directed by one mind, and placed himself at their head.

'This time Edward determined to make an end of his troublesome vassal, and to crush the independent power of the Welsh chieftain once and for all. Llewelyn prepared himself to meet the enormous English army which was marching against him, his mind filled with evil forebodings, and his heart heavy with sorrow at the recent death of his wife.'

The revolt broke out in the year 1282.

Edward gathered a great army. The Archbishop of Canterbury hurried to Wales, against the King's will and 'for love of Wales', as he put it, to threaten Llewelyn with the might of England and the disapproval of Rome. Llewelyn was offered an English estate and a pension. They were indignantly refused.

Then Edward entered Wales again, this time to stamp out nationalism for ever. Llewelyn and his shrunken council strove to meet the hopeless odds. One day, almost at the beginning of the campaign, Llewelyn went into the south to negotiate with his supporters. He went into a wood near Builth, while his bodyguard of eighteen Caernarvonshire men kept watch at a bridge-head. A party of English horse surrounded the wood. The Prince attempted to reach his own men. An English knight named Adam de Francton, who knew only that Llewelyn was a Welshman, ran his spear through his body and passed on. The Prince of Wales lay dying. He had enough strength to ask for a priest. A white friar administered the last rites of the Church.

Later that day de Francton returned to the wood to strip the man he had slain. Llewelyn was still breathing. His enemy learnt, to his joy, that he had slain the Prince of Wales. He waited until the breathing ended, and then, drawing his sword, he struck off Llewelyn's head.

Edward received the head of his foe when he was either at Conway or Rhuddlan. He paraded his army and sent the head mounted on a pike through all his divisions. Then some one remembered an old prophecy of Merlin's: that when English money became round in shape the Prince of Wales should wear his crown in London. The English coins of 1278 had been round. So in a few days' time the Prince of Wales wore his crown in London. The head of Llewelyn, mounted on a pole and crowned with ivy, was borne through London by a horseman. Trumpets and horns were sounded on the way. Then from the highest turret of the Tower of London the head of the last native Prince of Wales—a prince of one of the oldest ruling houses in Europe—rotted in the wind and rain for many a day.

The revolt collapsed. Edward remained in Wales for some years. In his footsteps grew up six shires after the English pattern. English settlers were encouraged to inhabit certain towns established under Royal Charter: Cardigan, Builth, Montgomery, Welshpool, Rhuddlan, Aberystwyth, Caernarvon, Conway, Criccieth, Harlech, Caerwys, Beaumaris and Newburgh. These towns were designed to become centres of English influence and round them, to protect them in time of trouble, grew up Edward's ring of concentric castles : Conway, Beaumaris, Caernarvon, Criccieth and Harlech.

So Edward I returned to London, leaving behind him a new map of North Wales.

§ 3

I met a superior person in the inn at Rhuddlan. He was clothed in waterproof coat and waders. He had an empty fishing-basket, a pocket full of reels and a cap full of trout flies. He was greatly incensed because a favourite fishing-rod which he had foolishly strapped to the running board of his car had fallen off somewhere on the road.

'I only hope that the fellow who finds it appreciates it,' he said, adding bitterly, 'but these locals seem to do better with their home-made rods.'

I gathered that he had endured the humiliation of fishing a lake or a stream with an expensive outfit while the next fellow caught all the fish with a hedge switch.

'There are some fine fishermen among the country lads round Bala,' he explained nobly. 'I'm not bad, but I've seen them pull out fish with a maggot when I've tried every fly in my book. And I consider myself a pretty good fisherman.'

This man seemed to have fished every river and lake in Wales ; in fact, he thought of Wales in terms of trout and salmon. He was scornful about salmon fishing in Scotland, which he described as a 'rich man's folly', and humorous about trout fishing in Ireland, which he called a 'poor man's slaughter'.

'There's no fishing like Welsh fishing,' he said ; 'and it's cheap, too, which is something in these days.'

'Do many English fishermen come to Wales so early ?' I asked.

'I'm not English,' he cried. 'I'm a Welshman ! I live here.'

I have yet to find a fisherman who is insensible to the beauty of mountain and stream, lake and woodland. My friend launched himself into an account of the glories of his country, and he interested me because he was a travelled man and had seen most of the famed beauty spots in Great Britain.

'Even if I were not a Welshman,' he said, 'I think I would put the view from Harlech looking towards Snowdon—on a clear day, mind you—as one of the finest in the world.'

The Welsh, like the Irish, are impulsive and friendly when they like you. One of the charms of the Irish is that they forget you immediately your back is turned. The Welsh also may share this virtue !

The fisherman and I were soon talking like old friends. He was anxious to take me to a lake where the May fly was rising. When I told him that I had to go on to Rhyl along the coast road to Conway, a look of disgust came to his face.

'Rhyl,' he said. 'Why do you want to go to Rhyl ? That coast isn't Wales—it's Lancashire ! It's been vulgarized by Liverpool, Manchester and Birmingham. It exists for them. . . .'

His eloquence was so great that I was nearly persuaded to take the road to Conway through Abergele and over the Denbighshire mountains to Llanrwst ; but, shaking off this superior person, I took the road to Rhyl.

§ 4

I like windy Rhyl. The tide was far out and the gold sands stretched for miles. It is one of the many seaside places in Great Britain which have grown up almost within modern times to satisfy the migratory instincts of great industrial cities. In May it has a lost, bereft appearance as of a place whose inhabitants have deserted it.

I soon found myself on one of the most fascinating and beautiful roads in Great Britain. Here is a Welsh Corniche Road serving a kind of Welsh Riviera. It is a road as beautiful in parts as the Antrim coast road in Ireland, and in parts even more beautiful than the Corniche Road. You have the sea on your right all the way ; on your left the highlands of Denbigh, and ahead of you—calling you on—the giants of Snowdonia.

Along the forty-odd miles of this road between Rhyl and Caernarvon are dotted some of the best-known and best-liked towns in the whole of Wales. This stretch of lovely coast is the playground of the industrial cities of the Midlands and the North. No true Midlander and no true son of Lancashire is entirely ignorant of it. It is a part of Wales designed by Nature and Man to capture the leisure moments of crowds.

Rhyl, Colwyn Bay and Llandudno are, of course, the big favourites on this coast-line, but between them are quiet little places, such as Pensarn, with Abergele and its woody hills at the back, and Llandulas where poor Richard II was betrayed into the hands of Bolingbroke.

It is not difficult to see why Colwyn Bay has become one of the most popular places in North Wales. Gold sands, a great half circle of sea, hills, woods and streams. The semi-circle of hills on the south and west give to this place what doctors call a ' local climate '. Like all these northern watering-places in Wales a large part of their charm and popularity is due to the fact that you can be tucked away in the town, but half an hour's walking takes you to hills and winds from the Atlantic.

I took one of these walks to a little place called Llanelian-yn-Rhos which in times past was one of the most feared names on the map of Wales. At the bottom of a hill is a depression in the earth which is all that is left of the cursing-well of St. Elian. These wells were magic wells common in Wales as recently as fifty years ago, but no other throughout the length and breadth of the Principality was so potent or so feared as that of St. Elian.

The saint was a noble of the sixth century who, becoming thirsty, lay down at this spot and prayed for water. A well burst forth at his feet. He then blessed the well and asked God to grant his wish that all who came to it with faith in their hearts should obtain their desires. It was then merely a wishing-well, one of thousands all over Great Britain. In course of time its character changed. It became a wicked well. Its power to cast spells and curses was so generally credited that several people are said to have died of fright in the belief that their enemies had sought its aid.

' When I was a boy,' said a man who was examining the site of this evil spot, ' we were frightened as children by the threat " mi 'th rof yn Fynnon Elian. . . ." Perhaps you don't know what that means ? It means : " I'll put you in Elian's Well ".'

' Do you know the history of it ? '

' It is well known round here. It was a very profitable well. A woman called Sarah Hughes, who kept it at one time, is said to have made £300 a year from people who came to curse their enemies and—from the cursed ones who paid to have the spells removed ! The most famous well-keeper was a man named John Evans, who died somewhere about 1850 or 1860. He made a good business out of it. The people who believed that they were cursed always paid more than those who did the cursing.

'If a man wanted to curse some one, Evans would write the enemy's name on a piece of paper, put it in a piece of lead and tie it to a slate with the initials of the man who made the curse written on it. This was thrown into the well and the curse recited in a special way. . . . Of course great care was taken to tell the person who had been cursed! He came to pay for its removal! The well-keeper then read out two Psalms to him, made him walk round the well three times and read the Scriptures. He took the curse in its leaden box from the well and gave it to the man who had been cursed. I have heard it said that sometimes whole farms were cursed at Fynnon Elian.'

'What was the end of it all?'

'I think a rector of the parish had the well drained in order to stop his people from trying to cast spells and so on. But long after it was drained the well was feared in Wales. . . .'

'How do you suppose it became an evil well? What changed it from a wishing-well into a cursing-well?'

'I don't know.'

Llandudno is a study in the psychology of success. It is true that there is no finer situation in the whole country for a big holiday town. It has all the virtues of an island. The sweep of its bay is as fine as that of Naples. Llandudno knows its job. It knows exactly what people want.

I wandered about its now fairly vacant frontage and noted the hotels and boarding-houses which are, in the month of May, dreaming of Manchester and Birmingham and Liverpool!

It is difficult, as you look at the graceful sweep of buildings round Llandudno's two bays, to believe that as recently as 1849 there was nothing on this shore but a few fishermen's cottages and two small inns! It was the opening of the railway from Chester to Holyhead that gave Llandudno its chance.

I hope that the thousands of Northerners and Midlanders who go to Llandudno every summer climb up the Great Orme to visit the little church of St. Tudno, from which the town takes its name. A church has stood there since the holy man came in the seventh century to escape from his fellows!

Llandudno shares with all its lucky sister resorts on this coast the combined virtue of sea-coast, country and mountain. A holiday spent in such places is three holidays in one.

§ 5

I am writing on the battlements of Conway Castle. An afternoon sun is falling over one of the most beautiful towns in the British Isles. Conway is exquisite.

No other town in the kingdom lies so snugly within walls which have sheltered it for seven hundred years. York and Chester have outgrown their walls. You walk round them and look down the chimneys of the outer suburbs. The walls of Conway, with their round towers for bowmen, rise up, weather-beaten and grey, exactly as they did when Edward I was swinging his heavy sword through Wales.

I look down from the high towers of the castle upon the estuary of Conway River, where white yachts ride at anchor in the harbour. Inland the blue outlines of the Caernarvonshire Mountains lift themselves against the sky. There is no sound but the cawing of rooks in the desolate towers and a hum of traffic from the bridge below. This bridge, which the great Telford constructed in 1824 when he made the London-Holyhead road, achieves what might have been considered the impossible. A suspension bridge has been made to blend with Conway Castle. It even forms a perfect approach to it. It is one of the best examples I know of good manners in architecture.

There is something, to my mind, very funny about this bridge. The scale of toll charges preserves an incredible sentence from the days of the stage coach. It is this:

> '*For every horse, or beast of draught, drawing any coach, chariot, brougham, clarence, sociable, chaise, Berlin, calash, landau, tandem, phaeton, gig, curricle, barouche, whiskey, buggy, or other carriage—6d.*'

I wonder how many of the Bridge Commissioners could tell the difference between a sociable and a whiskey!

Conway is like an illustration to a history of Wales. These great castles which rise up on hills all over this country are a lasting tribute to the fighting qualities of the Welsh.

Conway, with its fifteen-feet thick curtain walls and its fortified town, must have filled Welsh patriots with despair when they looked down on it from the distant hills. I walk round the walls gazing down into courtyards and roofless halls. I look down into the battered shell of this castle, and I note how the architect employed every cunning dodge of his time to protect the defender and place the attacker at a disadvantage: the arrow-slits, from the outside so narrow, but from the inside commanding so wide an angle of fire; the cleverly-designed doorways so impossible to rush; the spiral stairways which assisted the sword-arm of the man above; the narrow entrances, which would make it easy for ten men to hold a portion of the castle against a hundred.

All the energy and brains which we to-day put into a thousand trades and professions were poured, in old times, into the building of castles and churches.

There was nothing else in the world but War and Faith.

The first tourists of the year roam vaguely on the walls, trying hard to understand Conway's place in history, feeling that, like all old dead things that have influenced the present, it is important but dim and elusive.

They want to see the men and women who fought and suffered, failed or succeeded within these mighty walls; and all they see is something that might once have been a kitchen. . . .

The castle, which took eighteen years to build, was constructed by Edward I in his long and violent war with the last native Prince of Wales—Llewelyn.

But a man who seems to haunt Conway is not the stern builder, Edward, but a sad and hopeless man, Richard II, the Unlucky.

He was a weak and attractive fop, the victim of his defects, out of touch with his time. As a boy he had met a New Age with courage at Smithfield when he rode up to Wat Tyler and the rebels; but he learnt nothing from this encounter. He did not understand the time in which he lived.

After a reign of twenty years he made a futile expedition into Ireland, and during his absence a strong man came to England—Henry Bolingbroke. It was to the Welsh castles, and notably Conway, that Richard came in all the splendour of his extravagance to sleep on mouldy straw and starve.

Bolingbroke, marching with astonishing speed, crossed

England with 60,000 Londoners. In the ruined chapel of Conway Earl Percy swore on the Sacrament that he meditated no treachery when he advised Richard to leave Conway for Flint. He was taken out and handed over to his rival.

'And what do they want?' asked the King, pointing to the army of Londoners.

'They want to take *you*,' replied Bolingbroke, 'and carry you prisoner to the Tower, and there is no pacifying them unless you yield yourself my prisoner.'

The tragedy and humiliation of this journey is described by Froissart. It began with the King, mounted on the most miserable horse that could be found, setting south for London; it ended mysteriously one night in Pontefract Castle.

Richard's dead body was taken to London, where it lay in Cheapside with the face uncovered while 20,000 citizens filed past it. The story went that in a fight with Bolingbroke's assassins, Richard had received a fatal dagger wound in the head. When his body was exhumed in Westminster Abbey in 1871, it was seen that his skull was untouched by either knife or dagger.

So the old castle at Conway stands with its grey feet in the ruthless story of ambition which is history. . . .

I went out into the lovely little town. In the church I found a remarkable gravestone, that of a man called 'Hookes of Conway. Gent.' He died in 1639. This stated that Hookes was the forty-first child of William Hookes, and that he himself had been the father of twenty-seven children!

This is surely one of the most remarkable boasts in the country.

§ 6

Perhaps the most startling change of scenery in North Wales is the Sychant Pass that connects Conway with Penmaenmawr. In the twinkling of an eye you leave the friendly scenery of a river estuary and find yourself plunged into a miniature mountain gorge as grim in its way as anything in Scotland. It might be a little model of Glencoe.

The hills are strewn with great boulders which look as though a careless foot might send them crashing down on the narrow mountain road. The dark hills rise on either side and the wind comes through the Sychant Pass with that chill whistle which mountaineers know so well.

Then, almost as suddenly as it began, the pass ends, and you find yourself running into pretty Penmaenmawr, where people are playing golf and where at least one mansion guards the memory of Gladstone. . . .

What a road this is! I do not think it can be beaten for variety in the length and breadth of the kingdom.

§ 7

When you are passing Welsh schools you will often hear a magnificent burst of song. The choirs, sometimes girls' voices and sometimes boys', nearly lift the roofs from these buildings. I determined that next time I heard a school choir at work I would go in and see what was happening.

I entered a large school in Caernarvonshire and saw the headmaster.

'I suppose all these singing schools are practising for the Eisteddfod at Bangor?'

'Yes, indeed, and we have a wonderful girls' choir here. Would you like to hear it?'

'I'll come back if you will tell me when they are practising.'

'Oh, not at all. I will make them sing for you now! I must go and find the choir-master, Mr. Jones.'

He dashed excitedly from the room before I could stop him. This instant willingness to take any amount of trouble to satisfy a stranger's interest in anything Welsh is characteristic of the people. He was genuinely delighted that I, a casual wanderer, should wish to hear his school in full song.

After a time I heard the sound of many feet on stone stairways and the excited treble of many voices. The headmaster returned.

'We are ready.'

He took me to a large schoolroom. About forty little girls between the ages of twelve and fifteen sat at fumed oak desks. There was a raised platform at one end of the room, facing the girls, on which were several chairs and a piano. On the window-sills were glass jars full of bluebells. Above the platform was a life-size photograph of Mr. Lloyd George.

I was given a seat on the platform, where I thought, for the first time in my life, what an astonishing sight are forty small girls. They gazed at me with the frank curiosity of animals. Some of the girls thought I was funny and whispered something to the girl at the next desk, some of them gazed at me with embarrassing interest, some looked at me with the dull, glazed expression which I suppose is reserved for school inspectors and some looked at me brightly and expectantly as if I was the performer. I looked at them and thought how revealing is physiognomy. When you have forty small girls facing you it is possible not only to read character but to see the parents behind the children. Each face was stamped definitely with inherited characteristics. It was uncanny to realize as one looked at these long-legged, inky-fingered, spotty or peach-faced, funny little faun-like creatures that in another eight years some of them would be the wives and mothers of Wales. It was rather terrifying, like watching the manufacture of explosives.

The music-master, a dark young man who needed a hair-cut, gave out pieces of music, and when this was done the headmaster rose and made an astonishing statement.

'Girls,' he said, 'we have with us to-day a g-r-e-a-t musician who has come all the way from London to hear you sing.'

I writhed uncomfortably under the lie, for I know nothing about music.

'He has heard all apout you,' went on the headmaster, 'and he will be going back to London to tell all the people there apout you and your singing, so I hope you will sing well. . . .'

He gazed earnestly at me.

'He has paid us a g-r-e-a-t compliment by coming here to-day to hear you sing, and I want him to go back to London and say that he has heard the pest girls' choir in all Wales.'

He sat down next to me. I expected him to apologize for calling me a great musician, or at least to pass it off with a jest; but no, he did not refer to it. I began to wonder if I had said anything to give him the idea that I was a musician. It then occurred to me that he was not so much a liar as a dramatist. It was his artistic temperament coming out. Perhaps he has sometimes wished that Sir Edward Elgar or Chaliapine would drop in casually, as I had done, and pat him on the back about the choir. He was too imaginative, and had too great a sense of the dramatic, to pass me off as an ordinary visitor. I think the music-master believed the story, because I saw his cadaverous face gazing at me over the piano with marked respect.

'Now—one, two, three . . .' said the music-master, striking a chord.

The girls rose, holding their music-sheets, they opened their mouths and they let loose in that room a burst of enthusiastic sweetness such as I have never before heard. I had come out of curiosity and I was prepared to be bored, but in ten minutes those Welsh children fascinated me. Every one knows that the Welsh genius is the gift of song, and I was hearing it from the throats of small children. You cannot pretend to sing. You must mean it. And these children not only meant it but loved it. There was a sort of exaltation about it. They sang various songs in Welsh and then a queer, dramatic, sad song that attracted me.

'What is it about ?' I asked the master.

'It is about an accident to a slate quarryman. He is injured while they are blasting the slate and they carry him home on a stretcher.'

'Will you ask them to sing it again ?'

The commonplace theme became Homeric as these children sang it; their voices suddenly fell to a whisper and died into silence. It was as if the song mourned something old and unhappy on the Plain of Troy.

The choir then broke into a tune which I felt was a kind of Welsh 'Marseillaise'. It was a terrific march. It was savage. It sounded like the voice of old Wales defying Saxon, Norman and English. I began to feel like the enemy. It was like centuries of pride interpreted in sound.

'That,' I was told, 'is "Cymru'n Un" . . . "Wales United".'

I thought so. Why have the English no stirring songs like the 'Marseillaise' and 'Cymru'n Un' and 'Scots wha hae'? Our 'Rule Britannia' is just blatant and vulgar, and Elgar's 'Pomp and Circumstance' is merely a march with no national emotion behind it. I suppose a nation has to be defeated quite a lot before it can compose good national songs.

Another fine march was 'Captain Morgan's March', the words by Mr. Lloyd George. Then the girls, with the greatest ease, changed their language and sang in English. They sang two or three lovely Elizabethan madrigals. They sang them beautifully but a trifle sadly, I thought. It was Merrie England in a faint mist.

When the concert was over I looked at the children with respect and wonder. The ‘ great musician ’ was asked to say a few words, which he did with deep sincerity.

I went out with the knowledge that in an ordinary little schoolroom, presided over by Mr. Lloyd George and a few bluebells, I had heard the old romantic and darkly passionate voice of Britain.

CHAPTER FIVE

TELLS HOW I WENT TO BANGOR, ADMIRED A UNIVERSITY, HEARD A PAGAN DANCE ON THE HARP, SAW BARDS AND DRUIDS AT THE GORSEDD STONE, ATTENDED THE EISTEDDFOD, AND WAS PRESENT WHEN WALES CROWNED A POET

§ 1

BANGOR with an early morning sun over it is one of the freshest and most stimulating cities you can imagine. The term ' city ' is misleading because it is smaller than most English country towns. In fact, some writers, forgetting that it is a bishop's see, refer to it as ' a busy little town '.

Salt winds from the Menai Straits blow through its streets and behind it rise the blue mountains, fold on fold. Were I a Welshman I would rather be educated at Bangor within reach of Mona and Snowdon than anywhere on earth. In an age when men do almost inconceivably stupid things one cannot resist a feeling of gratitude towards those Welshmen of Victoria's day who chose Bangor from thirteen other Welsh towns and cities as a seat of education.

The Englishman in Wales is surprised and rather ashamed to learn that although the idea of a Welsh University was one of Owen Glendower's dreams in the Middle Ages (his letters about it are preserved in the French archives in Paris), the Welsh people had to wait five centuries before a Parliament sitting at Westminster established the University of Wales in the year 1893! Scotland had St. Andrew's University in the Middle Ages; Ireland had Trinity College in the time of Elizabeth; but Wales had to fight for higher education, and the story of that fight is, to my mind, one of the most heroic chapters in Welsh history.

I have often heard strangers make fun of the chapel-going Welsh and of the Welsh Sabbath, which is as the Scottish Sabbath was fifty years ago. But they seem to forget that these grim-looking buildings with queer Hebrew names like

'Ebenezer' and 'Horeb' carved above their portals have played the dominating part in the development—religious, political, artistic, educational—of the Welsh nation. Hideous they may be to the eyes of the tourist, but sacred they must always be to the Welshman who loves his nation.

And when the Welsh people, lifted by the chapel from the incredible spiritual squalor into which they were allowed to sink after the Reformation, demanded knowledge for their sons and daughters, it was from house to house and from chapel to chapel throughout the country that the collectors went, literally for pennies, to build a University. In London a handful of great Welshmen, forgotten by all except those of Welsh blood, fought for the scheme while the Welsh middle classes and the small farmers and the miners of the south gave so generously out of their humble means that in time the amazing sum of £60,000 had been found by a poor country.

The first college was established at Aberystwyth in 1872. How could it fail? It had been built by the self-sacrifice and faith of a nation. In 1883 another college for the south was opened at Cardiff and in the following year Bangor College was opened in an old hotel building. Still there was no charter of incorporation. There was no Treasury grant. None of the colleges was permitted to confer degrees. And it was not until 1893, after prolonged discussion and opposition from both Houses of Parliament, that the three colleges received their charter and were incorporated as the University of Wales. Since that time a fourth college—at Swansea—has been founded.

So in the morning I went down the hill and looked at the opposite hill on whose ridge Bangor College rises so proudly. The college soon deserted the old hotel. This cold but stately building was opened by the King in 1911 after the Investiture of the Prince of Wales in Caernarvon Castle.

It is strange that the English, who are reputed to admire a good fighter more than they admire most things, should never have paid adequate tribute to the pugnacity of the Welsh. The ancient Britons who inhabit these mountains have been fighting since Caesar's invasion: they have fought Roman, Saxon, Norman, English. When they were not fighting against the English they were fighting with them. The Welsh archers won the battle of Crecy. And in later times the

Welsh have fought for their religion, their language, their literature and their education.

Bangor College on its hill is a sign of victory.

§ 2

I was writing in the neat but uninspiring bedroom of a Bangor hotel when I heard quite near an unusually sweet sound of strings. Some one was playing an instrument a room or two away. At first I thought it was a harpsichord. When I opened the door to hear better, I knew that it was a sweeter, less mechanical sound. It was, of course, a Welsh harp.

On the landing I could hear quite well. The man or the woman who was playing was an artist. The air, which was played over and over again, was a queer plaintive thing like something sad and irrevocable that had happened long ago on a mountain-top or beside a waterfall. I have heard Arabs singing in the desert at night ; I have heard the queer little tunes that boys play on flutes beside the Nile when the moon is full, and I have heard the Gaelic songs that end in mid-air, like a bird that has rested for a moment in the beauty of its flight and then vanished, which men sing in the Hebrides. And the harp music had in it something of all this sadness combined with something that I felt was as old as the hills. It was an air that might have been played in a mistletoe grove.

The tune ended. The door opened and a young man came out. I asked him the name of the tune. He said something in Welsh which I did not understand. Fingers were swept over the harp-strings again as if uncertain what to play, and I knew that this young man was not the harpist as at first I thought him to be.

'Who is the player ?' I asked.

'My wife,' he said. 'She is playing in a choir of harps at the Eisteddfod and is practising. . . .'

Now it is not an easy thing to invite yourself into the room where a man's wife is practising for an Eisteddfod. But it can be done.

The Welsh, like all artistic people, respond to praise and, again like all artistic people, they enjoy an audience. I told him that I had never heard a Welsh harp before. He dashed me by telling me that it was an old French pedal harp.

I said that his wife had a most sympathetic and beautiful touch. He appeared pleased that I should think so. Then from inside the room, pricked out gently on the magic strings, came a tune I knew—the ' Bells of Aberdovey '. While we were talking about this melody the young man suddenly asked me to go in and listen.

I saw a young woman crouched in a bardic attitude beside a great gold harp. Her fingers moved in a determined yet leisurely way over the strings as she plucked the melody from them. It had never occurred to me before that the harp is the only musical instrument which does not offend the sight or make the player seem vaguely ridiculous. I might perhaps exclude the syrinx, or pipes of Pan, but this, of course, should be played in a state of nudity.

The players of all wind instruments look frankly comic. The trombonist is the comedian of a band, as is the man who plays the piccolo of an orchestra. Even the violinist is not a pretty sight as he sways with a little box of varnished wood tucked against his chin. And the contrast between the emotion which he creates and the means by which he creates it—the rubbing of horsehair over catgut—suggests to the sensitive that he should be invisible. The pianist is an acceptable sight merely from force of habit. We even enjoy the movement of a player's hands over the keys, but we have become so used to the piano as an article of domestic furniture that we never think of it as an exceedingly ugly and complicated affair with some resemblance to a coffin.

As I looked at Mrs. Jones—as we will, naturally, call her—plucking the harp-strings, I realized, with a sense of discovery, that the harp is the only dignified instrument and the only instrument that dignifies the player. Even a bad harpist, I reflected, must rouse admiration as he or she adopts an attitude as graceful to-day as it was in Ancient Egypt.

She rose from the harp and rubbed her hands together, saying that her fingers were cold and stiff. A spell was at once broken. She was just Mrs. Jones of Somewhere with a baby and a husband and a tiresome house to look after. She sat down again, spread out her hands, crooked her fingers and gently moved the harp-strings. Instantly, so it seemed to me, she became important. She became dramatic. It was as though the dignity of old things had shed grace upon her like a garment. Homer might have been standing beside her ready to chant the Iliad.

'Did you like that?' she asked.

'What do you call it?'

'"The Gentle Dove".'

She plucked a few chords and said:

'I will play you a very old Welsh dance.'

Her fingers moved quickly at the strings and out leapt a melody that brought me bolt upright in my chair. It was a mad and lovely tune. There were girls and boys in it and kisses, winking of eyes and tripping of feet, and, at the back of it all, was a gravity as if hill streams were joining in while the great blue mountains of Wales looked on.

And as I listened I knew that it came to me from a naughty pre-Nonconformist Wales. The man who wrote it and the people who danced to it had never seen a silk hat or a minister or a prayer meeting. It was Rabbie Burns in Welsh and set to music. It was a happy, pagan tune.

'How old is it?'

'Oh, I don't know,' she said, 'but very old.'

'What's the name of it?'

'"Eurwy'r Dyffryn"—"Golden Stream of the Valley".'

I was going to ask her to play it again and again but there was a horrid bump on the door, the sound of a woman's voice saying, 'Oh, do be careful,' and in staggered the hotel boots bearing another harp. . . .

I went back to my room and tried to write: but it was no good. The 'Golden Stream of the Valley' went dancing through my head. And I was astonished to think that in the old days there must have been Welsh nymphs and fauns. How otherwise could Wales have invented a tune to which Bacchus and Pan might have danced hand in hand?

§ 3

It is the morning of the Eisteddfod. Bangor is full of people. Every hotel is full. A stranger is vaguely conscious that he is moving about among celebrities. They look to him normal people, slightly formal, perhaps, in black morning-coats, but in no way to be distinguished in appearance from those who attend a large funeral. But now and then the hotel porter will whisper unhelpfully to the stranger:

'That's Pengoed, sir.'

And the stranger will look round the hotel lounge until he discovers an elderly clergyman sipping tea in a corner:

'Pengoed?' says the stranger. 'What do you mean?'

It seems impossible that such a solemn-looking cleric can be referred to so familiarly by an hotel servant. Why not 'Mr.' Pengoed or 'the Rev.' Pengoed. But plain Pengoed! Imagine an attendant in the House of Lords attracting a stranger's attention with:

'There's Canterbury!'

Eventually the stranger begins to realize that all these grave or vivacious Welshmen in dark clothes are either druids or bards.

The druids and the bards who are elected at each Eisteddfod are given druidic or bardic names by which they are ever afterwards known in druidic or bardic circles.

I have mentioned that the stranger is often able to identify the leading druids and bards with the help of an hotel servant. This is, I think, significant. It proves that a deep and intelligent interest in the Eisteddfod runs right through the social scale in Wales. Can you imagine an English hotel porter feeling the slightest interest in the Poet Laureate? He would certainly be more interested in Mr. Selfridge than in Mr. Masefield.

But the Welsh people, from the humblest to the highest, have an abiding passion for music and poetry, which makes the annual Eisteddfod perhaps the most nationally significant ceremony in the world. I do not know of any other event in a European country which brings together once every year on a basis of complete equality and competitive rivalry the most intellectual and the illiterate, the rich and poor, the university professor and the agricultural labourer, the divine and the coal-miner.

This meeting of a nation on a purely mental and artistic occasion is surely an outstanding characteristic of life in Wales. Amateurism in sport is one of England's treasured characteristics; amateurism in art is that of Wales. For twelve months thousands of Welsh people practise at the musical and poetic tasks which each Eisteddfod sets for the following year. There is not a city, town or village in the Principality which is unaffected. That is why the National Eisteddfod is such a grave, dignified and important thing. If it were merely a fashionable occasion, or if it were kept alive by the wealthy classes, it would become as unreal and unrepresentative as the Highland Games of Scotland.

But the Eisteddfod is the Voice of Wales.

§ 4

What is the history of the Eisteddfod? No one can attend this festival of song and poetry without wondering how it began.

The Celt has always loved song and music. Before Caesar landed in Britain a king of the second century before Christ was renowned as 'the King of Harmony'. Diodorus Siculus, who wrote about 45 B.C., says: 'Britons have poets, who, by their musical instruments, resembling lyres, chant forth the praises and censures of others.'

This instrument was, of course, the Welsh harp. The Welsh, unlike their cousins the Irish and the Highland Scot, have never enjoyed the bagpipe. A king of Wales, Gruffydd ab Cynan, who was contemporary with William the Conqueror, secured a brief place for the bagpipe in Wales, perhaps because of his Irish training, but it was never generally popular. The feeling of the ancient Welsh bards for the pipe was perfectly expressed in a satirical poem by Lewys Glyn Cothi which has been Englished by Mrs. Llewellyn. The poet describes how on a Sunday morning in Flint he attended an English wedding to sing his Welsh songs to the harp. But the gathering gave him what is known in theatrical circles as 'the bird'. Then Lewys sings bitterly:

Alas that through my cherished art
Boors should distress and wound my heart.

But at the wedding was a piper called William Beisir; and the harpist goes on to say:

For William Beisir's bag they bawl,
'Largess for him!' they loudly squall;
Each roared with throat at widest stretch
For Will the Piper—low-born wretch!
Will forward steps as best he can,
Unlike a free, ennobled man:
A pliant bag 'tween arm and chest,
While limping on, he tightly prest.

He stares—he strives the bag to sound ;
He swells his maw, and ogles round ;
He twists and turns himself about,
With fetid breath his cheeks swell out.
What savage boors ! His hideous claws
And glutton's skin win their applause !
With shuffling hand and clumsy mien
To doff his cloak he next is seen.
He snorted ; bridled in his face,
And bent it down with much grimace ;
Like to a kite he seemed that day—
A kite, when feathering of his prey !
The churl did blow a grating shriek.
The bag did swell, and harshly squeak,
As does a goose from nightmare crying,
Or dog, crushed by a chest, when dying:
This whistling box's changeless note
Is forced from turgid veins and throat ;
Its sound is like a crane's harsh moan,
Or like a gosling's latest groan ;
Just such a noise a wounded goat
Sends from her hoarse and gurgling throat.
His unattractive screeching lay
Being ended, William sought for pay ;
Some fees he had from this mean band,
But largess from no noble hand ;
Some pence were offered by a few,
Others gave little halfpence, too.
Unheeded by this shabby band,
I left their feast with empty hand.
A dire mischance I wish indeed
On slavish Flint and its mean breed ;
Oh ! may its furnace be the place
Which they and Piper Will may grace !
For their ill luck my prayer be told,
My curses on them, young and old !
I ne'er again will venture there ;
May death all further visits spare !

In Ireland and in Wales the bards formed a privileged class. They wandered, singing their songs, from chieftain to chieftain. In Wales they created public opinion as they sang their way round the country, much as the popular Press does to-day. In most of the rebellions against English rule—notably that of Owen Glendower—they played their part and revived ancient and stirring prophecies.

Every Welsh chief kept a family bard and, wrote Professor Rhys in *The Welsh People,* the custom had not in his time died out among the noble families of Wales.

Domestic harpers, he stated, were still kept in the Bute and

Londonderry families, while the late Lady Lanover (who died in 1896) always maintained quite a group of harpers in connexion with her house.

In addition to such stationary bards the country was full of minstrels who wandered from town to town, and there seems also to have been a recognized system whereby well-known bards toured the country much as a famous actor will undertake a provincial tour in our own times.

It is not unnatural that in a country where minstrelsy was like daily bread a national competition should have been organized. The Eisteddfod, which means 'a sitting' or 'session', is undoubtedly a very ancient ceremony, although no one seems to know when it was first held.

There are one or two records of princely feasts in Norman times when minstrels and bards were summoned from all parts of Wales to try their skill, but the first authentic Eisteddfodau seem to have been held at Caerwys in 1100 and at Cardigan in 1176, when the prizes were two chairs or thrones, one for the best poet and the other for the best performer on the harp, violin or flute. This custom of 'chairing the bard', or enthroning him, is still observed at the Eisteddfod. It is a custom which evidently goes back into the most remote antiquity—and incidentally suggests that the Eisteddfod is the oldest ceremony of its kind in the world—because rules for chairing a bard are set down in the Laws of Howel, the Welsh chieftain who lived about A.D. 940.

'From the person who shall conquer when there is a contention for a chair,' runs the rule, 'he (the judge of the competition) is to have a buglehorn and a gold ring, and the pillow placed under him in his chair.'

The early Eisteddfods seem to have been a regularly constituted court, a kind of artistic tournament, which any poet or musician might attend. It was advertised a year before not only in Wales but also in England, Scotland and Ireland. It had the practical purpose of setting a high standard in verse and music, and it had the authority, so to speak, of licensing bards to pursue their calling as professionals and to tour the country, billeting themselves on the nobility and gentry. This supervision was no doubt very necessary. In a nation which contained so much poetic and musical fervour there must have been an enormous mass of bad verse and worse music!

One of the most historic Eisteddfodau was that held at Carmarthen in 1451 by permission of Henry VI. At this gathering a poet called Dafydd ap Edmwnt, a native of Hanmer in North Wales, succeeded in imposing upon the bards two dozen complex and artificial metres. These metres have shackled the thoughts and style of many generations of Welsh poets. Even to this day the Chair poem at the Eisteddfod must conform to the tyranny of this dead and gone Flintshire bard.

It must be in the 'strict metres' imposed four hundred and eighty-one years ago, but the Crown Poem can be in any metre, even in *vers libre*.

We lose sight of the Eisteddfod, save for an occasional glimpse here and there, for several centuries. Welsh song is replaced by Welsh battle-cries; the harp by the long bow. With the coming to power of the Welsh Tudors, interest in the Eisteddfod again revived; but no longer was it a Golden Age of Welsh poetry; the art had declined and the bards were, apparently, quite out of hand! Read a sentence from Queen Elizabeth's commission for the holding of an Eisteddfod at Caerwys in 1568:

'Whereas it has come to the knowledge of the Lord President and other of the said Council in the Marches of Wales,' it runs, 'that vagrant and idle persons calling themselves minstrels, rhymers and bards are lately grown into such an intolerable multitude within the Principality of North Wales, that not only gentlemen and others by their shameless disorders are oftentimes disquieted in their habitations.'

The commission then goes on to order the calling of an Eisteddfod for the purpose of weeding out all the worthless bards, rhymers and minstrels.

This was evidently done, but in succeeding centuries the Eisteddfod became a casual and sporadic affair. It was not until the middle of the nineteenth century that the leading Welshmen of that time decided to revive it. They formed the National Eisteddfod Association. The meeting is held alternately in North and South Wales. Various local Eisteddfods are held during the year all over Wales. The successful competitors from these attend the National Eisteddfod. So every year the rank and file of the Welsh nation take part in an artistic parliament that links them with a remote past.

§ 5

It is early in the morning on the day of the opening of the Eisteddfod. I am told that I must rise before breakfast to see the ceremony of the Gorsedd. I have already noticed the druidic circle of stones which officials of the Eisteddfod have planted in a meadow near the road on the slope below the University. When I first saw them I thought that they were as old as Stonehenge!

I dress swiftly and am glad to see that the morning is, although misty, fine. On the hotel landing I collide with some one who appears to be either a female druid or bard. She is swathed in green draperies. She is not quite my idea of an ancient Briton because she wears pince-nez. I did not know that women are admitted to the sacred circle, which I always imagined to be one of the last strongholds of the male. I wonder, as some stray memory of a school primer comes to me, whether she is, perhaps, after all, a burnt offering. Possibly the druids are to place her in a wicker basket and sacrifice her to the Eisteddfod.

I discover in the hall downstairs a number of bards, druids and druidesses. I am told that these green-robed women are novates. The druids are elderly or middle-aged men robed in white. They are distinguished by a benevolence which rules out all theories of human sacrifice. The bards are robed in blue. They are younger than the druids. I am slightly worried by the trousers of bard and druid, which are visible for a few inches below their gowns. Father Christmas has this same trouble with his trousers.

I leave them as they chat together and go through the early morning streets of Bangor, which are already awake and excited.

The stone circle rises from the grass, surrounded by a large crowd. The entrance faces the east. In the centre of the circle is a large altar stone. The waiting moments are enlivened by the expert activities of those young men with a motor-car who broadcast ceremonies to the British Isles. They are just attending to their wires, speaking down telephones to distant colleagues and generally making certain that nothing will go wrong. The wireless van and the druidic circle are an amusing contrast. But something even funnier is to happen. A young man in plus-fours enters the circle, bearing in his hand what appears to be an offering for the high altar. It is a bunch of green leaves. He places it reverently before the altar stone, stands back from it and starts to address it. He might be intoning a prayer, but I know that he is speaking into a microphone which is carefully concealed among the leaves. What a touching tribute from the British Broadcasting Corporation to the age when druids walked the earth.

All is now ready. . . .

Soon we see the approaching procession. Men in scarlet gowns bear a litter on which is borne, like the Ark of the Covenant, the enormous Hirlas Horn, or the Horn of Plenty, which is normally to be seen in the National Museum at Cardiff. Behind, two by two, walk the druids in white, the bards in blue and the novates in green. They pause before they enter the circle and form a lane. Between the ranks strides a man in green bearing a great double-handed sword. Behind him comes the Chief Druid. He wears white robes and on his chest lies a replica of the Irish breastplate which Camden illustrated in his *Brittania*.

As the Chief Druid takes his place at the high altar, the attendant druids, bards and novates file in and group themselves round the circle. Now and again the irreverent wind blows aside the robes to reveal trousers of serge and tweed and pin-stripe. It is, alas, unfortunate. I spot one bard who has foreseen this. He alone of the priesthood wears white stockings and sandals. I, greatly daring, tap a druid on the shoulder and ask the name of this bard. He turns and, in the most friendly manner, informs me that the sandalled one is a bard named Cynan. He then adds for my better information :

'The Rev. A. E. Jones, you know. . . .'

I conclude that many of the priesthood are Welsh clergymen who are playing at being pagan for a day. But a glance at their trousers reassures me that it is all very respectable !

The ceremony of the Gorsedd begins. The great sword is

unsheathed. One by one the druids advance and place their hands on it. The Chief Druid lifts up his voice and cries in Welsh:

'Is there peace?'

He cries this three times. Three times comes a reassuring shout from the crowd:

'There is peace!'

A lady of beauty, who is not a green novate but a red lady who evidently represents the aristocratic laity, advances over uneven grass bearing the huge Horn of Plenty. She kneels before the Chief Druid and offers the relic to him. I expect him to drink from it, or in some way prove its plentifulness, but, as the horn is empty, he merely touches it symbolically and the lady bows and backs gracefully away with her burden.

The Chief Druid, mounted on the altar stone, then delivers a long speech in Welsh. I cannot understand one word of it. But I can tell that it is a good and well-prepared piece of oratory. The crowd love it. The words come rushing out like a stream in flood.

He is followed by other speakers. Some appear to be making epigrams at which the crowd laughs. There are prayers in Welsh. I imagine that the old gods of the Celtic peoples are stirring uneasily in their dim Valhalla. Then one by one, the newly-elected bards are led to the altar stone. These are young men and women singled out during the past year for some work of poetry, music or prose.

The Chief Druid shakes each one by the hand, calls them by their modern names and gives to each one a bardic name by which he, or she, will be for ever after known in the Gorsedd.

The ceremony is over. The procession re-forms. Druid, Bard and Novate go their solemn way. The great Gorsedd Sword moves slowly above the heads of the crowd. The Horn of Plenty shines a moment in a burst of early sun. The Eisteddfod is opened. . . .

A young man in plus-fours enters the sacred circle and steals out again carrying a bunch of leaves in which is hidden a microphone!

3a. AN OLD TIMBERED HOUSE, RUTHIN.

3b. RUTHIN CASTLE.

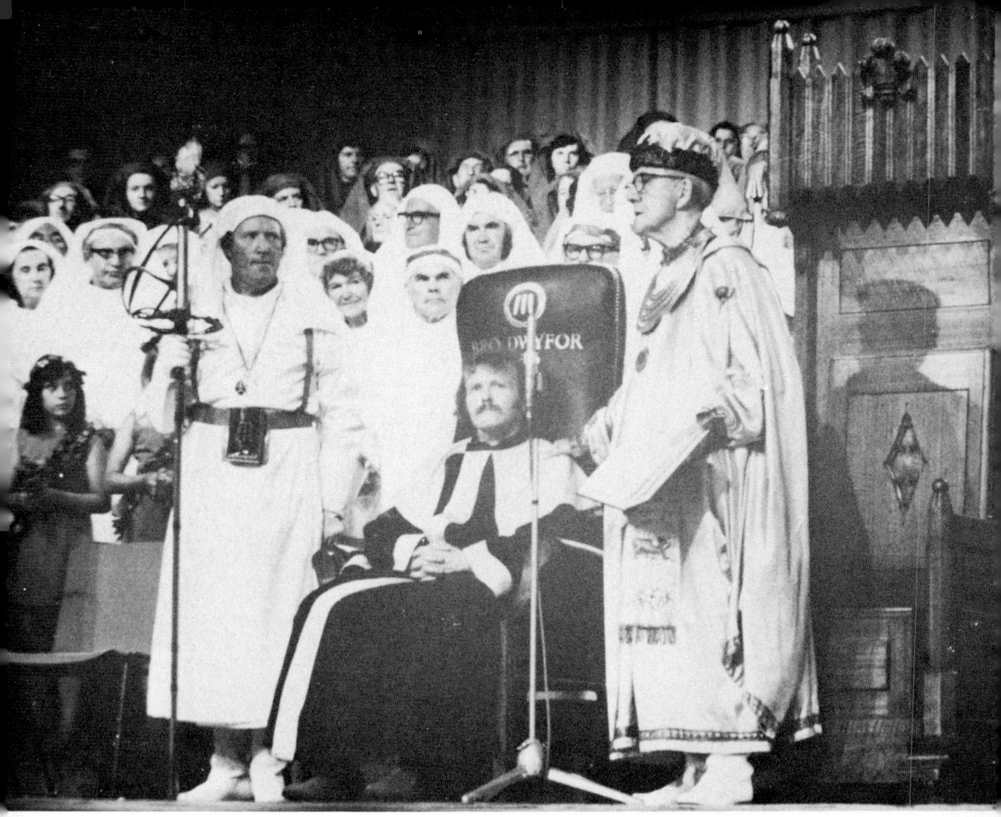

4a. THE NATIONAL EISTEDDFOD.

4b. BEAUMARIS CASTLE.

§ 6

An enormous wooden pavilion has been erected on the edge of the Menai Straits. Men boast that it holds ten thousand people, which is also said to be the capacity of the Albert Hall in London.

It has been built on grassland that slopes gently to a little harbour, and opposite, not more than half a mile distant, is the greenness of the Isle of Anglesey. Thus the druids and bards of the Eisteddfod hold their meeting in a part of Wales which is for ever sacred to the Celtic priesthood. It was over there in the little island once named Mona that the druids made their stand against the Roman; it was from these gentle shores that the great soldier, Suetonius Paulinus, turned the legions when news was brought to him that Boadicea was marching on London. . . .

I find the turnstiles besieged by an enormous crowd. Men, women and children from every part of Wales are present; so also are thousands of tourists. I hear Welsh spoken, I hear 'Lancashire' spoken, I hear 'Brummagem' spoken; but the Welsh leads.

The long grass is dotted with thousands of reclining figures. The pavilion rises up like some barn that has been enormously magnified. From within comes the sound of a brass band.

I sit down on the grass and study the people round me. Even my alien eyes tell me that I am at a gathering which represents North and South Wales. Every conceivable type of Welshman and Welshwoman is present. There are people from farms and factories; there are people from mansions and cottages; there are school choirs from cities and from villages and there are brass bands from the mining valleys of the south.

The National Eisteddfod is, I think, one of the most interesting ceremonies I have ever attended. I have seen kings crowned and I have seen them buried. I have seen nations in mourning and in times of popular rejoicing. I have seen crowds as big as this Welsh crowd whipped up into a dervish frenzy about sport; but never have I seen a crowd which represents all the lights and shades of an entire nation gathered together to sing, to play musical instruments and to recite verse.

A man in a neat and obviously Sabbatarian serge suit, who

lies next to me on the grass, asks me for a match to light his pipe. We fall into conversation. I put him down as a miner; and I am right. He tells me that he plays a cornet in a 'silver band'. He has come all the way from some dark valley in the south to help his town band to gain a laurel crown. He is voluble and intelligent, like all the Welsh, and he tells me how bad times are in the coal-fields and how expensive it is to attend an Eisteddfod in the north.

The brass band inside the tabernacle concludes its effort with a terrific crash; the doors are flung wide and I go inside and take a seat. The pavilion is full. Thousands of faces in hundreds of rows rise gently to the back of the immense building. There is a huge stage, rather bare in spite of the ferns and flowers that attempt to humanize it.

After a slight interval, about twenty men grasping band instruments stroll casually on the stage, place music on stands and prepare to lift the roof from the pavilion. They are obviously nervous. They have been practising a march tune for twelve months. Now the moment has arrived to deliver it to the musical Parliament of Wales. No wonder they are rather pale, shuffle a bit and blow apprehensively down the mouthpieces of cornets and trombones.

But where is the judge? He is nowhere to be seen! The Eisteddfod novice cannot but be amused by the elaborate precautions which are taken to ensure that there shall be no favouritism in the judging of brass bands. One of the first requirements is that the judge shall not be aware of the identity of the band to which he is listening. He is therefore hidden from sight in a green sentry-box. As soon as he is concealed, the bands draw lots for the order of their appearance. A shrill whistle from the hidden judge calls them on the stage one after the other. They all play the same competition march.

Watch a colliery band when the judge blows his whistle! The conductor lifts his baton, collects his men with his eyes, brings down his baton and there is an instantaneous crash of brass. An English Cup Final team could not be more grimly bent on victory than a colliery band at the Eisteddfod. The set of shoulders, the backs of necks, the nervous glances over music-stands all proclaim the fact that these men are playing for the honour of their town. The ears of their townsmen have been listening to them for a year. Every one in the town knows the tune by heart. This day, however, the eyes of the town are on them! There will be a stampede for the evening papers. It is a grim and fearful sight!

Woe betide the nervous trombonist who stutters midway in a note! Sheer undiluted hatred is written plainly on the faces of his fellow-bandsmen. As they continue to play with puffed cheeks, their eyes rove maliciously towards the malefactor, saying as clearly as possible:

'Just wait till we get you outside, indeed. . . .'

And, after all, how human it is! How terrible to think of a year's hard work being wrecked on one false note!

Band after band plays the same tune. I become frightfully bored with the tune but increasingly interested in the psychology of the various bands. I am more interested in the way they behave than in the way they play. Some have the superiority complex engendered by old victories; others have an inferiority complex due to an exaggerated respect for their opponents; and some are animated by a fearful ambition to snatch the laurels at any cost.

The bands go. Their place is taken by a series of young violinists from all parts of the Principality, girls and boys. They are followed by children under eighteen who sing to the harp. This is called Penillion singing, and it fascinates and enchants me.

The harpist plays the air while the vocalist sings the accompaniment; in other words, the technique of modern singing is reversed. It is a difficult art and the children, who excel in counterpoint, prove what an extraordinary part music plays in the ordinary homes of Wales. I felt again, as I felt when Mrs. Jones was playing airs on the harp, that I was listening to something old and dignified from the beginning of the world. . . .

The competitions continue all morning. Crowds continually leave and enter the great pavilion. Thousands lie on the grass awaiting their turn to perform. From distant places sound the tooting of cornets, the notes of a piano, the plucking of harp-strings as competitors put in an eleventh-hour practice.

The waters of the Menai Straits lap gently on the shore. Anglesey looks so near in the sunlight that you think it possible to shout across to it. And I suddenly forget that the crowds are all wearing the same dull modern clothes: I see only their faces and hear only their voices; and it seems to me that they are much the same kind of Britons who gathered in the old days to a feast in Gwynedd to sing their songs and chant their prose.

§ 7

The great event, and the so-called mystery, on the opening day of an Eisteddfod is the identity of the 'Crowned Bard'. He is the hero of the Eisteddfod. He is chosen beforehand, and in secret, by selected judges as the writer of the best poem. His name is technically a secret until it is called out in the pavilion, but—can anything be a secret when thousands of Welshman are gathered together! In England, yes; in Scotland, yes; but in Ireland and Wales, surely not! The Welsh have a proverb, 'Nid cyfrinach ond rhwng dau'—'it is no secret except it be between two'—and I am sure that more than two know all about the Crowned Bard.

I sit on the grass in the afternoon sunlight waiting for the great moment. Thousands of people are piling into the pavilion to witness the coronation of the poet.

A man, a young Welsh poet, sits down beside me.

'Is the Crowned Bard's name really a secret or not?' I ask.

'Oh, yes, of course,' he replies; then, dropping his voice, he says in a mysterious whisper, 'I believe it's Cynan. There he is. We'll ask him!'

The bard, Cynan, who turns out to be an extremely pleasant and amusing young man, sits down beside us and we pull his leg. Of course he knows all about it! Surely he has been warned to hold himself in readiness for the crown? No; he has not heard one word. He swears it. He drifts uneasily away. . . .

Other young writers and musicians join us. We continue to discuss the mystery.

'Whom do you think it is, Owen?'

Owen lowers his voice and whispers with a great air of secrecy:

'I'm told it's—Cynan!'

This, I think, is one of the most open secrets I have ever encountered.

'Look here,' I say, 'you don't mean to tell the poor ignorant stranger that this is what you call a secret in Wales?'

'Oh, yes, indeed, it is a secret. Only the judges know his name.'

'But surely,' I suggest, 'all Welsh critics are not entirely celibate, and as I conclude that Welshwomen are no different from the women of any other nationality, and that Welsh husbands make the same error of confiding exciting news to their wives, how can this be a secret?'

We are joined by other young artists. One of them bends down and whispers:

'It's Cynan. . . .'

'Of course, it has happened,' says some one, 'that the Crowned Bard has had to be warned to be present; in fact most of them are. That's why you always find him right at the back of the pavilion trying to look surprised when his name is shouted. . . .'

That, I feel sure, is a bit more like the truth of it!

We leave the sunlight and go into the dusk of the great pavilion to have the mystery made clear to us.

The huge place is packed with people. There is not one vacant seat. People are standing in the gangways. There is a sudden fanfare of trumpets. The big doors at the extreme end of the pavilion are flung open and we see, framed in sunlight, the Gorsedd of Bards in their full regalia, just as they officiated at the stone circle.

They walk slowly, two by two, down the length of the pavilion. They mount the stage and range themselves round a regrettably modern throne on which the Chief Druid seats himself. There is another fanfare of trumpets.

The Chief Druid rises and announces that the crown has been gained by a poet who has given himself the *nom de plume* of Morgan. If such a man is in the audience let him stand up and declare himself. Far off, at the remote end of the immense building, comes a burst of cheering. Thousands of heads are turned in the direction of it. Away at the back a blushing poet rises to his feet. He is a distant and indistinguishable figure. At the sight of him the cheering spreads all over the pavilion. Rarely do poets—and certainly never in England—enjoy such popular applause.

The Herald Bard and the Sword Bearer leave the platform and march slowly towards the mysterious ' Morgan '. They return, one on each side of him, to conduct him to his coronation. It is a pity that they have to hold him by the arm as if bringing him to his honours by sheer force, because to the irreverent it may appear that two early British policemen have arrested a drunk.

No sooner is ' Morgan ' half down the pavilion than I detect something familiar about him. It *is* Cynan! But I have been moving very obviously among the intelligentsia, because the thousands who fill the hall are undoubtedly taken by surprise.

The Bard is conducted to the platform, where he is garbed in a purple robe edged with white fur. He is seated on a throne. The Gorsedd Sword is held above him. And at this moment the Chief Druid advances and places on his head a crown that is slightly too small. The cheering bursts out again and the audience is told how and why the judges made their decision.

I try to get a translation of the poem, only to be met with the distressing information that it will not translate into English. This is true of most Welsh poetry. It is a door against which one beats in vain.

§ 8

In the evening every one goes to the Eisteddfod concert. This is distinct from the morning sessions, which are purely competitive.

If you wish to hear singing such as you will hear nowhere else in the world, listen to a mixed choir of Welsh voices. Such singing rouses wonder, admiration and respect. It is no secret that the Welsh have a natural genius for song, but it does seem to me intensely interesting that this should have been handed down to modern Wales from ancient times.

Giraldus Cambrensis, writing in the twelfth century, said of the Welsh :

' They do not sing in unison, like the inhabitants of other countries, but in different parts, so that in a company of singers, which one frequently meets with in Wales, as many different parts are heard as there are performers, who at length unite with organic melody in one consonance and the soft sweetness of B. Their children from their infancy sing in the same manner.'

One of the prettiest sights I have ever seen on a concert platform is a choir of harps. I listened to twelve maidens play twelve harps. According to the Welsh Triads, there are three things which a man should have in his home—a virtuous wife, a cushion on his chair and a harp in tune. Should the virtuous wife also play the harp, I consider that the Triads have been improved on and—only a fool would become pedantic about the cushion!

CHAPTER SIX

I EXPLORE THE GREEN ISLE OF ANGLESEY, SEE THE BIRTH-PLACE OF OWEN TUDOR, THE LOVER OF KATHARINE OF VALOIS, SIT ON A FARMYARD WALL AND REMEMBER ONE OF THE MOST ROMANTIC STORIES IN HISTORY, COME TO A FOREIGN TOWN CALLED CAERNARVON AND SEE ONE OF THE MOST MAGNIFICENT CASTLES IN THE WORLD

§ 1

THE Isle of Anglesey is separated from the mainland by a strip of water so narrow that a man with a loud voice could make himself heard from bank to bank.

On a sunny day the shores of the Menai Straits are unforgettably lovely. As I looked west over the green farmlands of the flat isle and back towards the mountains of Caernarvonshire, I thought that this spot is not only one of the fairest in Great Britain but in Europe.

The narrow strip of water can, given the right light, run in streaks as vividly blue as the sea round Capri, or as softly green as the sea that washes Iona. All the softness of Anglesey has marched down to the edge of the water, where it gazes across to the mountains of the mainland.

Surely one of the most difficult tasks that a man can undertake is to make a bridge in country such as this, linking the mountains of Snowdonia with the green fields of Anglesey. It would be easy to build an offensive bridge: it would, perhaps, be even easier to build a trivial bridge. Telford's bridge is a triumph.

Before he flung this mighty bridge into mid-air, the narrow waters of the Menai Straits formed a protective moat round Mona. Only a soldier grimly determined on conquest would care to lead an army across them. And when you see Anglesey for the first time you think of such a man, a man far off in the mists of time, but one whose campaign against the British druids brings Anglesey first into recorded history.

Tacitus, writing in the first century after Christ, tells us how the Claudian conquest of Britain was consolidated by Suetonius Paulinus, a distinguished Roman officer who, in the reign of Nero, was appointed general officer commanding the Roman expeditionary force in Britain. By subduing the mutinous Britons he hoped to equal the brilliant success of Corbulo in Armenia.

'With this view,' writes Tacitus, 'he resolved to subdue the isle of Mona; a place inhabited by a war-like people, and a common refuge for all the discontented Britons. In order to facilitate his approach to a difficult and deceitful shore, he ordered a number of flat-bottomed boats to be constructed. In these he wafted over the infantry, while the cavalry, partly by fording over the shallows, and partly by swimming their horses, advanced to gain a footing on the island.'

He then gives us a vivid glimpse of Anglesey as it appeared to the Roman legions, a picture which we cannot forget as we stand on these now peaceful shores:

'On the opposite shore stood the Britons, close embodied, and prepared for action. Women were seen rushing through the ranks in wild disorder; their apparel funereal; their hair loose to the wind, in their hands flaming torches, and their whole appearance resembling the frantic rage of the Furies. The Druids were ranged in order, with hands uplifted, invoking the gods, and pouring forth terrible imprecations. The novelty of the sight struck the Romans with awe and horror. They stood in stupid amazement, as if their limbs were benumbed, riveted to one spot, a mark for the enemy. The exhortations of the general diffused new vigour through the ranks, and the men, by mutual reproaches, inflamed each other to deeds of valour. They felt the disgrace of yielding to a troop of women and a band of fanatic priests; they advanced their standards and rushed on to the attack with impetuous fury. The Britons perished in the flames which they themselves had kindled. The island fell, and a garrison was established to retain it in subjection. The religious groves, dedicated to superstition and barbarous rites, were levelled to the ground. In those recesses, the natives imbrued their altars with the blood of their prisoners, and in the entrails of men explored the will of the gods. While Suetonius was employed in making his arrangements to subdue the island, he received intelligence that Britain had revolted, and that the whole province was up in arms.'

So to this island, the western limit of the Roman world, came the news of a woman who was marching on London with fire and sword—Boadicea. Suetonius, casting away his victory in Anglesey, marched his army back across Britain to face the furious tribes. Years afterwards Agricola subdued Anglesey. The fording of the Menai Straits under Suetonius must have become a well-known story in the Roman army, for we do not find Agricola advancing with a fleet of transports. He trained a special corps in swimming. This force could fight in mid-stream and manage its horses at the same time. The Romans rode down to the straits, swam across and took the isle by storm.

In a few minutes I had crossed those waters whose perilous currents had chastened the legions of Rome; and I found myself among fields, whitewashed farms, golden gorse bushes and quiet lanes. The first village, commonly and charitably called Llanfair, provides the stranger with an impossible task among Welsh place-names. Its title is:

Llanfairpwllgwyngyllgogerychwyrndrobwllllandysiliogogogoch

This is no joke. It is only too true! The full name, however, is never used; but it appears only slightly amputated in the Ordnance Survey maps. The postal name is Llanfair P.G. or Llanfairpwll.

I entered the first inn and said to those who were drinking in the bar:

'I will buy any one a drink who can pronounce the full name of this place.'

There was an ominous silence until an old man, finishing his beer, stood up and *sang* it! It is difficult to say it, but any one with an ear for music can sing it with a little practice.

'And what does it mean?' I asked.

'It means,' I was told, 'the Church of St. Mary in a wood of white hazel near a rapid whirlpool and near St. Tysilio's cave close to a red cave.'

I went out into one of the greenest and fattest parts of Wales. Anglesey is one enormous farm. They used to call it the 'Mother of Wales' because it was said all the corn needed by Wales could be grown there. The long roads run through flat, green country, linking quiet, stone-built little market towns together. Holyhead provides the one excitement—the arrival and departure of the Irish mails.

§ 2

Long before I had been in Wales, I remember asking Miss Megan Lloyd George if her knowledge of the Welsh language was useful when she fought her election campaign in Anglesey! I now realize what a silly question it was.

Anglesey is entirely Welsh-speaking. In the remote parts of the island there are still old people who could not carry on a conversation in English. Although the guide-books and the records of travel in Wales paint Anglesey as the very back of beyond, I think that the island must have changed during the last few years. Every Saturday the busy little town of Holyhead offers the doubtful blessings of a metropolis to the folk from the scattered farmsteads of the isle. There are shops as good as any in Bangor or Caernarvon, and also a 'talkie' theatre. The influence of this theatre is insidious! I went into a shop to buy some tobacco. The girl behind the counter was talking rapidly to a friend in Welsh. She concluded a Welsh sentence with 'O.K., kid'.

In the middle of the main street is a turning which you might easily miss. It leads to the covered .market hall. Here you will see Anglesey on a Saturday afternoon. The farmers and their families come in by motor-coach or by horse and trap to do their weekly shopping. Tradesmen from the mainland send over goods and spread them on trestle tables outside the market. These are mainly old and new clothes, women's hats, skirts, blankets, towels and dress materials. The farmers' wives and daughters prowl round the stalls, turning over the remnants, and sometimes making a purchase. In a corner of the market an unconquerable Cockney holds an outdoor auction on approved lines. He stands in his shirt-sleeves before an immense pile of blankets and sheets. He is surrounded by a quick-witted, canny crowd of Welsh people:

'Who says ten bob?' he shouts, giving a pile of blankets a vindictive smack. 'Come on now, don't all speak at once. . . . I'll tell you what I'll do because I'm in a good mood to-day.'

Then in a hair-raising voice he bellows:

'Eight bob!' and gives the blankets an even more savage smack.

The crowd is unresponsive.

'I'll give 'em away!' shouts the auctioneer in an excess of violent generosity. 'I'll chuck 'em at you! Seven and sixpence! No! Six bob? No! Five and six? You, lady!'

He keeps his word.

The blankets shoot through the air in the direction of a watchful young Jew assistant; and a farmer's wife gropes painfully in a small purse.

It is amusing to watch a crowd laughing at English jokes and talking together in Welsh.

Inside the market are the food-stalls. Old women sit beside baskets of eggs. Some offer about half a pound of home-made butter for sale. These small quantities of food brought from long distances, the meagre surplus, no doubt, of a more or less self-supporting farm-house, reveal in an eloquent manner the simple life and the modest means of many an Anglesey family. I suppose the old wives love a talk at the Saturday market, for it does not seem possible that the few pence earned by their produce can repay them for the trouble in making and marketing it.

I have never seen so many butchers in competition in a small market. There are perhaps fifteen or twenty butchers' stalls, some owned by mainland butchers, others the stalls on which Anglesey people display home-killed beef. Here again the quantities are diminutive. There is not a good joint to be seen. The meat is cut up into small, unpleasant looking gobbets of about a pound or half a pound in weight.

'The country people would never think of buying meat in the town,' one butcher told me. 'It is a custom to buy their meat from the market stalls.'

From which I assume that, during the week at any rate, the country folk of Anglesey are vegetarians.

Holyhead is an excellent place for a holiday. You have a mountain to climb from which, on a good day, you can see Ireland; you have bathing, fine cliff scenery, and all round you is excellent flat walking country with a supreme view to the east of the whole Snowdon range.

A straight road runs from Holyhead. It takes you through

gentle country where corn-fields lie against each other, where black cattle graze in fields among gorse bushes and the jagged outcrop of grey rocks.

There is the pretty country town of Beaumaris, which is pronounced Boo-morris or Bew-marris. The real Welshman of Anglesey regards Beaumaris as an English town! He is conscious of something that is subtly different when he goes there. And I suppose this is a legacy from those distant times when an English king planted his castle at Beaumaris and gathered round it those influences that made the town English while everything round it was Welsh.

You approach Beaumaris by way of lanes that dip down to it, with the silver gleam of the Menai Straits to your right hand. The trees arch themselves overhead, the stone walls, green with moss and fern, are almost as luscious as the walls round Killarney.

I liked Beaumaris, with the white yachts shining in the bay, the quiet, solemn little streets, the breath-taking view of the opposite mountains and the ivy-covered skeleton of Edward I's castle.

Edward built it after the death of Llewelyn to overawe Anglesey and watch Snowdonia. Nothing exciting seems to have happened to Beaumaris Castle until the reign of Charles I, when Anglesey became the meeting-place and refuge of north Welsh royalists. It is the most peaceful place you can imagine to-day when the sunlight falls over the ivy-covered drum towers and there is no sound but 'forty-love' from the courtyard, which is now a tennis court.

I found in Beaumaris a cosy inn and a great, stone hotel, both of which might have been a gift to Wales from any English market town.

But I found something else.

In a side street high up on a stone wall is a horrid door. It is not the kind of door which admits hay or corn to a loft. It is a sinister and improbable door.

'That,' said a Beaumarian, 'is where we used to have public executions until late in the nineteenth century.'

The wall is that of the now disused county jail. The door is that from which men condemned to death stepped out in full view of the assembled town.

This prison is now in charge of a pretty dark-eyed girl, who took me through heart-breaking cells. It is a real old nineteenth-century prison, haunted still by the ghosts of its former occupants. In a yard is an old wooden treadmill.

There was once a woman in prison there with a small baby. They made a hole in the stone floor of her cell and passed a rope down to the room below in which she worked so that, as she stood at the wash-tub, she could rock her baby in the cell above.

'And this is the condemned cell,' said the girl.

It looked like it.

'And here's the drop,' she said, opening the door.

I looked down into the street below. But this is the only grim thing in Anglesey. It is a cheerful, happy, green island that looks across to the mountains of Snowdonia knowing itself to be Welsh to the backbone.

§ 3

The main street of the little market town of Llangefni lies in a straight line among Anglesey meadows. Not far from it is a place called Ceint, which is a short walk from Plâs Penmynydd. This old manor-house, like many in North Wales, is a mass of old and new stone. Here and there you see above a lintel a coat of arms or an initial which tells of grander days. The farm-house, which is still occupied, is a terra-cotta building, small and solid, and round it on sloping meadowland stand the cow-sheds and the barns.

As I sat on a stone wall and looked at Plâs Penmynydd I remembered one of the greatest romances in the history not only of Wales but of Great Britain; the rise of the House of Tudor. This quiet and humble farmstead was the birthplace of Owen Tudor. The rose-bush that flowered in the Elizabethan age was grown in Wales, and from this soil in Anglesey sprang the most spectacular period in the history of Great Britain.

A man sitting on a wall in Anglesey must see, as in a cloud over Plâs Penmynydd, the Battle of Bosworth Field, the discovery of America, the Field of the Cloth of Gold, the Reformation, Mary and Elizabeth, the defeat of the Armada and the varied richness of that age in which the national destiny, like a ship on the slipways, glides slowly into the modern world on the flood-tide of the Tudor age.

I have always thought that the secret love-affair of the

Welshman, Owen Tudor, and Katherine of Valois, widow of Henry V, is a plot for one of the most perfect novels in English history.

In the month of May, 1420, young King Henry V entered the church of Notre Dame at Troyes clothed in a suit of burnished armour, and in his helmet, instead of a plume, he wore the brush of a fox. He was met at the high altar by the Queen of France, the notorious Isabeau, consort of the mad Charles VI, and Katherine, her daughter.

Henry and Katherine were, unlike many royal lovers before and after them, really in love with each other. He had for years followed up his slaughter of her countrymen with proposals of marriage. He was thirty-two; she was just nineteen. She was a beautiful girl, with dark hair, dark eyes, an oval face, a fair complexion and a small mouth. She had also 'a most engaging manner'.

As soon as the Treaty of Troyes was signed, Henry fell on his knees before the altar and asked the young princess if she would marry him. She 'timidly assented'. He immediately took her hand and placed on her finger the ring worn by the queens of England at their coronation. In the following month Hal and his 'sweet Kate' were married with great magnificence. They had only two years together. They crossed to England, where Katherine was received 'as if she had been an angel of God'. She was splendidly crowned at Westminster. Henry took her on a royal progress through the north in order that England might see her beauty. Just before the birth of her child he was forced to return to his army in France. When he was besieging Meaux, news was brought to him that Katherine was delivered of a son at Windsor. He then remembered an old prophecy about the ill-luck of a prince born at Windsor Castle and he cried to his chamberlain:

'My lord, I, Henry, born at Monmouth, shall short time reign and get much. But Henry born at Windsor shall long reign and lose all!'

In a few months' time Katherine was summoned to attend her husband's death-bed. 'Katherine the Fair' was twenty-one when she crossed the Channel with the dead body of Henry V.

Now, among the Welshmen who followed King Henry to the French wars was a man of Anglesey known as Owen Tudor. These tough warriors, under the command of Davy the One-eyed, the brother-in-law to Owen Glendower, did gallant service at Agincourt. There is a tradition that Owen Tudor was made a squire of the bodyguard for his bravery at Alençon.

It has been said that Owen Tudor came from humble stock and that his father was a brewer in Beaumaris. But no Celtic clansmen are ever really humble: there is always a prince from whom they claim descent. So it was with Owen Tudor. He was probably, at the time he took service with the King of England, an ordinary small landowner in Wales. He certainly did not possess £40 a year at the time of Henry's death or he would have taken up his knighthood.

We see him in attendance at Windsor Castle on the beautiful widowed Queen. He was at this time thirty-seven years of age, a tall, good-looking and undoubtedly amorous Welshman. There is a story that on one occasion when he was on guard in the Castle he was asked to dance before the Queen. In his anxiety to show himself off, he performed a rather too ambitious pirouette and fell into Her Majesty's lap! The manner in which the Queen excused the unsteady Welshman told the sharp eyes of her ladies in waiting quite a lot, for it seems that they chided her, telling her 'how much she lowered herself by paying any attention to a person, who, though possessing some personal accomplishments and advantages, had no princely, nor even gentle, alliances, but belonged to a barbarous clan of savages, reckoned inferior to the lowest English yeoman'.

That was the opinion at the time of the man who sired Henry VII, Henry VIII and Queen Elizabeth!

Katherine replied to the criticism 'that being a Frenchwoman, she had not been aware that there was any difference in race in the British island'.

How Owen first made love to the Queen we shall never know. We know, however, that she thought very solemnly about him, because she tackled him on the question of his humble origin. That argues a certain closeness. He replied, like a good Welshman, that he was descended from a race of brilliant princes. She asked him to produce some of them for her inspection at Windsor.

'Whereupon,' writes Sir John Wynne, 'he brought into her presence John ap Meredith, and Howell ap Llewellyn, his near cousins, men of the goodliest stature and personage, but wholly destitute of bringing-up and nurture (education); for when the Queen had spoken to them in divers languages, and they were not able to answer her, she said "they were the goodliest dumb creatures she ever saw"; a proof that Katherine knew several languages, but had no skill in Welsh.'

A proof also that she was in love with Owen Tudor.

We can surmise a certain amount of whispering behind hands at this time, because in the sixth year of the reign of her infant son a law was passed threatening with dire penalties any man 'who should dare to marry a queen-dowager, or any lady who held lands of the Crown, without the consent of the king and his council'.

It has been said that Katherine and Owen were secretly married before this law was passed; but we can never know how a woman of her position, surrounded by other women, could have kept her love-affair a dead secret. It is one of the mysteries of history. But she managed to do so. Owen was Clerk of the Wardrobe. It was his duty to guard the Queen's jewels, to discuss new clothes with her and to buy the materials for her gowns.

She bore him, in secret, three sons. The first was Edmund of Hadham; the second Jasper of Hatfield; the third Owen of Westminster.

No one in England—obviously no one who mattered—knew that a new royal house had been founded under the Tudor rose!

But something went wrong towards the end of the summer of 1436. To employ a vulgar but eloquent Americanism, it was too much to hope that a queen-mother and her Welsh courtier 'could get away with it'. Katherine at this time was only thirty-five and her 'husband' was fifty-one. They had known fourteen years of secret love; and therefore, I suppose, cannot be pitied. But the storm broke over them. The still young widow gave birth to a daughter, Margaret, who lived for only a few days. The death of this child, and probably years of mental anxiety, drove Katherine into an illness. She entered the Abbey of Bermondsey as a modern woman would enter a nursing home, or, as some say, she was sent there under restraint by order of the Duke of Gloucester.

She remained very ill at Bermondsey during the autumn. Meanwhile the news of her marriage with Owen Tudor must have leaked out. Her three Welsh sons were taken from her by order of the Council and placed under the care of Katherine de la Pole, the Abbess of Barking.

Owen Tudor was arrested and placed in Newgate. His royal wife and lover died while he was in prison. She was buried with the pomp and ceremony proper to her station in Our Lady's Chapel in Westminster Abbey. Her son by the royal marriage erected a Latin epitaph, which was, in the process of time, to be replaced by one erected by her equally royal grandson by the secret marriage. Her first epitaph was:

Death, darling spoiler of the world, has laid
Within this tomb the noble clay that shrined
Queen Katherine's soul; from the French king derived
Of our fifth Henry wife; of the sixth
Henry, mother. As maid and widow both,
A perfect flower of modesty esteemed.
Here, happy England, brought she forth that king,
On whose auspicious life thy weal depends;
And, rest of whom, they bliss would soon decay.
Joy of this land, and brightness of her own,
Glory of mothers, to her people, dear,
A follower sincere of the true faith;
Heaven and our earth combine alike to praise
This woman who adorns them both e'en now.
Earth by her offspring; by her virtues Heaven!
In the fourteenth hundred, thirty-seventh year.
First month's third day, her life drew to its close,
And this queen's soul, beyond the starry sphere
In heaven, received for aye, reigns blissfully.

Not one word, you notice, about Owen Tudor. Not one word about the second marriage or the children whose descendants were to be kings.

Katherine died in February. In July Owen had escaped from Newgate and was at large in Daventry. Young King Henry summoned him to court, saying, 'that he willed that Owen Tudor, the which dwelled with his mother, Katherine, should come into his presence'. Owen cannily refused to present himself. He entered London, however, and took sanctuary in Westminster. His old friends tried to lure him out 'to disport himself in the tavern at Westminster Gate'. But Owen was not to be lured.

One day, hearing that the King was listening to evil reports of him, he took his courage in both hands and appeared suddenly before the Privy Council. He defended himself with such verbal skill and with such spirit that Henry VI set him free.

He retired to Wales. He was pursued by his enemy, the Duke of Gloucester. He was recaptured and again flung into Newgate, with a priest (probably the priest who had married him to the queen-mother) and a servant. But Owen was an old soldier and a man of undeniable nerve. Had he not carried on an intrigue with Henry's widow under the very eyes of the court? He broke out of Newgate a second time with his companions ' after wounding foully their gaoler '. He fled again into Wales.

Years were to pass before the Welsh lover of the dead Queen of England was to be accepted in court circles. But the time came. In the rejoicings which followed the birth of an heir to the throne—Owen Tudor was summoned to London and given an annuity of £40 out of the privy purse. His two sons—the half-brothers of Henry VI—were declared legitimate and accepted into the ranks of the nobility. Edmund Tudor was created Earl of Richmond, and his younger brother, Jasper, was made Earl of Pembroke. But the father, the gallant Owen, received no title: he was merely made ' park keeper of our parks in Denbigh, Wales '.

It was through the influence of the King that his Welsh half-brother, Edmund Tudor, was married to Margaret Beaufort, heiress to the house of Somerset. When this child was little more than thirteen years of age she gave birth to a son at Pembroke Castle on June 26th, 1456. That boy—the grandson of Owen Tudor and Katherine de Valois—was to ascend the throne as the first Tudor—Henry VII.

What happened to Owen Tudor, the squire of Plâs Penmynydd in Anglesey, the soldier of fortune, the Clerk of the Wardrobe, the Queen's lover? At the age of seventy-six this man led a Royalist army against the Yorkists. He was defeated at Mortimer's Cross. His aged head fell to the headsman's axe in Hereford Market Place.

When his grandson, Henry Tudor, defeated Richard Crookback on Bosworth Field and entered London as Henry VII, he devoted a deal of time and thought to his pedigree. He caused the verses extolling the marital virtues of his mother, Katherine, to be taken away from her tomb in Westminster Abbey. Its assertion that she died the widow of Henry V, and its scrupulous neglect of his grandfather, Owen, must have been rather embarrassing. So the first of the Tudors substituted the following lines, which have been preserved by John Stow:

Here lies Queen Katherine clos'd in grave
The French King's daughter fair
And of thy Kingdom (Charles the Sixth)
The true redoubted heir.
Twice joyful wife in marriage match'd
To Henry Fifth by name;
Because through her he nobled was,
And shin'd in double fame.
The King of England by descent,
And by Queen Katherine's right
The Realm of France he did enjoy,
Triumphant king of might.
A happy Queen to Englishmen,
She came right grateful here,
And four days space they honoured God,
With mouth and reverent fear.
Henry the Sixth this Queen brought forth
In painful labour's plight;
In whose empire a Frenchman was,
And eke an English wight.
Under no lucky planet born
Unto himself nor throne;
But equal with his parents both,
In pure religion.
Of Owen Tidder after this,
They next son Edmund was,
O Katherine, a renowned prince,
That did in glory pass.
Henry the Seventh, a Britain pearl,
A gemme of England's joy;
A peerless prince was Edmund's son,
A good and gracious roy:
Therefore a happy wife this was,
A happy mother pure;
Thrice happy child; but grand-dame she
More than thrice happy sure.

So the first Tudor, that great but cold-blooded man, tried to link himself to his royal grandmother by an epitaph.

It is impossible to leave the romantic story of the Tudors without some account of Katherine's mummy. When

Henry VII was buried, the body of fair Katherine was exhumed. Henry VIII did not possess his father's reverence for Katherine de Valois, or perhaps he was too sure of himself to feel self-conscious about Owen Tudor. However that may be, the body of Katherine, most marvellously preserved, was not re-buried. It lay about Westminster Abbey and became one of the sights of London for at least three hundred years.

Weever in his *Funeral Monuments* describes it as he saw it in the time of Charles I:

'Here lieth Katherine, Queen of England, wife to Henry V, in a chest or coffin, with a loose cover, to be seen and handled of any who much desire it, and who, by her own appointment, inflicted this penance on herself, in regard to her disobedience to her husband, for being delivered of her son, Henry VI at Windsor, which place he forbade.'

In the reign of Charles II poor Katherine was shown to the curious for twopence. Samuel Pepys, who could be a ghastly little vulgarian, describes how he saw the Queen's body, adding the boast that he had 'this day kissed a queen'.

It was not until the reign of George III that the bones of once lovely Katherine were decently interred in the vaults of Westminster.

So upon a wall in Anglesey a man may dream of a true story that is like romantic fiction. Neither Katherine nor Owen knew that their dangerous love-affair would in course of time blaze itself across the pages of history. I wonder what Owen Tudor would have said could he have foreseen that day when the Crown would be picked from a thorn bush and placed upon the head of his grandson.

Five centuries have passed over the world since the Tudors farmed in Anglesey, but any day you can see the smoke still rising from the chimneys of Plâs Penmynydd and you can hear the lowing of the cattle as they are driven home in the evening.

§ 4

I entered Y Gaer yn Arfon—the Fort of Arfon—or Caernarvon, in the early evening. It is a town of over eight thousand people, all of whom, it seemed to me, speak Welsh. At first I thought that it was rather an undistinguished place, and then, gradually, its peculiar atmosphere began to affect me. It has a character of its own, different from anything I had so far met with in Wales. I felt exactly as I did one evening some years ago when I entered Galway on the west coast of Ireland. On that occasion I thought to myself: 'There is a strange wind blowing through this town, and it is an Irish wind. In Dublin I was only half a foreigner; in Galway I am completely alien.'

Caernarvon on this evening was supremely Welsh. A wind as Welsh as the Galway wind was Irish blew through its stone streets. I felt alien and alone.

It had been a market day and a big crowd waited to catch motor-omnibuses in the square. It was a tired but talkative crowd. I stood in it and listened to the vivid and vivacious language, the sudden jokes, the whispered scandal, the funny treble voices of children speaking Welsh; the deep voices of the men; the sharp managing voices of the women. I would have given anything to have understood them. I wondered how long it would take me to learn a little Welsh—just enough to admit me into the secret. When I listened again to the quick sing-song of it I knew that I would never be able to learn it. Even Borrow, who prided himself on his knowledge of Welsh, made a great fool of himself as he stormed through Wales, startling people with what he considered to be their native language. How queer it was to stand in a crowd and listen to people, who had perhaps been buying gramophone records or a new valve for a wireless set, chatter, as they waited for the homeward omnibus, in the tongue of the Ancient Britons! Welsh, like all living languages, must have passed through many phases in its long history, and I wondered how much of this talk a Briton or Caerleon would have understood. Perhaps only a word here and there.

A strange feeling came to me in this crowd. When you stand in a Spanish or an Italian square you are always conscious that you have a passport in your pocket and that behind that passport is the Foreign Office. But this Welsh crowd gave me a faint feeling of insecurity. I knew perfectly well that had I turned to the man next to me and asked him a question in English he would have answered me with charm and courtesy in that language; yet some vague kind of race memory, perhaps, made me uneasy. These Ancient Britons were, to me, much more foreign, even more dangerous, than Frenchmen or Italians. I might have been a Roman spy in a British town of the first century—a member of Claudius Caesar's C.I.D.

The omnibus swung round the corner with place-names in English on them; but the conductors answered the crowds in Welsh. . . .

I went in the fading light towards the castle. An outline that took away my breath lifted itself against the dead sunset. I saw vast dark walls, machicolated battlements, turrets, and a gateway, locked and barred, behind which, so it seemed to me, all the horror and all the splendour of the Middle Ages might be sleeping. What a place!

It looks as though a great flourish of trumpets has just died over it. You feel that if your ears were keen enough you might hear the echo flung back by the hills. It has an air of arrested life. It is alike magnificent and terrible: magnificent in its strength; terrible in the grim ambition that lies like crumbling mortar between its stones. So Caernarvon Castle—the most splendid ruin in Great Britain—lifts its dead battlements to the sky. It is astonishing that anything so complete and stern in purpose should have survived into our time. It is like a strong will frozen in stone.

I went through the now darkening streets, mourning the fact that if I went in search of companionship to that unfailing source of information and amusement in England—an inn or a bar parlour—I would hear only the Welsh language, which delights and exasperates me, and I would also be regarded with suspicion as a stranger. However, I thought that I would risk it.

The public-houses of Caernarvon are not very attractive. I detest the Victorian drink-shop, with its vile movable little windows designed to hide the face of the hypocrite from that of the publican. And the bars of Caernarvon seemed to be of that kind. After looking at so many with a critical eye,

I became really thirsty and returned to one that had particularly revolted me and went inside.

There was a warm smell of beer and sawdust. Advertisements for beer and whiskey hung on the walls, and beneath them, at small round tables, sat a number of men. Some were speaking in Welsh ; some in English. They were, I judged, farm labourers and quarrymen from Llanberis.

The door opened and in walked a man in a railway uniform, blue serge coat and a pair of mechanic's overalls. He was a popular character, because a volley of greetings met him and conversations stopped. He sat down next to me. He answered the questions that were shot at him in a humorous way and then buried his cheerful face in a mug of ale. He was apparently a Socialist and an atheist. He made a few pungent remarks about Welsh chapel-going and Welsh parsons, which caused half the assembly to look exceedingly uncomfortable and the other half to roar with laughter. He chaffed a rather too neat young man in an unmerciful manner. I gathered that neat one was a noted Lothario. He appeared confused under the railwayman's satire, and for a moment I thought that he might lose his temper. There is something almost Sadistic in the Celtic temperament. I have seen Irishmen torture their friends with their tongues in precisely the same way. Nothing is so deadly as ridicule when it is biting—a trick which I imagine the ancient bards knew very well.

There was a sudden exodus due to the arrival of an omnibus bound for some distant place. All the men, whom I took to be quarrymen, left the room. But the farmers remained. I fell into conversation with the young railwayman. We talked about the War. He had served in the Welsh Regiment. He was a southerner. He had many vivid memories of the Ypres Sector.

When he told me that he came from the south I knew why he was different from the northern farmers. He had begun life in a pit near Cardiff.

As a second pint of beer worked in him, he suddenly rose up and became an actor. He crouched down and moved his arms as if they held a pick. He was telling me in the most graphic way what it feels like to strike a good seam of coal. He described the tearing sound as the seam is found, and it all worked up to a magnificent climax when the miner shouted ' Stand clear ', and the coal came crashing down in the dark.

He spoke also of coming up from the darkness of the mine to the darkness of the sky on the midnight shift, packed in the ' cage ', too tired to say good night ; just a body going home. . . .

The dramatic fervour of this young man held us spellbound. And the big farmers from Caernarvonshire and the Isle of Anglesey, their brown hands holding mugs of ale, sat listening fascinated to the story of a life so strange to them.

So North Wales met South Wales.

I said good night and went out into the streets of Caernarvon. I walked to the castle and saw it high against the stars, cold and lonely, with salt water lapping at its walls.

§ 5

He was standing at the entrance to Caernarvon Castle. My first impression was that Mr. Lloyd George had been Eton-cropped. He was the same height, about the same age, he had the same expression, the same kind of voice, the same gift of description. He wore the blue uniform of the Office of Works. He was Mr. Rees Hughes, Sergeant in charge at Caernarvon Castle. The usual lost sheep who haunt all historic ruins gathered timidly in the shelter of his authority. He grasped a walking-stick and led us off.

Now Caernarvon Castle is the most magnificent thing of its kind in the British Isles. We have all known it from photographs in railway carriages since we were children, but no one who has not seen it can have the faintest conception of its size and grandeur.

Here is a great mediaeval castle that is outwardly intact but inwardly a ruin. Approach it from the sea, stand under its great walls, and it looks exactly as it did to the Welsh of the Middle Ages. It is only when you pass under the great gateway that you see close-cut lawns and battered arches, walls that begin nowhere and end in mid-air. It is one of the corner-stones of Wales . . . ' that most magnificent badge of our subjection ', as Pennant, who was a Welshman, called it.

Mr. Hughes lifted his stick and began to tell us about the castle.

There are guides who send you to sleep, guides who drive

you to despair, guides who fill you with contempt and guides who just make you laugh. I have met them all. But Mr. Hughes is one of the rare guides who has identified himself with his castle. He knows every stone of it. He has read all the books on it and has checked them up on the spot!

And he imparts his knowledge in the high, sing-song voice of the Celt. It is the voice of the bard reciting some epic thing that happened long ago.

He chanted to us about Edward I.

This castle was built to subdue the Welsh who were getting a bit tired of hiding in the mountains. The stern king was determined to put down the armies of Wales. He spent much of his time travelling round that chain of castles which was once the sorrow but is now the pride of Wales—Conway, Criccieth, Harlech, Bere and Beaumaris. But the biggest of them all was Caernarvon.

Mr. Hughes swept his walking-stick round the courtyards and rebuilt the castle for us in words. He showed us the place teeming with life. We saw the cooks carrying steaming dishes from the kitchens, the men-at-arms lounging round the gate-houses, the sentries pacing the walls.

'And here,' said Mr. Hughes, indicating a lawn that had been newly mown, 'was the royal dining-hall. There the king sat while archers stood on duty, ready for trouble. Notice that the entrance to the hall was so narrow that only one man could enter at a time.

'Why? Because if the castle were rushed the archers could pick off men one by one as they entered. The entrance would be jammed with dead bodies. In the confusion the king could escape down that stairway over there—it's now blocked up—which leads to a little tunnel in the rock where a boat was always waiting. . . . Now, come along, if you please.'

He took us up winding stairs to that little room in the Eagle Tower which is associated with one of the most famous stories in Anglo-Welsh history. Whether it is true or not is another matter.

We were told how Edward's queen, Eleanora of Castille, was sent to Caernarvon to bear on Welsh soil an heir to the throne.

In this little dark den of stone, twelve feet long by eight feet wide, the queen is said to have given birth to the unlucky child who became Edward II. He was born towards the end of April. The king was at Rhuddlan Castle. He was so overjoyed to hear of his son's birth that he knighted the messenger on the spot and gave him wide acres.

Edward hurried to Caernarvon to see Eleanora and his heir. Three days later all the chiefs of North Wales assembled at the castle to pay their final homage to the conqueror. Then took place that historic episode which created an English Prince of Wales.

The Welsh chieftains begged Edward to appoint a Prince of Wales to rule over them in his name, a man who could speak neither French nor English.

Edward agreed to this. They swore to obey this prince if his blood was royal and if his character was above reproach. Then the king presented his infant son Edward. He was born in Wales, said the king, his character was unimpeached, he knew no French nor English, and his first words should be in the Welsh language!

The mountaineers, conscious that they had been tricked, knelt and kissed the child's hand. In a few moments the small body was carried on a shield to the castle gates and proclaimed 'Edward Prince of Wales.'

A visitor ventured to suggest that he had read somewhere that all this is pure legend. Mr. Hughes was almost annoyed.

'Some say one thing and some another,' he replied sternly; 'but until we can definitely say that it did not happen that is the story we shall tell. . . . Now this way, if you please. . . .

'When any one was condemned to death in this castle he was taken to this chapel, which you will see is very thoughtfully designed in the shape of a coffin. Now—come this way! In this room he was placed on this stone. Below was an eighty-foot drop. The tide came in and washed out the bodies. And those were the good old days. . . .'

Mr. Hughes had some harsh things to say about those travellers who admire antiquity so much that they must take a bit away with them. The Americans are, he told us, the most passionate collectors. He pointed out in one room various breakages in Caernarvon Castle. His indignation was so great that he began thinking in Welsh and talking in English.

'No matter,' he cried, 'if they came clothed in gold with

Rolls Royces waiting outside, out they'd go at the double if I caught them!'

No English official of the Office of Works could have composed that sentence!

If you go to Caernarvon Castle, slip away from the crowd when you decently can and climb the turret of the Eagle Tower. You will notice that the builders placed stone men on guard there to deceive the Welsh. (You can see the same trick on the gates of York.)

The view looking down on the inner and outer bailey and beyond them over the smoky roofs of Caernarvon to the hills is superb. Westward lies the low green shore of Anglesey over a narrow strip of water.

And you can climb down and think, if you like, how time takes its revenge. Edward's great castle now wrings tribute from the English, and Caernarvon, once an English town, is now perhaps the most Welsh town of its size in the Principality!

CHAPTER SEVEN

IN WHICH I VISIT ST. BEUNO'S CHURCH, EXPLORE THE 'LAND'S END' OF WALES, SEE CRICCIETH, MEET MR. LLOYD GEORGE IN A LANE, GO THROUGH THE PASS OF LLANBERIS, VISIT THE GRAVE OF GELERT, CLIMB A MOUNTAIN OF SLATE AND LEARN SOMETHING ABOUT TAFFY AND HIS FAMOUS LEG OF BEEF

§ 1

THE excellent book I was reading in bed told me that the Lleyn Peninsula, that Cornish-like arm which thrusts itself westward below Anglesey, is one of the last provinces of Arcady. The Land's End of Wales, a place called Aberdaron, is, I read, a remote wilderness seventeen miles from a railway station. The inhabitants live in happy ignorance of this modern world. Their only link with fame is a half-crazy wanderer named 'Dick', who, for no apparent reason, had learnt an unnecessary number of foreign languages. ('Simple lodgings might be obtained at the village inn'.)

Now this is exactly the kind of place I like, but I have long despaired of finding it away from the west coast of Ireland or in the remote north-west Highlands of Scotland. In the morning, however, excited and stimulated by thoughts of Aberdaron, I took the road south and soon came to a village among trees, with a church, on low ground, whose weathered tower rose up to the right of the road. The name of this village is Clynnog Fawr, which, I think, means 'a hiding-place'.

I could see the waters of Caernarvon Bay to the right and, ahead, was a great mountain, the Rivals, standing in the sea, with its three peaks towering against a blue sky.

The church at Clynnog Fawr drove all thoughts of Aberdaron out of my head. It is like no church I had seen in North Wales. It is a lovely Tudor building, its stones mellowed by the winds and rains of centuries. I walked through the lych-gate down a steep path between gravestones and ancient trees.

Every one should visit this church, because not only is it an unspoilt relic of the sixteenth century but it also has a quality rare in Welsh churches: the past lives so securely in its shadows that you expect to see the ghost of that almost inconceivable character, a Welsh monk, moving about a chancel designed for the Mass.

The building is full of old oak. The nave slopes upward to a decorative rood-screen that separates it from a square, high chancel. The Late Perpendicular windows are magnificent, and when they were full of stained glass must have been really exquisite. In a land which worships God in surroundings as severe and practical as those of a town hall, this church in Clynnog Fawr seems unreal and alien. I found myself wishing that I could attend a service there. I feel sure the spirits of St. Beuno's monks mock the Welsh Protestants on Sunday, and I am surprised that there is no legend of some night wanderer in Clynnog who, peeping through the now clear windows of the church in the still hours, saw the altar blazing with candles and heard the monks reciting the Little Office of the Blessed Virgin. That is the impression St. Beuno's church makes upon me: a haunted church in a land of chapels.

St. Beuno, of whom I suppose few Englishmen have ever heard, was a saint second only in godliness and power to St. David. At least six North Welsh churches are dedicated to him. He lived in the sixth century, when the memory of Roman Britain was still a live thing in the hearts of men. He planted an oak tree which slew every Saxon who passed beneath it, but a Welshman could walk by unharmed! That is eloquent of the age in which he lived. It is supposed that after the great battle of Chester in A.D. 615, when an invading army of Angles, after beating the Britons, separated for ever the Welsh of North Wales from the Welsh of Strathclyde, St. Beuno arrived in Arfon. His first church, a building probably of mud and wattle, occupied a site now covered by a little sixteenth-century chapel which is to-day connected with the larger church by a curious stone-vaulted passage-way. The monastery that grew up round Beuno's chapel is mentioned in the Laws of Hywel Dda as a community almost as famous as that of Bangor.

In the Middle Ages, church after church had been built on the site, pilgrims visited the tomb of St. Beuno, which had become one of the miracle-working shrines of North Wales.

The saint was reputed to have raised the dead. The sick and ailing would visit the chapel to spend a night near the tomb. Pilgrims were in the habit of scraping his tombstone and making from the dust an eye lotion that faith alone could have prescribed. When Pennant toured Wales in 1776 he saw a feather-bed lying on the tomb, on which was a poor paralytic from Merionethshire. The unhappy creature had first been dipped in the holy well of St. Beuno and then placed in the church to spend a night above the holy relics. It is strange that when St. Beuno's chapel was excavated in 1913 no bones were found in the place which tradition claimed as the resting-place of the saint.

In a glass case in the church is Cyff Beuno, or the chest of St. Beuno, a tinder-dry, worm-eaten old box with a formidable lock. It is made of one solid piece of ash. The lid was sawn off and then a hollow scooped in the block of wood, much as primitive races fashion their canoes. In the old days the chest had three locks, which accounts for the old Welsh proverb, 'You might as well try and break open St. Beuno's chest,' a task that was considered impossible.

On Trinity Sunday the farmers of Clynnog Fawr were in the habit of driving into the churchyard all lambs and calves born with 'St. Beuno's Mark' on them; and the sale money was given to the monks and placed in the chest. The Nod Beuno, or mark, was a little slit occasionally present at birth in the ears of Welsh cattle. Mr. Alun Roberts of University College, Bangor, has stated that it was known less than a generation ago to cattle farmers in Carmarthenshire and Pembrokeshire, but it is rarely met with now. It has been suggested that the monks cunningly introduced cattle from France which bore this distinctive mark, knowing well that a percentage of their offspring would also bear it and add to the revenue of their community.

Another object of interest in this church is a pair of dog tongs, or Gefail Cwn. These tongs, rather like ordinary coal tongs but with toothed extremities, were formerly quite common in all the Welsh country churches. In those days sheep-dogs used to follow their masters to church and would curl up in the pews and sleep through the service as peacefully as any English squire. Now and then, however, the devil would enter into one of them and a fight would take place. The dog tongs would be taken down and, while the service was suspended, the offender would be seized and forcibly ejected. There is a story about a Welsh parson who used to take his dog Tango to church with him every Sunday. The dog would go to sleep in front of the lectern. One day he spied an enemy, a farmer's dog, and a terrific battle took place just as Tango's master was about to read the Lesson. The fight was so violent that the dog tongs were no use, and it was so exciting that the vicar and his congregation forgot about the service! Above the roar and snarl of battle the worshippers heard their shepherd cry in a loud voice:

'Three to one on Tango!'

I remembered this unholy story as I examined the dog tongs of Clynnog Fawr and, shaking myself free from this haunted building, I took the pilgrims' road to Aberdaron.

When I had left Pwllheli—which is a very ordinary little sea-side town set in the curve of exquisite Tremadoc Bay, with a heavenly view of the Merionethshire mountains over the water—I struck inland.

I was now in the very heart of the Lleyn Peninsula. The roads became lanes. The uncultivated land was black and peaty. Smooth, round-backed hills brooded darkly over the land. Black cattle grazed behind stone walls in fields that rose in hummocks like waves. And over this land was something weird and unheard that reminded me of Ireland.

I noticed, as I went on, that dogs ran away from the car. Horses took alarm. I was in a part of Wales that, until the coming of the motor-omnibus, had always been remote and isolated.

A steepish hill took me down into the pretty little village of Sarn, where I entered the inn to drink beer and ask the way to Aberdaron. I was evidently suspect as a stranger, although the young Welshman who served me and answered me reluctantly was reading an English morning paper printed the previous night in Liverpool. He was polite and non-committal; but still I had the feeling that until my business was known I would be told no more than common courtesy demanded. It is easy to understand this attitude of mind. He was not even superficially voluble like the majority of his race: he was as dour and suspicious as a Norfolk rustic.

The fields and the moors fell away towards Aberdaron, the

5. CAERNARVON CASTLE.

6a. HARLECH CASTLE, LOOKING TOWARDS SNOWDONIA.

6b. MOUNT SNOWDON AND LLYN LLYDAW LAKE.

most remote village in Wales. I could see before me the blue sea sparkling, but instead of the holy isle of Bardsey, which I expected to see, was a high green hill that closed the view.

I ran down to a pretty village of whitewashed cottages that nestles in a cove of Aberdaron Bay. There was a stream and a stone bridge, and behind the village the grassy hills rose steeply, while, to the right, headlands fell sharply to the sea. So this was the Land's End of Wales.

The church, the last halting-place for pilgrims to Bardsey Isle, is built almost on the crescent of white sand, and so near the sea that in winter time the spray must drench its stones. It is an ancient church, low and Celtic in design, cold and bleak inside, and the fine Norman doorway is weathered by centuries of salt winds. For hundreds of years this little church sheltered the saintly and the repentant, for two pilgrimages to Bardsey Isle, four miles out to sea, had the virtue in the eyes of the Catholic Church of one pilgrimage to Rome.

I walked past the score or so of white cottages. People looked at me with interest; but I was not satisfied that I was in Arcady. I heard children running down the hill at the back on their way from school shouting to each other in Welsh; but still I had my suspicions. I am sure that, when the book was written that sent me to Aberdaron, every other chimney did not sprout a wireless mast! And can any place be considered an Arcady when the big joint-stock banks hire front rooms in cottages and place between lace curtains a card bearing the information that Mr. Barclay will be doing business there on the following Monday? I am afraid that Aberdaron has linked up with the world.

Instead of the simple quarters in the village inn, I discovered a good little hotel.

'Two gins and It!' was the first remark I heard as I entered.

Two young men in golf clothes were sitting in the lounge talking to a girl who stood in a perfectly sophisticated bar. And this was Aberdaron, the place in which I expected to see ancient Britons clothed in skins!

'It is really frightfully unspoilt,' said one of the young men as he drank his gin and Italian. 'Do you know, we were walking on the hill there the other day and we found a child who could not speak a word of English.

'It's a fact,' said the other young man. 'A kid of about

six or seven. Nothing but Welsh is spoken in the cottages here and the children have to go to school to learn English.'

'But people come here for their holidays?'

'A few.'

'Still, I didn't expect to find people drinking cocktails at the end of the world.'

'Progress,' said one of the young men in a sudden flash of inspiration.

I walked for two miles or so uphill to get a view of Bardsey Island. The steep headlands slope down to the sea. Sheep graze on the heathery moorland, and, four miles off in the sea, is an island like a huge mouse. Bardsey is a gentle, dome-shaped hill with a long tail of flat land flung out behind it.

There are, I believe, about forty-eight inhabitants on it, all of whom live by farming or fishing. Although they are within sight of the mainland, no people in Great Britain live in greater solitude. The four miles of sea that separate Bardsey from Aberdaron are among the most dangerous round the coast of Britain, and it often happens that the community is cut off from the world for a month at a time.

I would like to have made the voyage, but the boatmen in Aberdaron said that while we might land there in safety we might be marooned on the island for days, because a gale was on the way! This happens even in the height of summer.

Like all the islands off the British coast, Bardsey was claimed early in history by an anchorite whose only thought was to retire from the world. He was St. Cadvan, who in the year 516 planted there an abbey dedicated to the Virgin. Its peculiar fame during the Middle Ages was due to the legend that twenty thousand saints were buried there. This legend has, no doubt, a certain historical background, because after the battle of Chester over a thousand monks who escaped from the huge monastery of Bangor-Iscoed sought refuge, and a new life, on Bardsey Isle.

I walked back to Aberdaron and, after eating fish as fresh as you eat it in a North Sea trawler, took the road back from 'the end of the world' towards Pwllheli and Criccieth.

§ 2

I wish to see nothing finer than Criccieth on a sunny afternoon. A high grass-covered rock lifts itself from the sea, and on its summit is the gate-house and bastion of an ancient castle. When the tide is out there are yellow sands, rock pools and great boulders green with weed. There is a modern town, neat, precise—a delightful mixture of streets and fields and parks—but you never notice it because in clear weather it is impossible to take your eyes from the opposite coast. I have never seen anything more magnificent than the incredible panorama of sea and mountains that faces Criccieth across ten or fifteen miles of blue-green water. On this afternoon the mountains of Caernarvonshire and Merionethshire stood up clear of mist against a pale blue sky. The only cloud was a gold halo to the north, lying as if anchored on the peak of Snowdon. The mountains were grape blue and pale blue and dove grey. They seemed to rise straight from the sea. What a magnificent picture: to the north Snowdon, in the centre Harlech Castle on its rock, on the south the vast outline of Cader Idris. In the stillness of afternoon this blend of sea and blue mountain was like a vision from another world.

The tide was rolling in over the yellow sands of Criccieth when I set off towards the little town, and I think I have never turned away from any view with greater reluctance. I soon realized that I was in the town sacred to Mr. Lloyd George. A tradesman from whom I was buying tobacco was talking to a customer in Welsh. The only words I understood were 'Lloyd George'.

'Is Mr. Lloyd George in Criccieth now?' I asked.

'Oh, yes, indeed, he is in Criccieth.'

I took the Caernarvon Road, turned up Arvonia Terrace and soon came to a modern house whose white walls make it a landmark for miles. This was Bryn Awelon, the Welsh home of Mr. Lloyd George. Fame carries with it unpleasant penalties. The ruined castle and Mr. Lloyd George are the only 'sights' in Criccieth. Those who visit Criccieth in the summer are not happy until they have seen Mr. Lloyd George and even, perhaps, thrust their cameras through the gate.

The result is that he has been forced to surround himself with a protective wall and to plant a thick hedge.

A lane opposite Bryn Awelon runs between fields and woods to the village of Llanystumdwy, where Mr. Lloyd George went to school as a small boy. This village is perfect. It has a soft and gracious beauty which one associates with Devon and Somerset. A stone bridge spans a river on the banks of which are grey stone cottages and an old grey church.

It is a hushed, quiet little place; the only sound is the music of the stream as it moves over its pebbles. On this evening the waters were slow and unruffled by the wind. I leant over the bridge, admiring the trees reflected in the calm water and the green ferns that grow on the piers and between the stones of the bridge. Children were playing on the footpath by the stream, trying to make a small dog leap in after a stone. From the cottage chimneys came a faint smell of wood smoke.

Nearly opposite the Feathers Inn are two cottages. One of them has a small lean-to building at the side of it. This is the cottage in which Mr. Lloyd George was brought up by his uncle, a shoemaker. No matter whether a man is Liberal, Labour or Conservative, he must agree that the Welsh wizard is one of the greatest personalities of our time. In days to come men and women will still visit this quiet village to see the cottage so intimately associated with the Welshman who took charge of the destinies of the British Empire during the darkest moment in our history.

Most people would tell you that Mr. Lloyd George was born in Wales. He was born sixty-nine years ago at Chorlton-on-Medlock, near Manchester. His father, a schoolmaster and a native of Fishguard, gave up schooling and took a farm near Haverfordwest, in Pembrokeshire. When David was less than a year old his father died and the family was cared for by an uncle, Richard Lloyd of Llanystumdwy.

Audacity has been the watchword of Mr. Lloyd George's career. It is true that he became a rebel quite early in life, but many of the stories attributed to his infancy are no doubt apocryphal. It is said that when this blow fell upon the family, the young Lloyd George encouraged his sister to pack the garden gate with gravel in the hope that unpleasant men would be prevented from seizing the household gods! This first wile of Ulysses is, of course, too good to be true!

In Llanystumdwy he was brought up in a stern, religious atmosphere by a relative who was a local preacher. He attended the village school, and at the age of sixteen he decided to apply his wits to the law. He became an articled clerk to a solicitor in Portmadoc. When he qualified as a solicitor at the age of twenty-one, he was too poor to buy his robes, which cost three guineas. In Wales a solicitor has to appear in robes before he receives an audience.

The event which brought the name of Lloyd George first before the public has now been forgotten. It was known all over Wales as the 'Llanfrothen burial case'. A quarryman, a Dissenter, died expressing the wish to be buried in the local churchyard near the grave of his child. There was some dispute about this, and Mr. Lloyd George, taking the part of the dead quarryman, advised the local people to break down the churchyard wall if the vicar refused to open the gates for the coffin. This was done. Fines for trespass followed, which on appeal were quashed, and after the litigation the name of Lloyd George was known from one end of the Principality to the other.

It was this case which led to the young solicitor's adoption as Parliamentary candidate for Caernarvon boroughs. He was elected by a small majority and became known—how strange to think of it now—as 'the Boy M.P.' He went into Parliament not so much as a Liberal but as a Welsh Nationalist and Nonconformist. He gave the world a taste of his future qualities when he declared, on his election, that 'the banner of the red dragon had been borne aloft in triumph'. Westminster looked at him and realized that something new had happened.

Those of us who are not yet forty can, if we come from Tory families, remember Lloyd George as some kind of political ogre. Our fathers used to call him 'that damned little Welshman'. We can probably remember, as small boys, hearing a gathering of the old guard work itself up into a state of incoherent fury about death duties or land duties, or something. We did not know what it was about, but at the bottom of it all was, one gathered, a very small Welshman—almost a 'nihilist', that was the word—who used extremely ungentlemanly language to dukes. Our generation was to know him much better. His voice came like a strong wind in the war years, the old fighting voice of Wales, and we who were too young to care about 'Billingsgate' knew that one man in Great Britain could feed the guns in France.

I was walking back from Llanystumdwy, not far from where the road leads to Bryn Awelon, when I saw, coming towards me down the lane, a man in a brown tweed suit. His picturesque silver hair was visible under a tweed hat, and his blue eyes looked keenly at the world from a nest of good-humoured wrinkles. It was Lloyd George. I told him that I had been to Llanystumdwy. We began to talk about Wales. There is something patriarchal about Mr. Lloyd George. He really looked like the father of his country as he stood there in the lane.

There is also something boyish about him, something lovable and tender, something quizzical and something gentle. It is difficult to think of him as the relentless political warrior. I suppose all Welsh warriors have been a strange blend of bard and fighter ; mystic and materialist.

We talked about the Welsh landscape, Welsh history, the Welsh Nonconformist revival and the Welsh language.

'It is difficult to express oneself in Welsh when one has been in England for a long time,' he said, 'I am making a speech in Welsh very soon because the people who will come down from the hills to hear me would be bitterly disappointed if I spoke in English. When I speak in Welsh I think in Welsh. It is a magnificent language. It is a splendid language for an orator. It is a dramatic language. In English I would say the same things but in a different way.'

He looked at me with his quick blue eyes :

'What impresses you about Wales ? ' he asked.

'I like to watch the difference between the Welsh-speaking people and visitors from England. I was in an inn parlour the other night. As soon as the Englishman had left the room the Welsh spoke in their own language and became different men.'

'Yes,' said Mr. Lloyd George, 'and better men.'

He laughed when I told him how I had been claimed as a great musician by the schoolmaster.

'You are right,' he laughed. 'That is the dramatic Welsh temperament. And by describing you as a musician he also inspired and encouraged his class. Yes, we are a dramatic people.'

He told me a story of the great preacher, John Elias. On the night before he preached in a country chapel, Elias found the caretaker and ordered him to light a number of candles in the chapel. He then mounted the pulpit and ordered certain of the candles to be extinguished until only a few were left burning. These few were lighted on the night of his sermon. He worked up his audience to a pitch of fervour and then, as he spoke about the Finger of the Lord, he flung out a hand and pointed at his audience. They saw with something like terror an enormous shadowy finger printed by the light of the candles on the walls of the chapel :

'It must have been terrific,' said Mr. Lloyd George.

I watched him go on down the lane with the feeling that he is in direct descent from the Welsh champions of old. Some one described him once as a 'country-bred elf'. This elfishness was a quality attributed to Glendower.

§ 3

The dark hills narrow on either side. A thin rain is falling. The water shines on the rocks. There is no sound but the plaintive bleating of mountain sheep and the rush of streams falling from the hills. This is the Pass of Llanberis.

The stone walls twist round, following the line of the road ; sheep hide from the sweeping rain in the shelter of them ; high up on the hill-side great rocks are poised as if they had been left there from some old battle of giants. And against the sky the dark hills take in queer shapes.

I would hate to see the Pass of Llanberis in the height of summer-time, when the charabancs go through it. On a wet spring day it gathers into it all the loneliness, all the sadness, all the brooding melancholy which are at the heart of Celtic countries. It might be in Ireland. It might be in Scotland : it could never be in England.

The memories that live up in the black Valhalla of the Welsh hills are memories strange to the English mind. They are of kings who were half poets, and poets who were half kings ; of queer things that happened in the dark, and in the half light ; of swords and struggle and failure in an age so remote that it ended where our history begins.

And the right time to see these sad places is when the rain falls over them, and the wind cries in them like something that has been lost since the beginning of the world.

I came up to the top of the pass where two inns stand near together in mist, friendly as all places are which promise fire and food in the mountains. They are interesting inns. Their kind in Scotland have improbable trout and salmon stuffed in the hall with the name of the man who caught them in 1889. But these inns at the foot of Snowdon, preserve other relics. They have shelves stocked with enormous nailed boots, ice-axes, ropes.

Their halls ring to the tramp of mountaineers and in the evening men talk of nothing but 'couloirs' and 'chimneys' and 'glaciers', and other things which mean nothing to men who do not venture into high places. The shadow of Snowdon is always on the Pass of Llanberis.

When you come to the top of the pass a great valley sweeps down to the right and the brown hills lie against the sky. It is like coming out of darkness into light. On the hill-sides are tiny farms scratched with the most desperate courage from the hard rock. The Welsh farmer in the mountains round Snowdon, working with his sons as most of them do, tills land that would break most men's hearts.

This peasant determination to survive and make the best of a bad job is seen all over the mountains of Wales as in the west of Ireland.

The ruined clachans on the hills of Scotland prove also that the same courage existed there before the Highlanders emigrated or were driven overseas.

A sign-post says 'Bettws-y-Coed'.

You need more courage than I possess to take the road that leads away from it! This waterfall has been sanctified by centuries of sightseeing. I went on to it with the faint feeling that I was being bullied by Ruskin.

A young woman stood beside a post-card kiosk dressed in the national costume of Wales. She wore a high top-hat and a red cloak and a check apron over her skirt. I believe the Welsh top-hat dates only from Stewart times. It is exactly the same kind of hat that Guy Fawkes wore.

'Is that an old hat?' I asked.

'No,' she said, taking it off.

Inside was the name of a well-known London hatter!

The history of the red cloak is interesting. In 1797 three French frigates landed a force of six hundred soldiers and eight hundred convicts near Fishguard. Their surrender was due four days later to the belief that a large force of British soldiers was approaching, but these were Welshwomen in their red cloaks!

The fall at Bettws-y-Coed deserves all the nice things that have been said about it. It is a magnificent cascade.

§ 4

If you would see a pass that is as friendly as Llanberis is gloomy, take the road through Aberglaslyn to Beddgelert. The river runs between steep hills covered with fir-trees, and its music goes with you all the way. It leads to one of the most beautiful villages in Wales. It is a place that teems with stories preserved largely by the splendid work of William Jones, who spent his life behind a draper's counter and his leisure in writing the folk-lore of Wales.

The legend of the faithful hound is, of course, the best known. Gelert, it is said, was a hound which was presented by King John to his son-in-law, Llewelyn the Great. The hound was a great hunter, and his prowess has been embalmed in four lines of Welsh poetry which were idiotically translated during Victorian times as follows:

The remains of famed Gelert, so faithful and good
The hounds of the cantred conceal,
Whenever the doe or the stag he pursued,
His master was sure of a meal.

On one occasion, however, Llewelyn, who was possibly not hungry, dispensed with the services of Gelert and went off to the chase, leaving the hound to guard the hunting-lodge. Llewelyn's infant son was in a cradle in the lodge. When the prince returned, his dog, with joyful cries and much wagging of the tail, ran out to meet him. Llewelyn noticed that his coat was covered in blood. This alarmed the prince, who rushed to the nursery, where he saw an overturned cradle and more blood. Instead of turning the cradle to see if his child had been harmed—as you or I would have done—the impetuous chieftain drew his sword and thrust it into the body of Gelert, on the assumption that his hound had killed the child. Only after poor Gelert had been slain did Llewelyn turn over the cradle to discover his infant, safe and sound, lying beside the dead carcase of a wolf. Then Llewelyn knew that Gelert had been wounded himself in defending his young master.

This story is told every year to thousands of people. Millions must know it and believe it to be true. It is almost a pity to spoil it. But the truth is—as Joseph Jacobs and other folk-lorists have pointed out—that the legend was unknown in Beddgelert before the year 1798. The higher critics believe that it was imported by David Pritchard, the landlord of the Goat Hotel in the eighteenth century. This man came full of excellent stories from South Wales. Among them may have been the story of Gelert or of some other hound who was slain by a prince, for similar tales were current all over Europe in the Middle Ages and were known, as the Rev. Baring-Gould proved, even in Thibet!

The innkeeper of Beddgelert, being a wise man with a sound sense of publicity, erected a stone in a field near by. He called it 'Gelert's Grave'. It became the custom for all Victorian travellers in Wales to go there and shed a sentimental tear. They were greatly assisted in their sorrow by a well-known and unconsciously funny poem written in Wales under the influence of the legend, by the Hon. W. R. Spencer. The last lines are:

And now a gallant tomb they raise
With costly sculpture deck'd,
And marbles storied with his praise
Poor Gelert's bones protect.

There never could the spearman pass,
Or forester, unmov'd;
There oft the tear-besprinkled grass
Llewelyn's sorrow prov'd.

And there he hung his horn and spear,
And there, as evening fell,
In fancy's piercing sounds would hear
Poor Gelert's dying yell.

And till great Snowdon's rocks grow old,
And cease the storm to brave,
The consecrated spot shall hold
The name of 'Gelert's Grave'.

The grave is still shown to tourists in a field at the back—from which, by the way, there is a marvellous view—but whether the young men and maidens who dash through the Pass of Aberglaslyn in motor-cars are as sentimental, or as credulous, as their grandparents I cannot say.

§ 5

Llanberis, as millions of people know, is at the foot of Snowdon. Every one who has been there will remember the grotesque mountain of slate that rises on the opposite bank of the lake. It glitters in sun or rain.

It is a queer, improbable mountain. Men have been attacking it for generations. They have bared it to the spine. It stands among the untouched hills, the victim of man's energy, a vast blue-grey mountain that cooled into slate ages before Life appeared on the earth.

Slate is one of the oldest of rock formations. Its intense hardness is due to the great pressure that has acted on it for millions of years, and also to the bands of molten rock which, in volcanic ages, have been shot up through the slate-beds, submitting them to an incredible heat.

Welsh slate (as every architect, but not every houseowner knows) is the hardest and best slate in the world. It will outlast any house. Leicester Town Hall was roofed with Welsh slate in the reign of Henry VII, and the slates are still as good as new.

If any proof were needed that Welsh slate is the hardest in the world, you have the word ' Cambrian ', which geologists have given to the oldest and hardest of all rock strata. Cambria was, of course, the Roman name for Wales.

When I arrived at the Dinorwic Quarry I was taken to the manager's office, where a map of the great North Wales slate quarries was shown to me. Slate is to North Wales what coal is to the south.

' There are about twenty slate quarries in Caernarvonshire and Merionethshire. The Dinorwic Quarry is the most spectacular. It is not only the biggest quarry in the world : it is also the largest man-made excavation.

On the mantelpiece were lumps of rock and abnormal chunks of slate. I picked up one of them.

' Why do you keep this ? ' I asked.

'Oh, that lump killed a man.'

'How?'

'We blast the slate from the quarry and every one takes cover, as you will see. One poor fellow put his head round the shelter to watch the explosion, and it was probably a million to one, but—that small piece hit him. . . .'

I went out to explore Slate Mountain.

There is nothing, except, perhaps, the Isle of Portland, quite like the Dinorwic Quarry.

The mountain rises to a height of 1,400 feet. It has been quarried in terraces. One glance at the mighty face of the mountain tells you that the system is to work the slate away evenly all over the mountain in order to avoid under-cutting.

It is a pyramid with a broad base that is being continually reduced.

As you look at the great gashes in the mountain, some of them vast enough to hold St. Paul's Cathedral, it seems to you incredible that Man with his white little hands could have visited such ruin on Slate Mountain.

'And, look!' said my guide, 'although we have done so much we have barely scratched the face of the mountain. We have enough left to roof the world for untold centuries. . . .'

And I glanced up to the summit of Slate Mountain, where miles of rough grass and rock have never known Man.

Over fifty miles of railway run through the Dinorwic Quarry. Small, toy-like engines pull long trains loaded with slates.

You stand gazing up at steep precipices of slate. The mountain is an amazing study in colour. Seams of sea-green slate lie next to bands of grey and purple-grey; slate almost the colour of claret lies next to slate that is almost blue.

'There is not a fossil in that mountain,' I was told. 'You are looking at rock that formed ages before there was any life on earth. . . .'

The slates come down from the mountain on a steep little railway. The trucks are attached to steel-wire ropes with a breaking strain of thirty tons. They come slowly down the long incline, and, as one loaded chain of trucks descends, a line of 'empties' goes up on a double line.

This line runs up into the heart of the mountain. It is a main line which communicates with every 'gallery' in the quarry.

'Jump in!' said my guide.

We caught a chain of 'empties' and sat on the little trucks. We were pulled up slowly for fifteen minutes over a gradient that was sometimes one in two.

We came to a level junction. We walked some way and saw before us another steep track leading up to another junction. We caught another train and so we went on for half an hour.

We stepped out half-way up the mountain-side, where the air was already colder. Here were sheds and workshops. Slate from 'galleries' miles distant was coming down to this place to be cut and trimmed before going on to the ground level.

On the edge of an appalling drop I stood and looked down. Slate everywhere. Great gullies of bared slate. Steel-hard ravines of slate. Far below, the little slate trains, the engines no bigger than a lump of sugar, puffed noiselessly over the lines. The lake looked like a saucer of blue water.

Suddenly a harsh siren blew, echoing all over Slate Mountain.

'Come on, take cover!' said my guide. 'It's the signal for blasting.'

We could see men in a near gallery stop work and enter a stone hut. We had hardly taken cover before the first explosion occurred.

'Boom!'

The explosion cracked in a hundred valleys, and went rolling to the sky. I peeped through a hole in the hut and saw far up on the mountain-side a belch of smoke and a sudden fall of rock. It was extraordinarily like an artillery bombardment. Explosion after explosion shook the quarry. Some were near, some distant. I felt they were getting our range!

In every gallery where slate was being quarried, men working with rock drills had set their charges of powder. In every stone safety hut the workers were watching their own blast. Should it fail to go off they would be forced to signal and remain under cover for half an hour.

But to-day there were no misfires. Twenty or twenty-five

high velocity shells seemed to be registering hits on Slate Mountain. One was so near that we could hear the splitting of tons of slate and then the dull sound of its fall. Silence followed. We waited for five minutes. The siren blew.

'All clear,' said my guide. 'We can go out.'

In the nearest gallery we saw the result of an explosion. Tons of beautiful green slate had been torn from the mountain. Some of it had been hurled in masses to the earth; some of it lay poised forty feet up on the face of the quarry, some of it had not fallen, but remained cracked and ready to be dislodged.

Quarrymen with ropes round their waists then let themselves down the steep flanks of the 'gallery'. They worked with picks at the slate that had not fallen. Great slabs of it came crashing down. It was quickly cut into tombstones about five inches thick, loaded on trucks pushed by two men, and taken over a branch line to the little funicular railway. We followed it into the workshops.

The splitting and dressing of slate blocks is one of the most fascinating sights of the kind I have ever seen. Slate is the only stone that is capable of being split longitudinally into smooth flat layers without losing the hardness of the original block.

The skill with which the worker tackles five-inch thick slabs of slate, splitting them and again splitting them, is something that cannot be learnt quickly: it can be acquired only after years of apprenticeship. Slate working is something like an hereditary occupation in North Wales. It looks easy; but try, as I did, to split a slate with a mallet and—see what happens!

Men sit at circular saws, in long workshops, grey with slate dust. The huge blocks are pushed up to the teeth of the saw. In a few moments a long slab is cut into lengths, each about one inch thick. Watch an expert worker take an inch thick piece of slate. He has a fish-tailed chisel and a mallet. He places the chisel on the edge of the slab, gives two or three light taps with his mallet, and in a second he has pressed a slate from the slab.

It is possible to divide an inch thick slab into nine slates, but actually no slates are made less than one-sixth of an inch in thickness.

When the slates have been split, they are trimmed. This

is done by hand and by machinery ; the hand-trimming is, of course, more interesting.

Men and boys sit with piles of rough slates beside them. They put the slate on a sharp edge and with incredible speed and complete accuracy of judgment give a series of sharp blows with a knife-blade and—a slate is squared !

In workshops all over the blue-grey flank of Slate Mountain, men cut up the slate into various sizes. They have queer names for them. The largest slate is a 'Queen', the next size a 'Duchess' ; and so they go on through Debrett until you get the sixteen by eight-inch slate, which is a perfect little 'Lady'.

The men employed in this trade are a fine type. They come from miles round Llanberis. They have an open-air look, and they laugh easily. I imagine that if the Welsh slate industry was not working on short time it would be perfectly happy. The quarry contains an interesting personality in a man who is seventy-one, and feels like a boy. He has a name which sounds like a piece of Welsh history—Owen Griffiths Jones. He is a deacon, and one of the best slate-makers in the quarry. And he cannot speak a word of English !

I talked to him with the help of an interpreter, but I am afraid I missed all his jokes.

Mr. Jones left Wales once to visit London during Queen Victoria's Jubilee. He has a vivid memory of a London that has gone for ever. He stayed only a day, but he seems to have seen everything.

'How on earth did you get on without English ?' I asked him.

'Ah,' he replied in Welsh, 'two Welsh girls met me.'

He remembered the cabs and hansoms in the Strand !

We caught a train of 'empties' and set off on the steep journey to earth.

'By the way,' I said, 'I have seen every kind of roofing slate, and even a slate mantelpiece, but I have not seen one slate pencil or one writing-slate.'

'That side of the industry is absolutely dead,' I was told. 'In the old days millions of pencils and slates were made. They provided a great amount of work. The writing slates had to be polished and framed. But now Health Authorities have banished the writing slate from schools. They say it is not hygienic.'

We slipped down over the edge of the mountain. I kept looking up at galleries and terraces whose slate now roofs buildings in London, Paris and New York. I was reminded of the Isle of Portland, where they point to steep valleys and say:

'That's where St. Paul's came from!'

The Dinorwic Quarry can point to its blue-grey caverns and its gashed valleys and say:

'That's where the best roofs in the world come from. . . .'

§ 6

There was a middle-aged man in the Llanberis inn who interested me because he was Welsh and because he was always writing. Some men write unostentatiously, some write casually, some write imperceptibly. But this writer was a glutton for pen and ink. He obviously adored the sensation of putting his thoughts on paper. He would pause in mid-sentence and gaze upward for a moment as if some god were handing him the right word. Then, when a sentence took his fancy, a pleased little smile would come to his face and he would put in a comma or two, cross a 't' and proceed with the utmost self-satisfaction. I hated the sight of him.

One night we were alone in the inn. I was reading and watching apprehensively for that moment when he would move over to a writing-table and enjoy himself. When that moment arrived I was determined to go out and drink beer with a ploughman. Then a surprising thing happened. He got up, touched a bell and said:

'Will you join me in a drink, sir?'

I thought to myself, 'Good heavens, he is now going to bore me with a long account of the book he is writing. How can I get out of it?'

'Thanks,' I heard my good manners reply.

So we sat down together, and, after talking about the usual drivel that men discuss to hide mutual suspicions, the iniquities of the weather and the Government, the state of the roads and the crops, we became more human and talked about Wales and the Welsh. I began to like him. After a discussion about Ogham stones I discovered that he was a member of a Cambrian archaeological society. He told me that he had been preparing a lecture on stone circles. I ordered another drink at once and apologized for the unworthy suspicion that he was some self-centred and intolerable author.

'What interests me about the Welsh,' I said, 'is their sensitiveness.'

'Yes: we are a sensitive nation. All conquered nations are sensitive.'

'But you are not conquered.'

'Not spiritually maybe; but do you remember what Ossian said: "They went forth to war but they always fell." That is the history of the Celt everywhere except, latterly, in Ireland.'

'Are you a Welsh home-ruler?'

'No, I am old-fashioned enough to believe in the cultural nationalism we used to talk a lot about. I believe in home rule for the intellect!'

He then began in his turn to interview me.

'What do you think about Wales?' he asked.

'That too much is known about it and too little.'

'That is true.'

'What I mean is that too many people come to Wales, look at it and go home without the slightest idea that they have encountered an alien culture. Thousands of industrialists invade you every year unconscious that they are exploring a tribal territory. When the Welsh don't behave as people behave in the Black Country, they go back and call you surly or mean or lying. And the thing that will make the Saxon and the Briton honestly and sincerely like each other has not yet been discovered!'

My friend laughed loudly.

'There is a deal of truth in that.'

'What would annoy me intensely if I were a Welshman is the ignorance and patronage of tourists. You have enough philosophy to take the cash and let the credit go, so to speak; but it is irritating. Here in the North you live two lives: one in Welsh and one in English. I have not the slightest idea what the Welsh side of it is like, but I imagine that it is more interesting and intelligent than the English. By the way, a thing that has done the Welsh more harm than anything is a rhyme that every English school-child knows. . . .'

'"Taffy was a Welshman, Taffy was a thief" . . .' cut in the archaeologist.

'What is the right version?'

He then recited the following:

Taffy was a Welshman, Taffy was a thief,
Taffy came to my house and stole a leg of beef,
I went to Taffy's house, Taffy was from home,
Taffy came to my house and stole a marrowbone.

'There is another ending to it,' he said. 'It goes like this:

I went to Taffy's house, Taffy was in bed;
I took a marrowbone and broke Taffy's head.

'Is it true,' I asked, 'that this rhyme goes back to the Border warfare, that the leg of beef represents the cows that the Welsh raiders took from Shropshire and the marrow, or mutton bone, represents the sheep stolen in a return raid?'

'That is the commonly accepted origin,' he replied. 'But there is another one. It is possible that this rhyme has nothing whatever to do with Wales or the Welsh! I believe that this was C. H. Bellenden Ker's explanation. His theory was that this rhyme is an ancient Low Dutch lampoon on the greed and selfishness of the priests. The word Taffy is a corruption of the word "Tayf", which was the term for the high black caps worn by the Dutch priests at all outdoor functions.'

He took a piece of paper, and I watched him, with a certain sinking of the heart, pull out a fountain-pen and begin to write. He handed this to me:

Tayf je was er wee helsch m'aen, Tayf je was er drief,
Tayf je gee em t'oom hye huys een stoel er leeck af beefe.

'Do you mean to say that this is Low Dutch?'

'That, I believe, is the origin of the rhyme. I have no idea at what date it became popular in England, but it is not difficult to see, if Ker's theory is right, how simple it was to corrupt Tayf into Taffy and pin the lampoon to Wales.'

On the strength of this we had another drink.

The archaeologist told me that centuries ago it was a commonplace along the Border Marches that the cry of the wood-pigeon was:

'Take two cows, Taffy, take two . . .'

This was obviously a relic of Border raiding.

'Next time you hear wood-pigeons cooing, listen and you will be able to fit these words to the sound,' said my friend. 'And you will also notice that, like a determined raider, the pigeon, if disturbed and silenced, will resume his cry where he left off. For instance, if he stops at "Take" he will begin next time with "two cows, Taffy. . . ."'

I promised to listen for this on the next opportunity.

'Why is the leek the national emblem of Wales?' I asked.

'It is not really known,' he said. 'There is a tradition that its use originated at the battle of Meigen in the seventh century. This was a battle between Edwin and his Angles and Cadwallon and his Britons. Another legend states that when King Arthur won a great victory over the Saxon invaders his Welsh troops were, by the orders of St. David, distinguished by leeks, which they wore in their caps. . . .'

'Is that to be found in any of the early chronicles?'

'No, I believe not. I think I am right in saying that there is no mention of the leek as the Welsh national emblem before Shakespeare's time. The daffodil? Yes, that also is the Welsh emblem. It is associated with St. David. . . .'

That night I was led by this talk to pick up a book I had with me called *Shakespeare and the Welsh*, by Frederick J. Harries. I came by a happy chance to a good story about the leek and the daffodil. It is as follows:

'Henry VII, in exile, remembered that the bards were for ever proclaiming anew the old prophecies that a Cymro should yet wear the crown of Britain. By stealth he came to Wales to stir up his countrymen to realize the old dream of deliverance, and he succeeded.

'In two places we get track of him in this wandering. In Mostyn Hall the window is still shown through which he escaped to the mountains while the troops of Richard were hammering at the door to take him. At Corsygedol, in Ardudwy, the same chance favoured him, and he set sail for

Brittany again from Barmouth, all his plans laid and his friends ready. It was during this wandering that the seed of our national emblem was sown. As grandson of Katherine of Valois, Harry Tudor used the green and white of Valois in his coat of arms. As a sign to each other his partisans used the green and white for a test. They did not carry it about with them. If they met each other in the field they simply pulled up a blade of grass, a wild hyacinth, a daffodil—anything that showed a green stem and a white root. If they met in a house they could lift a leek or an onion or any other vegetable which showed the two colours. And so we wear the leek, or scorn it for the daffodil in forgetful remembrance of that day.

'At the installation of the Prince of Wales at Caernarvon in July, 1911, the daffodil was substituted for the leek, and the Welsh Insurance Commissioners have also decided to prefer the dainty flower above the humble vegetable.'

I went down to breakfast full of pride and conceit to inform the archaeologist of my discovery, but, alas, to my sorrow, he had departed in the dawn towards some distant monolith.

CHAPTER EIGHT

IN WHICH I FAIL TO CLIMB SNOWDON IN A TRAIN BUT SUCCEED ON MY FEET, IN WHICH I ADMIRE THE GENIUS OF THE WELSH SHEEP-DOG AND THE MOST PERFECT VIEW IN WALES, ENDING WITH A GLANCE AT BARMOUTH AND A MARKET DAY IN DOLGELLY

§ 1

LIFE in Snowdonia has the charm of variety. You can catch small, speckled trout in hill streams, you can walk over bleak moors for days without meeting a soul, you can climb some of the most impressive mountains in Great Britain and gloom beside little black, dead-looking lakes; you can lose yourself in woodland, in open country and in terrifying nooks and crannies of the hills; or you can just sit outside an hotel and wonder why people, who look more or less sane as individuals, appear incredibly stupid when seated in a charabanc.

In midsummer I believe that this part of Wales would drive me away as cold iron drove the fairies into Ireland. Even in Maytime the first Saxon hordes begin to make the time-honoured tour of the Snowdon district. The pneumatic tyres of their saloon coaches follow the same roads and stop at precisely the same 'beauty spots' once sacred to the four-horse Victorian brake.

I love the silence of night, with stars burning above the hills and shining in still lakes. I like the dark lanes that lead to prim little Welsh mountain villages and small, warm inns where, often by light of gas or oil, a group of labourers or quarrymen will, when they have silently sized you up, become friendly and gentle, as most Welsh people are when they like you.

It is amusing to sit in a corner and watch some worthy man, whose life has been spent among crowds in Manchester or Birmingham, doing his best to cultivate the native. He wants to be friendly, and they accept the drinks for which he generously pays simply because they do not wish to offend him. In his attempt to be friendly he becomes loud ; in his desire to be interested he becomes inquisitive, and he is not conscious of the barrier which must for ever separate him from these hill people.

He talks to a man who can see corpse-lights as if he was talking to a mechanic in his factory. He does not know that his mind, outlook and background are as different from theirs as oil from water. But they know it. They protect themselves from the things they do not understand about him by wild and apparently friendly rushes of words. He thinks he is getting along splendidly. They tell him the things they think he would like to hear. It is a kind of spiritual parry. It is so easy to be extravagant in a language that is not your own ; rather like spending some one else's money. And when the ardent tourist discovers that some of their statements are not exactly accurate, he goes home and says that all Welshmen are liars. They tramp home through the dark lanes, speaking about him in Welsh. I wonder what they say. . . .

§ 2

You may think this is rather a silly story, but Welshmen who know the climate of their country will realize that it is a true one.

At six a.m. it was a heavenly morning. The sun was shining from a blue sky. All the hills were singing with their heads in the light of morning. The lake was like blue glass. The mountain burns, swollen by days of rain, gushed in their rocky beds, and it seemed that Wales had met summer. I decided to climb Snowdon. I spent a long time with maps. I decided to go through Llanberis and tackle the Old One from Pen-y-Pass and come down him another way into Beddgelert.

While I was eating breakfast, a few clouds appeared. I dressed for the ordeal, put on the right boots, took the right stick, packed the right rucksack, and, as I was leaving, I said to the hotel boots :

' It's a grand day for Snowdon ! '

' Yes, indeed—perhaps,' was his mysterious reply.

The Welsh, unless they know you very well, are too polite to contradict you. I now realize that this remark translated into good Scots would be :

' It isna a guid day, man—ye're mad.'

It was nearly noon when I reached Llanberis.

Oh, what had happened to the morning? The sky was grey. The sun had vanished. A thin mist hid the hills.

'You will see nothing at all,' said a local authority. 'I should give it up.'

This made me more determined than ever. So I hung about Llanberis waiting for the day to make up its mind. At the end of the village I came to a surprising little station—the kind of station you see in the window of a toyshop. A toy engine slid out of a shed and attached itself to a long, open coach. In this coach sat about fifteen men and women. One man wore a bowler hat. Most of the women were in black. They looked as though they were going to some aerial funeral.

As I stood there in the mist thinking how strange it all was, a man in uniform came up, and seeing, perhaps, that I was a mountaineer, offered to sell me a railway ticket to Snowdon.

When I tell you I was revolted, I am putting it mildly! I love mountains and respect them. I am still young enough to climb them. I know what it feels like to win a summit with a beating heart and feel that you own the earth. Would I take a ticket to Snowdon? I was insulted!

The conductor told me that a gale was blowing over the mountain, that no one with an ounce of sense had climbed it, and that his train could not get to the top. He would, however, sell me a three-quarter-way ticket for eight shillings.

'And why can't you get to the top with your foul train?' I asked.

'There is the Saddle,' he said. 'It is very narrow, and on either side is a drop of thousands of feet, yes, indeed. We should be blown over in this wind.'

'Well, when do you start?'

'We are waiting for a telephone message from the top.'

'Is there a post office there?'

'Oh, yes, indeed there is.'

'And an hotel?'

'Yes.'

'Then give me a ticket. It's all thoroughly immoral.'

So I fell.

I took a seat right in the front of the Snowdon express, where the conductor works the brakes. Behind me was a glass partition, and the coach in which sat the saddened tourists.

As soon as I was committed to this sinful journey I became happy. Most of all, I loved to think of the hearty men with whom I have climbed mountains: Whipcord Fordie, who goes up Ben Nevis like a goat; the Pilgrim Father from Partick, who climbs solemnly; the wild doctor who sweeps through the Larig like an angry clan. How I wished these Three Musketeers could walk on the station at Llanberis and see me sitting in the train; how I would have enjoyed their horror. . . .

A man came up the platform with the message from Snowdon. The engine, which was behind the coach, gave a startled squeal and began to push us slowly up the mountain. In half an hour we were in the clouds. Now and then, as the wind blew a hole in them, we looked down on many miles of green valley and stone walls. We puffed on over the narrow rail and it became colder. The wind waited for us round corners and came at us like a charge of cavalry.

The mourners in the coach behind were now suffering great discomfort. Some of them lay full length on the seats to escape the wind. Two women tried to let down the canvas flaps. This stopped the train. The conductor got out and warned them that if the flaps were down we might blow over if we got to the Saddle.

As we mounted, the clouds were blown straight up at us from below. It was one of those days on a mountain when you find shelter and stay near the path. The wind began to reach gale force. A man who sat next to me and had not said one word bellowed in my ear:

'It's a verra unfortunate day. . . .'

'What part of Scotland?' I shouted at him.

'Stirling,' he yelled.

'What are you doing here?'

'Having ma holidays,' he shrieked.

At this point the train stopped. We could see nothing on either hand. The wind was terrible. We could feel the train shaking gently. It was icy cold. The conductor held a consultation with the engine-driver and announced that we must turn back.

'Nonsense, man!' shouted the Scotsman. 'Get on wi' ye. . . .'

'I have been here for over thirty years, look you,' said the conductor, 'and it is not safe to cross the Saddle to-day.'

I got out to look at the Saddle, but I could hardly stand. Into the mist stretched a track perhaps ten or twelve feet wide, and on either side was a sheer drop of several thousand feet.

When I got back the Scotsman was still trying to persuade the train to go on to the top! But no; the conductor said that the train always played for safety first, and he would never cross the Saddle in a gale while he was in charge of it!

'I've no' had ma money's worth,' said the Scotsman; then he shouted at me, 'and we can get a drink at the top.'

However, to the relief of the tourists, we reversed and started back. One old lady, utterly unmoved, sat with folded hands, her spectacles glistening with condensed cloud, exactly as if she were at home in a parlour at Wolverhampton.

As we slid back to earth the clouds thinned. The sun was trying to shine. We looked up and saw a mighty cloud over Snowdon. All the devils that haunt great mountains were going mad up there. I conceived a great respect for Snowdon—though I felt none for myself! I swore that I would climb it on a better day. . . .

We stamped about Llanberis Station trying to get warm. The conductor told us that a sudden storm had swept up from the west. The Scotsman was still unsatisfied.

'Man,' he said to me, 'did ye pay eight shillings for yon ticket?'

'I did.'

'Ye should hae got a reduced one like mine,' he said, and went off happily.

§ 3

You meet him everywhere in Wales. He is the presiding deity of the narrow lanes. He is a small, black-and-white fellow with a foxy little body and the manner of a senior wrangler. They call him a sheep-dog.

When the sheep move like a grey wave over the road he cruises on the fringe of their stupidity, never hurting them, just watching and doing the right thing with the quiet certainty of a woman.

The shepherd clumps behind, smoking his pipe and thinking whatever shepherds think, until you become tired of waiting and sound an indignant hoot on a motor-horn.

Now, if the shepherd were alone, this is what would happen: the flock would panic. The awful sense of physical disaster which, perhaps, centuries of onion sauce have bred in these poor, scatter-brained creatures, would drive some forward, some backward, while the majority would stand frozen in terror and indecision.

The lambs would become separated from their mothers. They would leap about, seeking the safety of a sheltering flank ; and if you had the heart to prolong this rout you would drive the headmost for half a mile and scatter them to hedge and field.

No man with a stick could prevent this. The greatest general or the finest organizing genius would be helpless.

Only the little fellow on four legs can handle the situation. He looks back at you with his quick, brown eyes, runs forward, heads the flock, holds them with the authority of his eye, makes a path for you ; and as you go by he looks up at you with a grin :

'I know my job,' he seems to say. 'I was born and bred for it.'

Welsh shepherds and farmers love their dogs.

I gave ten shillings for him,' said one shepherd, 'and I would not sell him for ten thousand pounds ; I would not, indeed. . . .'

'That is a lot of money,' I said, knowing that he did not realize how much it was.

'Well, indeed,' he replied, 'I would not sell him for twenty pounds ! I could not do my work without him.'

From the Llanberis road I saw a sheep-dog perform without any fuss an act of rescue which no man could have accomplished. Two sheep had somehow become lodged on an outward ledge of rock far up on the mountain-side. The shepherd and I could see them through field-glasses, standing on the edge of a precipice.

The shepherd thought carefully before he decided to risk his precious dog on the enterprise.

'He will do it,' he said at last, handing the glasses back to me ; but I could tell that he hated to send the little fellow off on the adventure.

The dog streaked off over the hill. He appeared above a dip and turned to receive instructions. The shepherd gave a long whistle.

The dog ran through the heather, and, looking up, saw the sheep. He crouched down and considered the situation. He ran one way and found that he could not reach them ; he ran another way and found himself facing an unclimbable face of rock. Then he disappeared.

We saw him in a few minutes cautiously approaching the sheep from the top. One indiscreet move on his part and the creatures might in their panic have fallen to certain death. But the dog knew !

He slithered down the rock like a ferret. He lay there flat on his stomach. The sheep, aware of him, turned towards him. He lay there and seemed to mesmerize them. They were incapable of action.

Then, holding them in his power, the brave little thing worked his way to the precipice, stood between them and the drop and—barked. After a desperate battle between brain and fear, he won. The sheep, in their crazy terror, leaped upwards over the rock into safety.

In a few moments they came running back over the hill, behind them the grinning little friend of shepherds. He crouched down in the grass and smiled.

'That is a good dog,' said the shepherd.

The dog knew that he was being praised. He leapt up and came running to his master's feet.

Every one who has seen the miracles of intelligence performed at a sheep-dog trial must have wondered how these animals are trained.

On the Welsh hills I saw a black-and-white sheep-dog pup taking his first lesson in discipline. He was chained by the collar to his father.

The old dog was an expert. He could be sent over miles of country by either a wave of the arm or a whistle. He could be made to wheel to left or right ; he could be told to single one sheep from a flock ; he could be instructed to drive them to the left or right of a hurdle. He was the finished product.

The pup had no idea what was happening. When a whistle sent his parent off over the field he hesitated a moment and was dragged after him.

He joined in the game. He thought it was great fun ! A second whistle and the old dog dropped like a stone. The young one did not understand. He was dragged down. So it went on time after time. More than once, the parent nipped the young one to bring him to earth.

'It will not take long,' said the shepherd. 'He will soon know the signals. His father and his grandfather are the best sheep-dogs in these parts.'

In the day's work of the countryside there is nothing quite like this partnership between man and beast. It is a lovely thing to see because there is no cruelty in it. The dog respects and obeys his man, and the man knows that his best friend in spring, summer and winter is the little shadow on four feet who fulfils his lightest wish as if he were a god.

§ 4

The Welsh name for the summit of Snowdon is *Y Wyddfa*, which is sometimes wrongly translated as 'the far-seen'; but the original name was *Y Wyddfa Fawr*, which is said to mean 'the great burial-place'.

Snowdon, although it is 846 feet lower than Ben Nevis, is a more sublime and impressive mountain. Its cone-shaped summit, like that of a dead volcano, lifts itself in majesty above the five attendant peaks, and on a clear day it dominates the scenery of North Wales.

Nature shrouds its great head in cloud, and man has woven around it a cloud of legend. Imagination is part heredity and part environment. A man born of Kentish parents and brought up on the gentle chalk downs, and among the sweet meadow-lands and hop gardens of the southland, will have a different outlook from one born of a race of mountaineers whose first memory is a great thunder-storm in the hills. Our first attempt to reconcile ourselves to our surroundings is made by way of legend and story. English children hear tales of fairies and goblins, none of them cruel, some mischievous like Puck, but on the whole nice friendly fairies that would never startle you, the creatures of lovely woodland or broad acre or gracious river-bank. The Scottish fairy is a lost pagan hiding in the land of John Knox. You could not talk to him as you could with an English fairy, or if you did he would put a spell on you and you would awaken a century hence like Rip Van Winkle or the two pipers of Strathspey. The same may be said of the Irish fairy. They pipe on the hills, but you listen to their music at your peril. Good Catholics put their fingers in their ears. In other words, where a country is hard and cruel the fairies are dangerous;

where it is kind and soft they are capable of good deeds and generosity.

The Welsh fairies are more interesting than any others because, it seems to me, they have their roots in England. There are two kinds of fairies in Wales: the dangerous ones who live in all mountains and the pretty ones who hide in fox-gloves and come to dance in the moonlight. There are thousands of stories about these good fairies who dance in the mushroom rings, just as they do in England, who make beautiful music, who, like Robin Goodfellow, sometimes want to play with milk-pails. I wonder if the Welsh Goodfellows are the old fairies of Roman Britain who were driven west into the mountains when the Saxon war-bands came raiding so long ago.

You have only to spend a day walking through the Pass of Llanberis or climbing the mountains of Snowdonia to know that the oldest fairies in this part of Wales must be malicious and terrifying. If you found a kind one in this wild place I think you could safely trace his ancestry back to a softer land.

The legends of Snowdon are of giants and demons, of terrifying battles in the clouds, of giantesses hurling red-hot stones into the valleys and of horses whose hoof-beats were like thunder.

Four giants ruled the mountains round Dolgelly: they were Idris whose 'seat', or Cader, was the mountain-top; Yscydion, Offrwm and Ysbryn. Idris was the chief giant. On Snowdon lived the most powerful of all giants, Rhitta, who wore an unpleasant garment made of the beards of kings whom he had slain. The act of cutting off a man's beard was the most deadly insult that could be offered in the old days.

Rhitta seems to have exercised a restraining influence on the nobility of early times. Two kings, Nynniaw and Peibiaw, were once boasting on the slopes of Snowdon.

'See what a vast field I possess!' said one.

'Where is it?' asked the other.

'There it is,' replied the first, pointing to the sky.

'Do you not see my countless flocks and herds?' asked the second.

'Where?'

'All the stars.'

'They are grazing in my pastures,' said the first.

So a great war was declared. Rhitta, the Giant of Snowdon, intervened and, according to his barbarous practice, cut off the beards of both kings. The news of this outrage spread over the land and twenty-eight kings of Britain marched to Wales to avenge the insult. Rhitta took them captive and, before reaping their beards, observed grimly:

'This is *my* extensive field!'

Snowdon is haunted by both Merlin and Arthur.

The magician, Merlin, appears first on the dome-shaped hill of Dinas Emrys, between Beddgelert and Capel Curig, when Vortigern was building a great castle. But in the night the stones that had been erected during the day were cast down. Vortigern demanded that his wise men should explain this. The chief was told to search for a lad without a father and to sprinkle his blood among the foundations of the building. Some time after, in the streets of Carmarthen, a boy, who was being taunted by his playfellows because he was fatherless, was captured and taken to Dinas Emrys. This lad was the great and fearsome Merlin of the Arthurian legends.

When he was questioned he displayed so great a knowledge that not only was his life spared but the inferior magicians were put to death. Merlin then gave to Vortigern his version of the phenomena.

'Two dragons,' he said, 'one red and one white, live in a subterranean cave beneath the hill. They sleep by day and fight by night, and the fury of their quarrel causes the half-built walls to fall down.'

The Red Dragon symbolized the Britons; the White Dragon the Saxons. As long as the struggle continued the castle would never be completed. And this was true.

The White and the Red Dragons fought for centuries. The White often seemed to win, but the Red Dragon was never beaten to the earth.

And to the solitude of Snowdon comes that most mysterious hero, King Arthur. Perhaps nothing will ever be known about this hero of romance. His fame has spread over Europe. Countless poems have been made, and continue to be made, about him. Two of his contemporaries, Gildas and Aneurin, do not mention him. Bede had never heard of him. Taliesin and Llywarch Hen mention him casually. Then centuries after his lifetime, he gradually dawns on history as the exterminator of the heathen Saxon, the gallant king who symbolized the heroic resistance of the Welsh, or Britons, to the invader from over the sea.

Some historians even doubt his existence ; others see him as a Roman soldier, or as a Romanized Briton, who, when the legions left this island, remembered enough of organized warfare to be a tower of strength in the bloody days that followed.

That is how I see him. Imagine a retired British colonel, who finds himself abandoned in a British province from which all regular troops have been withdrawn. Imagine that province to be attacked by invading savages. What would the colonel do ? Surely he would put on his uniform, try and remember as much as he could about drill and tactics and organize resistance modelled on the methods of the vanished British army ? In time, given a few good fights, his memory might become idealized. He would have identified himself so thoroughly with the ambitions of an oppressed people that he would be remembered as their champion.

Surely Arthur was an ex-officer of Rome who by means of his superior military training defeated the Saxons in twelve battles. Six hundred places in the British Isles claim some memory of him. The higher critics call him a ' culture myth ', a sun myth or a racial totem. It is, I think, more reasonable to think of him as a real man : a Roman soldier who rose up among the ruins of the crumbling Western Empire and for a little time tried to drive the barbarians towards the sea.

The unreal Arthur is, of course, the Arthur of Malory, and the even less creditable Old Etonian Arthur of Tennyson. This prince was destined to return to his native land, centuries after his death, with a French accent and clothed in the plate armour of mediaeval Europe.

But Arthur remains for ever essentially the hero of Wales as Alfred is the hero of England. M. Gaston Paris has given reasons for his belief that Welsh bards travelled England and the Continent in pre-Norman and Norman times singing their songs of Arthur, so that to Wales is partly due the sowing of that fertile seed of romance. But the memory of Arthur, the hero and national leader, lived on in the minds of the Welsh people for centuries. It was believed as late as the reign of

Henry II that he would return, hale and hearty, from the Isle of Avallon to lead his countrymen to victory against the English as he led their ancestors against the Saxon.

The Welsh believed this legend so firmly that Henry II considered it necessary to destroy the legend before he could conquer Wales. That is why in the year 1189 the obliging monks of Glastonbury suddenly discovered the bones of Arthur and his queen, Guinevere, among the tombs in their monastery!

What has become of Arthur's coffin? Giraldus Cambrensis, who was alive at the time, gave the inscription on the sarcophagus as: 'Hic jacet sepultus inclytus rex Arthurius, in insula Avallonia, cum Wennevereia uxore sua secunda.'

The Welsh, however, were not impressed. They continued to believe that their hero was biding his time. And stories were told over the fire-side how now and then Arthur and his men had revealed themselves to some simple shepherd on the slopes of Snowdon. They would be seen playing at chess in a great cave in the inaccessible ravines of the mountain, or they would be lying asleep, their shields and swords beside them, and sometimes a man lost in that wild place would come upon them leaning on their spears with closed eyes waiting for the sound of the bell of Destiny.

The very winds of Snowdon still breathe the name of Arthur, and when the Welshman, Henry Tudor, became Henry VII of England, he called his first-born Arthur. This unlucky prince died to make way for his more robust brother—who became Henry VIII—but for centuries the virtues of Prince Arthur were sung by the Welsh.

§ 5

It was six o'clock and a fine, clear morning.

I looked at the sky and the hills. The sky was clear, the sun was bright and the hills lay hushed in the white mists that had gathered about them in the night. White veils had dropped down into the valleys to lie there like smoke. Clouds hung anchored to the mountain-tops.

Mountains turn the thoughts of man towards God, and in no mood are they more ominous and awe-inspiring than in this still morning time. Jehovah did not proclaim the Law upon the sands of the Sinai desert but on a shrouded mountain-top to the terrifying sound of those trumpets which, it seems,

7a. THE PASS OF LLANBERIS.

7b. BALA LAKE.

8. ST DAVID'S CATHEDRAL.

might at any moment ring out when sky and mountains meet. And as I looked at the mountains of Snowdonia I felt that their shrouded gullies and hidden pinnacles might hold who knows what pagan mysteries: the old Gods of Britain, perhaps, discredited, anaemic deities long starved of blood, gathered together in the hidden solitudes to remember the smell of roasting flesh.

Even as I looked the mists moved, stirred by the growing heat of the sun. They moved like sleepers awakened by the day. They stirred uneasily and stole, steaming gently, up the great flanks of the hills. And soon the sky was a pale blue.

At about ten o'clock I set off to climb Snowdon. This is the easiest mountain to climb in Great Britain: it can also be the most dangerous. You can go up by train or pony from Llanberis, or you can take one of a number of well-known routes to the summit.

I left the road at Gorphwysfa, at the top of the Llanberis Pass, and took a cart track that led me gently towards a lake called Llyn Teyrn. I left this lake on my left and in half a mile or so came to a long, narrow strip of water that lies 1,500 feet above the sea. This was Llyn Llydaw. I was in wild mountain land. All round, except to the east, the arms of Snowdon lifted themselves in grim and fearful majesty. The lake was ruffled by a slight wind. Right ahead of me, its lower slopes cut across by the shoulders of lesser heights, was Snowdon. What a splendid mountain it is! It stood up on this bright morning clear against the sky like some dead volcano. I looked at its chasms and precipices. The sun picked out ledges of bare rock that shone wetly like silver. The winding path I was to take was utterly lost in the immense bulk of the mountain's base.

I sang with joy to think how lucky I was to find Snowdon at last without his cloud cap. As I crossed the lake by a rough stone causeway, I watched a hawk cruising in the sky over the opposite ridge. He hung in space and then dived like a gannet.

The path went along the northern shore of the lake for some time and led sharply over desolate rocks to another little lake lying cupped in a hollow of the hills. The wind grew colder.

Now I began to climb in real earnest. The path that had

been wide enough for a car or a cart suddenly ended; and before me stretched a steep, zigzag mountain track winding its way over loose scree towards the distant summit.

I began to suffer gloriously, and to think of iced beer. I plodded onward denying myself the luxury of a rest. I promised myself that I would lie down for a while when I topped a ridge ahead of me. When I got there, I discovered a rather fat man sitting, very red in the face, in his shirt-sleeves. Vanity urged me onward. For an hour I forced my steps upward with my heart beating and the mountain wind cold in my hair. I wondered whether Snowdon was harder to climb than Ben Nevis. Its moral effect is more destructive. On a clear day you can see the awful cone towering above you in distant and aloof glory, but on Ben Nevis, the goal of your ambitions being mercifully hidden, you plod on hoping that the worst is over. I looked back over the way I had come and took heart. Behind me lay an awful wilderness of rock; before me the track, at times invisible, ran on, twisting and turning, rising all the time into deeper solitude.

I was now well on the monster's flanks. Somewhere above me his head towered like a challenge. And it grew still colder.

Behind a distant rock, where I had promised myself a rest, I discovered two Amazons lying on their backs. One was fair; the other was dark. The fair one wore decent tweeds and the dark one wore indecent khaki shorts. Two unnecessarily immense packs lay beside them. They sat up and instinctively tidied their hair, then, remembering they were he-women, paused and smiled.

'By God,' I said, 'this is a mountain!'

They looked embarrassed, and I knew that they lived in some nice suburb.

'Have you read *The Ballad of the White Horse*?' I said.

'Yes, I have,' replied the dark one. 'It's ripping.'

'"Before the gods who made the gods had seen their sunlight pass,'" I quoted, '"the White Horse of the White Horse Vale was cut out of the grass . . .'"

'Oh, how does it go on?' she said, wrinkling her forehead.

'It goes on like this: "Before the gods that made the gods had drunk at dawn their fill, the White Horse of the White Horse Vale was hoary on the hill. Age beyond age on

British land, aeons and aeons gone, was peace and war in western hills, and the White Horse looked on ".'

'Yes; isn't it ripping?' said the dark one, while her fair friend ate a piece of chocolate and thought me mad.

'No one should climb a mountain without *The Ballad of the White Horse*.'

'You haven't got it,' said the dark one pertly.

'It's in my head.'

'Oh; I think it's ripping,' she said. 'Do say some more!'

So I did, until I noticed that the fair one showed signs of distress.

It is as interesting to encounter people on a mountain as it is to meet them in a thick fog or on a ship. I decided to write a story about a man who met a girl on a mountain and thought she was the most wonderful thing in creation until he saw her in the valley among other human beings.

'It's a topping day for Snowdon,' said the fair one.

'Simply ripping,' said the dark one.

'Do you know Moseley?' said the fair one suddenly.

'Oswald?' I asked.

'No. Birmingham?' she said.

'Oh; Moseley, Birmingham,' I said. 'I knew it before you were born. I probably passed you in your perambulator.'

'How old are you?' asked the fair one.

'Nearly forty,' I cried proudly.

'I'm eighteen,' she said.

'You look much older; almost a hag.'

'How ripping, Joan,' said the dark one. 'I shall call you the hag!'

So in this fatuous way we flirted on the slopes of Snowdon, watching the cloud shadows glide over the remote earth. Women have a way of lying about that is extraordinarily graceful and lovely. Tigers and leopards also have it; it is impossible for them to be ugly. And the sudden beauty of women in moments of which they are unconscious is so much more appealing than their million calculated tricks of beauty which so often miss the mark. I tried to think of the artist who could best have painted these girls with their generous legs, their brown arms, their clear eyes, the fair and the dark hair wind-blown, and behind them the high wilderness of barren hills. There were no horses, or A. J. Munnings would have been good. He would have caught the play of light, the sparkle of morning and the contrast between their laughing youth and the ageless gravity of the hills.

The girls from Birmingham told me that they were on their way down the mountain. They had reached the summit in cloudless weather. They had seen Anglesey lying out at sea like a green ship ; they had seen over the Irish Sea to something dark on the limits of the sky that might have been the Wicklow Hills in Ireland. They had looked north along the coast-line of North Wales ; they had looked over miles of mountain to the green Vale of Clwyd.

'It was absolutely—ripping,' said the dark one. She stood up and looked back towards Snowdon. I do wish women would leave shorts to footballers and those thin, exhausted men with hairy legs who pant unaccountably in the dusk through the streets of cities.

'The clouds are coming on!' she said.

I leapt up and said good-bye. They waved me off, and how obscurely comforting it is to be waved off by women even if you have never seen them before!

And now the path rose and twisted like a snake through the loose stones. I felt in the air about me the cruel harshness of desolate high places : a feeling that always comes to man if he is alone on a mountain. I had been climbing for perhaps half an hour when I felt mist cold and clammy on my hair and face. I ran into the ragged edge of a cloud. It would be nothing. It was a passing cloud drawn from the sea towards the cap of Snowdon as steel is drawn to a magnet. But it made it hard in places to follow the track which, here and there, was marked by little stone cairns. The path joined another. I turned to the left and knew from the chilly air and from the indescribable feeling of emptiness that I was nearly at the end of my journey. The mist grew thicker.

I came suddenly upon the silhouette of a human being. It stood before me, grey and queer, becoming, as I approached it, an elderly woman with a red nose who grasped an open umbrella. What an odd sight on the summit of Snowdon! A company of witches would not have surprised me ; a flight of shrieking furies would not have been out of place. But this very solid matron with her umbrella was almost incredible. Other forms grouped themselves about the woman with the umbrella. I saw shivering men and women, miserable and unhappy creatures who had come up by train.

On the very crest of Snowdon is a small, wooden hut. I went inside. Men and women were standing before a friendly stove drinking hot coffee. I noticed the train conductor.

'This cloud will blow away soon ?'

'You'll see nothing to-day,' he replied. 'There will be no view whatever.'

Outside the hut the mist moved thickly and the wind came over the top of Snowdon to the sound of an eerie moan. There was a little man stamping his feet and swinging his arms like a frozen cabman. He wore a thin, grey overcoat, a cap, and spectacles on which the mist had condensed.

'Rot, I call it, coming up here,' he said petulantly. 'Catch your death of cold.'

He made me howl with inward laughter. He was so absurd.

'You can 'ave it,' he said to me suddenly.

'Have what ?' I asked.

He waved his arm round at the mist.

'The whole bloomin' mountain—Snowdon. It's yours! You can 'ave it.'

He went, almost whimpering, to the conductor and asked when the train was going back.

It was like a nightmare. Queer figures developed from the mist. I found an elderly clergyman standing in the cloud wearing a worried expression. If he believed that heaven is in the air he was probably nearer to it than he had ever been, yet he looked terribly unhappy. I found an old woman, frail and brittle, who could not have walked a hundred yards of Snowdon. She stood there on the head of the monster blinking into the cloud. There was a young man from the north country who thought the adventure was a huge joke. Everything he said was hailed with shrill peals of feminine laughter.

And the devils who live in the clouds on all mountains entered into me and I wished that something really shocking might happen to us. Failing an onset of fiends, I would have liked a terrific thunder-storm.

There was a burst of laughter from the hut, cries of 'Come on!', and figures began to move towards the train, led by the little man who had presented the mountain to me. There was the noise of the train starting; then silence deep as death.

I went down through the cold mist. It became brighter.

Once or twice the wind blew holes in it and I saw for a second a brilliant picture, far away, of green fields and lakes lying in sunlight. Then the mist closed in again. I walked out of the mist into a summer day. Turning, I saw the edge of the cloud moving at my back, steaming a little round boulders, grey and ghostly.

I went down. I watched a hawk cruising. I came to green grass and rock. I heard a choir of larks in the sky. I came to the ruined mine buildings by the little lake. I looked back from Llyn Llydaw and saw a cloud no bigger than a man's hand resting on the very tip of Snowdon.

§ 6

This is the impression which Snowdon made on George Borrow when he climbed the mountain one abnormally fine day with Henrietta, his stepdaughter :

'There we stood on the Wyddfa, in a cold bracing atmosphere, though the day was almost stiflingly hot in the regions from which we had ascended. There we stood enjoying a scene inexpressibly grand, comprehending a considerable part of the mainland of Wales, the whole of Anglesey, a faint glimpse of part of Cumberland ; the Irish Channel, and what might be either a misty creation or the shadowy outline of the hills of Ireland. Peaks and pinnacles and huge moels stood up here and there, about us and below us, partly in glorious light, partly in deep shade. Manifold were the objects which we saw from the brow of Snowdon, but of all the objects which we saw, those which filled us with most delight and admiration, were numerous lakes and lagoons, which, like sheets of ice or polished silver, lay reflecting the rays of the sun in the deep valleys at his feet.

' " Here," said I to Henrietta, " you are on the top crag of Snowdon, which the Welsh consider, and perhaps with justice, to be the most remarkable crag in the world ; which is mentioned in many of their poems, amongst other in the ' Day of Judgment ', by the illustrious Goronwy Owen, where it is brought forward in the following manner :

' " Ail i'r ar ael Eryri,
Cyfartal hoewal a hi.

' " The brow of Snowden shall be levelled with the ground, and the eddying waters shall murmur round it.

'"You are now on the top crag of Snowdon, generally termed Y Wyddfa, which means a conspicuous place or tumulus, and which is generally in winter covered with snow; about which snow there are in the Welsh language two curious englynion or stanzas consisting entirely of vowels with the exception of one consonant, namely, the letter R.

'"Oer yw'r Eira ar Eryri,—o'ryw
Ar awyr i rewi;
Oer yw'r ia ar riw 'r ri,
A'r Eira oer yw 'Ryri.

'"O Ri y'Ryri yw'r oera,—or âr,
Ar oror wir arwa;
O'r awyr a yr Eira,
O'i ryw i roi rew a'r ia.

'"Cold is the snow on Snowdon's brow.
It makes the air so chill;
For cold, I trow, there is no snow
Like that of Snowdon's hill.

'"A hill most chill is Snowdon's hill,
And wintry is his brow;
From Snowdon's hill the breezes chill
Can freeze the very snow."

'Such was the harangue which I uttered on the top of Snowdon; to which Henrietta listened with attention; three or four English, who stood nigh, with grinning scorn, and a Welsh gentleman with considerable interest. The latter, coming forward shook me by the hand exclaiming:

'"Wyt ti Lydaueg?"'

'"I am not a Llydauan," said I; "I wish I was, or anything but what I am, one of a nation amongst whom any knowledge save what relates to money-making and overreaching is looked upon as a disgrace. I am ashamed to say that I am an Englishman.'

'I then returned his shake of the hand; and bidding Henrietta and the guide follow me, went into the cabin, where Henrietta had some excellent coffee, and myself and the guide a bottle of tolerable ale; very much refreshed we set out on our return.

'A little way from the top, on the right-hand side as you descend, there is a very steep path running down in a zigzag manner to the pass which leads to Capel Curig. Up this path it is indeed a task of difficulty to ascend to the Wyddfa, the one by which we mounted being comparatively easy. On Henrietta's pointing out to me a plant, which grew on a crag by the side of this path some way down, I was about to descend in order to procure it for her, when our guide springing forward darted down the path with the agility of a young goat, and in less than a minute returned with it in his hand and presented it gracefully to the dear girl, who on examining it said it belonged to a species of which she had long been desirous of possessing a specimen. Nothing material occurred in our descent to Llanberis, where my wife was anxiously awaiting us.'

§ 7

The road runs south from Beddgelert towards sea and wide, sandy estuaries that at high tide are filled with salt water. The mountains stand back some way from the sea and gaze down bleakly at a strip of greenness as flat as Holland, cut across by stone walls and dotted with small farms. This is the Morfa Harlech which centuries ago was washed by the waters of Cardigan Bay.

So I crossed from Caernarvonshire into the adjoining county of Merioneth. Both these counties were shired after Edward I had beaten down Llewelyn's rebellion, but the name of Merionethshire takes us back another eight centuries into Welsh history. Meirion was one of the many sons of Cunedda who in A.D. 420—during the chaos that followed the Roman evacuation of Britain—swooped down from Strathclyde and possessed himself of this territory.

What a county is this! It is just a wilderness of great mountains, embroidered towards the sea with a thin edge of marsh-land. And across these mountains run roads, or the ghosts of roads, which are to me more eloquent of the Roman power than even the Great Wall of Hadrian that lies across England for eighty miles between the Solway and the Tyne. Those indomitable conquerors cut their way over the Welsh highlands to the silver and the lead-mines of this county. You can stand in the mountains and, on such relics as the Roman Steps behind Harlech, imagine the long lines of slaves mounting into the wildness of the hills bowed down with baskets of ore. These steps, about two thousand, rise in irregular flights and have been for many years a mystery to archaeologists. Some say that they are Cymric, others Roman; and the Royal Commission on Ancient Monuments recently declared that they are mediaeval. This need not worry you: it was over a path exactly like this that the Roman legions slowly found their way through the hills of Cambria.

In a few miles I came to Harlech.

§ 8

If you asked me to pick one view which sums up Wales, I would take you to a high wall above the sea and ask you to look north to Snowdon.

This view seems to me as Welsh as the cliffs of Dover are English, as the Valley of the Tweed is Scottish, and as the Kerry Hills are Irish: it is one of those unforgettable landscapes which print themselves for ever on the mind; it is a memory of home which must have pained and consoled countless Welshmen and Welshwomen in every part of the world. This is the land of the Men of Harlech. . . .

A wide half-moon of bright sand sweeps in a huge curve for miles. The waves come on slowly in great semi-circles to turn over in white foam on the sand.

On the extreme right Harlech Castle rises on a stern outcrop of rock, the most defiantly placed of all Welsh castles, a ruin that might spring to life at the sound of a trumpet, a castle that seems still to remember the whistle of arrows and the movement of lances against the sky, a stronghold whose very silence seems to whisper of King Bran the Blessed, who once perched there like an eagle, and of his sister, Bronwen the White-bosomed, who became a queen in Ireland.

Far below is a green vale that was once the sea. The great castle faces the horizon like a knight who has fallen asleep on a hill. Miles away are the mountains of Snowdonia, hung up like a blue screen in the north.

When I looked at Harlech the mountains were in parts grape blue. Snowdon raised his head clear of cloud. The lower hills that fold themselves in long curves at his feet were a lighter blue; and away to the east and the west his companions, Moel Hebog and Moel Siabod, lifted themselves above the valleys as if cut in blue velvet.

What a view of Wales! It is the finest thing I have seen in

this country! To a Welshman it must seem like a national anthem. In those blue hills the Welsh spirit hid itself, suffered, strove and survived.

'Men of Harlech in the hollow.'

Every one knows this magnificent song. It is sung every day by people who have never seen Harlech and will probably never see it.

The air is traditional, but the words are by Ceriog Hughes, the farmer's son who became a clerk in a railroad office in Manchester and spent his later life as stationmaster in North Wales. He was the Burns of Wales, but his reputation does not rest on this song. It was inspired by the gallant defence of Harlech Castle when held by Dafydd ap Ivan against a force under Sir Richard Herbert. This was during the dreary Wars of the Roses, when Wales was torn between white and red.

Harlech held out for the red rose of Lancaster while the Yorkist troops battered at its gates for months. When the brave garrison was asked to surrender, Dafydd ap Ivan replied: 'I have held a castle in France until every old woman in Wales heard of it, and I will hold a castle in Wales until every old woman in France hears of it!'

So the siege went on. At last the castle was starved into submission, but only after Edward IV promised a pardon for Dafydd and his 'Men of Harlech'. The King tried to go back on his terms when the castle had surrendered, and it was not until his commander, Sir Richard Herbert, threatened to replace the garrison within the castle walls and begin the siege all over again, that the royal word was kept. That is the story which has given the world one of its grandest marches.

Harlech, like many another Welsh town and village, is anchored to the past, while it flings a life-line to the future. This life-line is Harlech College. The ambition of this college is to be the centre of working-class education in Wales. It is more like a mediaeval monastery than anything should be in a Nonconformist country! Its resident tutors go out into town and village spreading knowledge and the thirst for knowledge. They work closely with the Welsh University and the Workers' Educational Association, and other similar organizations.

The working-class scholars who are in residence have either

won scholarships or have received grants from unions or educational associations.

Harlech College is as typical of modern Wales as the castle is of mediaeval Wales, for Wales resembles Scotland in its passion for knowledge. A respect for scholarship runs right through the life of the Welsh people, and the history of their educational system is that of a popular, democratic demand for opportunity. The self-sacrifice of the older generation who slaved to educate their children, just as the Scottish farmer slaved, has given to the world many great scholars. Most of the celebrated Welsh preachers of the past century were born in small farms or in workmen's dwellings. Men like Sir O. M. Edwards, Sir John Rhys, Sir Henry Jones, and Mr. Lloyd George, were sons of the people who seized the opportunities for which their fathers strove so wisely and so well.

Harlech College should be visited by every one who goes to Wales. It expresses the fine Welsh spirit of equality. And it is also the latest manifestation—for it is only a few years old—of the Welsh belief that opportunity is half-way to achievement.

§ 9

The variety and richness of the west coast of Wales, the blend of sea, marsh, mountain and woodland, makes it almost impossible to prefer one place to another. No sooner had I put down the view of Harlech with its blue screen of mountains to the north as the most perfect sight in Wales, than I found myself at Barmouth. The town, I think, has suffered, like all Welsh towns, from its architects, but on a day when the sun is bright over Barmouth and the sails of yachts move in the harbour, you might be looking at some smaller, less exotic Gibraltar.

The long wooden bridge that crosses the wide Mawddach Estuary is, with Plymouth Hoe, perhaps the finest artificial promenade in Great Britain. You look inland, where the salt tide swirls and eddies, towards the mountains round Dolgelly. They lie folded against one another in long, gentle lines, flaming with gorse, green with grass, the darker belts of woodland climbing in the hollows. It is an unforgettable blend of water, mountain and wood, a view of its kind unsurpassed among the Highlands of Wales. . . .

And the road runs inland to Dolgelly, up and down hill through a paradise of glens with the mountains rising all round, their heads in the sun. You lose the estuary and see the gleam of its water again, narrowing as it thrusts its way into the land. On your right is a stupendous view of Cader Idris and his satellites. The cloud shadows ride his broad flanks. A cloud passes him, steaming like blown smoke, and sails on into a blue sky. At Penmaenpool, where the wooded hills are reflected in still water, is a bridge ; and soon you come to a grey stone town with grey smoke rising from its chimneys and behind it, rising sheer from its back gardens, is Cader Idris.

The town is Dolgelly.

§ 10

It is Saturday afternoon in Dolgelly.

I sit on a green seat in front of the hotel which faces the square, and I think that I have reached the most foreign corner of Wales. Caernarvon, it is true, was alien, but Dolgelly might be in the Austrian Tyrol.

The square is crowded with mountaineers. It is a crowd as masculine as that which you will see at an Irish fair. The men stand about in dark groups. They are farmers and farm labourers. They wear breeches and leggings, caps or bowler hats. Most of them carry rough sticks or switches cut from a hedge. Some of them are shaggy as mountain ponies ; some fair, some small and dark as Spaniards, some tall and fair, rawboned as Highlanders. Now and again local girls, walking two by two, pass and re-pass among the herd of men, and occasionally they turn to smile back at some chance remark in Welsh which is flung at them.

The village policeman parades his authority on this day of days. He stands among them, a strange and isolated figure in his blue uniform, as queer and out of tone with his surroundings as those swarthy men in blue who control the traffic in the streets of Gibraltar.

Dolgelly is a hard little mountain town. Its houses are made of the mountains. They look, like Highland houses, as though they were made to endure for ever. And right at the back of the square the slopes of Cader Idris lift themselves to the clouds, bright green and sage green and brown, scarred by gullies, cut across with thin mountain paths.

It is from such wild country that these quick-spoken, slow-moving men have come. I look at them and miss the mountain ponies on which, I feel, they should have ridden to market. But they have come in from miles around on motor-omnibuses. It is a grotesque thought. They stand for hours looking exactly like the mountain levies of Llewelyn the Great or Owen Glendower; looking, in fact, as though they are waiting for them instead of for the homeward omnibus that will take them over the mountains to Bala or south to the green valley through which the Dovey pours itself into the sea.

The sight of the Welsh mountaineers in the square of Dolgelly is, no doubt, as ancient as Wales. They know each other and their families unto the third and fourth generation. Many of them are perhaps related by marriage. Their lives separated by miles of mountains, their homes hidden by towering peaks, they can seldom meet except at this weekly gathering of the clans beneath the smooth flank of Cader Idris. That is why they have so much to talk about as they move from group to group. This is how news spreads through mountains. I wonder how many of these hill-men take in a daily newspaper. Perhaps not one of them! They hear all they wish to know of the world—their world—in the little stone square of Dolgelly. . . .

There is a slow parting of the crowd as a big omnibus swings into the square. There is a rush for it. The mountaineers pile in and lose in the act whatever of picturesqueness they may have held as they stood leaning on their sticks. There is a volley of farewells in Welsh. Gradually the square empties. In the mountains about, these men who so lately stood there are climbing towards the light of farm and cottage. Dusk falls. A bell rings. It is the curfew. They ring it every night from the church of St. Mary. The mass of Cader Idris grows darker, fading from sight until you can tell the broad curve of it only by the line of stars that burn above it.

§ II

In Dolgelly, in strange contrast to the sombre but solid Calvinistic chapels, is a little Roman Catholic church hardly bigger than a barn. It is not generally realized that Wales was for a long time after the Reformation the most Catholic part of the British Isles. The whole of Wales produced only three Protestant martyrs in the reign of 'Bloody' Mary.

'Catholicism stood for more than the old religion,' writes Mr. W. Llewelyn Williams in *The Making of Modern Wales*. 'It stood also for Welsh nationality. Protestantism was an alien plant fostered by English or Anglicized officials. Men looked back to pre-Reformation days as a time when Wales was not a mere part of England, when the Welsh language was not tabooed in the courts, and when Welsh laws and customs were still observed. All that was best and noblest in Welsh story was intertwined with the history of the roofless abbeys, which remain to this day monuments of Welsh piety and art. . . . Each parish church, called after a native saint who had no place or meaning in the Protestant economy, led the Welsh mind, with its insistence on the living influence of the past, back to the earliest dawn of Christian civilization in the land. Everywhere within sound of the monastic bell had reigned peace and contentment. The Church had given free education to the brightest sons of the poor; it had dispensed its kindly charity in the homes of the aged. . . . With the Reformation came strange doctrines and strange laws. Gone were the kindly landlords of the monastery, and in their place stood needy adventurers, unmindful of the past and uncertain of the future, only anxious to make the most of the present.'

Mr. Williams has something rather interesting to say about the unconscious survival of Catholic custom in Protestant Wales:

'Relics of Catholic practices and beliefs have survived to our own days,' he says. 'Mari Lwyd still cheers the winter nights of rural Wales, though few know that it represents the mystery play of Holy Mary. Children, the truest conservatives, even yet make the sign of the cross when seeking to avert an evil omen or taking upon themselves a binding oath. The "gwylnos" survives, in Puritan setting, to mark the permanence in the human heart of that pathetic care for the departed which gave rise in ancient times to the practice of saying masses for the dead. The beautiful custom of strewing flowers on the graves of friends and relatives on

" Sul y Blodau " testifies to the abiding, if unconscious, influence of Catholicism on the faith and practices of Welshmen. These are small matters, it may be, but that they have survived at all, after two centuries and more of the sternest and straightest Puritan discipline, is surely significant of the strong hold which the old faith had taken on the Welsh people.'

So in Dolgelly, which looks as hard and Puritanical as a town in the Highlands of Scotland, the faith which meant so much to ancient Wales exists side by side with the Nonconformity on which modern Wales is spiritually founded.

There must have been a frightful cry of ' No Popery ' when the little Catholic chapel was opened in the July of 1927. There were only five or six Catholics in the congregation. Since that time, I am told, the numbers have grown to about twenty-five, drawn from the Welsh, English and Romany communities.

I imagine that only the very poor, who have nothing to lose socially or economically, will go to Mass in Dolgelly. There is something about that stone market square on a Sunday morning, when the bells of Calvin are ringing, that tells me it would be easier for a rich man to pass through the eye of a needle than for him to walk from his shop past the Nonconformist chapel to the little church where the candles burn.

That, perhaps, is the sensation for which Dolgelly seems to be waiting.

CHAPTER NINE

I GO TO BALA, REMEMBER FAMOUS WELSHMEN, HEAR THE STORY OF KING ARTHUR, SEE THE MAKING OF WELSH TWEED, ENTER ABERYSTWYTH, TALK ABOUT AGRICULTURE WITH PROFESSORS, SET OUT IN SEARCH OF A WIZARD AND FIND—THE BIRMINGHAM WATER WORKS

§ I

SO many people had told me that I must see Bala Lake that one afternoon I went off over the pretty road from Dolgelly. I was disappointed. I was more interested in Bala than in its lake. This stretch of water, the largest natural piece of fresh water in Wales, is, in my opinion, neither so fine as Loch Lomond nor so beautiful as Killarney, but it has a placid majesty of its own. On a fine day, when the sun is shining on the green foothills and on the mountains beyond—Cader Idris, Arenig Fawr and the Arans—this lake is undoubtedly one of the beauties of Wales.

Bala itself is a short, wide, tree-lined street with a calm, leisurely, well-washed air about it. It has atmosphere and dignity. I was just too late to hear a law case in the local court, but I sat in the lounge of the hotel opposite and watched the witnesses come out. They had assumed black and solemn garments, and looked as though they had been to a funeral. Apparently a motorist had run into a flock of sheep at night, slaying two and nearly killing the farmer. Every one was very worked up about it.

It was in Bala that George Borrow actually found some ale which he could praise : " Rich and mellow, with scarcely any smack of the hop in it.' I had a glass of ale which resembled this very closely (without the richness and mellowness), but it came from Burton-on-Trent. And it was in this town that Borrow noted the inevitability of the name Jones. It has occurred to me so many times in Wales that the Joneses should hire Salisbury Plain and have an annual meeting of the clan ! It must be very confusing to live in a small town in which nearly every one is called Jones. The name Jones, by the way, is a corruption of John, or Ieuan.

Welsh names are interesting and peculiar. In England there are thousands of us who take our names from localities, like the Hills and the Woods, or from occupations, like the Smiths and the Coopers and the Taylors and the Bakers, or from personal characteristics like the Whites and the Browns and the Blacks; but in Wales the surname is nearly always patronymic. So many Welsh names begin with either the letter p or b. This is a relic of the Welsh word 'ap'—son of. Ap Harry (the son of Harry) has become Parry. Ap Hugh (the son of Hugh) has become Pugh. Ap Richard (the son of Richard) has become Pritchard; ap Howell has become Powell; and so on.

It is said that Robert Lee, Bishop of Lichfield, who was President of the Marches of Wales in 1535, was the first to abridge Welsh names. Pennant in his *Tour in Wales* states that 'Thomas ap Richard, ap Howel, ap Ievan Vychan, Lord of Mostyn, and his brother Piers, founder of the family of Trelaere, were the first who abridged their name, and that on the following occasion: In the reign of Henry VIII Lee sat at one of the courts on a Welsh cause, and, wearied with the quantity of *aps* in the jury, directed that the panel should assume the last name or that of their residence, and that Thomas ap Richard, ap Howell, ap Ievan Vychan should for the future be reduced to the poor dissyllable Mostyn, no doubt to the great mortification of many an ancient line.'

Bala is a place which every one who is really interested in Wales must visit, because it has played a great part in the history of Welsh Nonconformity.

'In the making of modern Wales two men stand out pre-eminent and without rivals—King Henry VIII and the Revivalist, Howel Harris,' writes W. Watkin Davies in *Wales*. 'The former gave to Wales the opportunity of playing an equal part with England in the life of the Empire. The latter roused Wales from its mediaeval lethargy into clear realization and appreciation of the opportunity which lay within its grasp. In the darkest hour of its history, in 1916, the British Empire entrusted its fortunes to the care of a Welshman. That Welshman had been made possible by Henry VIII: he was produced by Howel Harris.'

Harris was one of the most extraordinary characters in

Welsh history. The Welsh-speaking people in his time—the middle of the eighteenth century—were probably the most backward in Europe. This passionate mystic was obsessed by the desire to awaken the people of Wales to spiritual salvation. He was dauntless. He courted death at the hands of his enemies. Whole districts were stirred up against him ; but he did not care. He was beaten, stoned and shot at with guns. Some of his meetings were riots. Women in his congregations were, in the violent frenzy of the moment, stripped naked.

This indomitable man preached throughout the length and breadth of Wales. He rode sometimes a hundred miles a day and had to preach secretly on mountain-tops to evade his persecutors. On one occasion he slept in his clothes for seven nights.

'Yesterday was a glorious day,' he wrote on one occasion. 'I was at a great feast, and chose to oppose the devil on his own ground ; and we discoursed within a few yards of a public house, where diversion was to be. I never tasted more power. I believe some were cut through ; many wept, and one fainted ; others felt a great trembling, and all were filled with awe.'

That was the kind of man he was. Very soon the whole of Wales was ablaze with the Revival. Other preachers took the field. The movement was well launched that within a century was to transform a faithless peasantry into the most God-fearing section of the British Isles. At the very height of the movement the amazing Harris suddenly retired from the world ! He formed a community whose members had to place all their possessions into a common fund. The 'Family', as it was called, was religious and industrial. They picked wool and made knitted goods. They bought a printing press. They improved land cultivation. And this was at a time when steam power was arriving in England and the first signs of the Industrial Revolution were already visible. It was this queer community of Howel Harris that first voiced in Wales the main precepts of the Industrial Revolution.

One incident in the stormy career of Howel Harris is almost incredible. In 1759, during the war with France, he joined the local militia ! He was evidently as good a volunteer as he was an evangelist. He was made an ensign and soon after promoted to the rank of Captain-lieutenant. Alas, he got no further in the war than Yarmouth, or we might have heard a lot more about him ! His last years were spent in the bosom of his community. Fifteen clergymen administered the Sacrament to a congregation of twenty thousand people who attended his funeral.

He takes a foremost place among the heroes of Wales, and no life in the long history of Wales would respond more readily to the treatment of a competent biographer.

It is to Harris and his great successors, one of whom the Rev. Thomas Charles was a pioneer of the Sunday School movement in Wales, that Bala owes its position as a religious centre. Here is the Bala Theological College.

Harris and Charles are as exciting and as interesting as Llewelyn and Glendower ; and the most casual visitor to Wales should know something about them. The Welsh chapel and the Sunday School mean more to Wales than any stranger from England, Scotland or Ireland can imagine. The intellectual life of Wales has grown up in these by no means beautiful buildings. The chapel in Wales is not merely a church : it is a club in which all the religious and social activities of a community are focused. Lectures are given in the chapel, concerts are held there, literary and debating societies are formed among its members.

Charles of Bala, who founded the Sunday School—and the Welsh Sunday School is for adults as well as for children—was the opposite type to fiery Harris. Harris and the Revivalists whipped the people into religious responsibility. The men who followed on, like Charles of Bala, were students and organizers. He has been called the ' Wesley of Wales '. His Sunday Schools, which began simply to teach people to read, have meant, and still mean, much to Welsh life and literature, because in them the Welsh language was cherished and preserved.

The romance of the Welsh chapel and the Welsh Sunday School is part of the long and glorious struggle which is Welsh history.

§ 2

The little farm in which I am staying is planted firmly in the shadow of a hill. The living-room is a large dark kitchen paved with great slabs of blue slate. Hams hang from hooks in the ceiling. In this room old Mrs. Evans polishes, sweeps and busies round a huge fire-place all day long. The door is never closed except at night, so that often a cockerel escorted by his wives stands with lifted foot on the threshold and gazes curiously into the dimness.

My bedroom is a queer place, because although it is in the farm it is not of it. It does not quite belong to it. It might have come from some small villa in Penmaenmawr. That is because in the summer-time old Mr. and Mrs. Evans eke out their slender earnings from the soil by boarding visitors from the cities. In course of time this bedroom has assumed the appearance of all rooms that are 'let'. There is a trivial insincerity about it so different from the almost harsh reality of the farm. The bed is of fumed oak, and there is a wicker-work arm-chair upholstered in chintz. My companion in this little room is the safe ghost of a thin female pupil-teacher with glasses. At some distant date Mrs. Evans, in the course of making this room right for city folk, picked up several pointless ornaments during a rare visit to Shrewsbury. One is a china youth in eighteenth-century costume heavily spotted with gold, who exists in an attitude of debonair deference directed towards a companion figure, a girl, who has lost her nose. There are two pictures in the room. One, probably gathered with the china, is the death of General Gordon; the other is that of an exceedingly soft and silly girl with long hair, which the artist, in a wild flight of imagination, called 'Fancy Free'.

In contrast to the unreality of this are three black-edged cards framed and hung over the door. They are the funeral cards of various relatives of the Evans family. The only literature in the room is to be found under the cushion of the wicker-chair: three copies of *Weldon's Fashion Journal*, dated the previous year, abandoned, no doubt, in some reckless moment of departure by the pupil-teacher.

When I look out from the window of this neat, clean little feminine box of a room I can see the pigsties, which occupy the life of Mr. Evans, and the hens and ducks and geese which occupy a portion of the life of Mrs. Evans. A stream brawls down from the hill and runs right across the farm, making the land very wet and boggy but providing a swimming-pond for the ducks and the geese.

Mrs. Evans is a dear. Years of simple labour and elemental

sorrows have carved hundreds of lines on her face, and these might have made a sad map had they not been illuminated, as it were, by an absolute faith in the goodness and the wisdom of God and in a life in a world to come.

'It's all for the best, whatever,' is a phrase that has become habitual with her. I suppose she said that, after a time, when her two sons died in France.

That, of course, is the tragedy of old Mr. Evans. He has to work his little farm not with the help of his own flesh and blood but with the casual labour of two local youths. When he dies there is no one to carry on with the land. There is a married daughter in England; but that is not the same thing. And so these two old people, alone again and their lives nearly ended, live in the kitchen with the slate floor while two young men in the uniform of the Royal Welsh Fusiliers look down at them out of the dusk above the mantelpiece.

Mr. Evans is a vivacious, elderly little Welshman with quick, humorous, grey eyes. Although his face is like an old nut, his eyes are the eyes of a young lad. The only books he has consistently read are the Welsh Bible and the Welsh Hymnal. Yet his knowledge is extremely wide and varied and his head is full of Welsh stories. He has a Celtic respect for all poets and writers. He likes to see me writing by the light of the oil lamp on the kitchen table at night, because he thinks it is wonderful to spin words. When I say unpleasant things about poets and writers, which I do very frequently, he becomes vaguely hurt and annoyed; so that I turn it off with a joke and make him laugh. I suppose some ancient Welsh respect for the office of the bard lingers in a corner of his mind.

One day when I insisted on helping him to clean out a pigsty, because, as I told him, writing was work for short-haired women and long-haired lunatics, he was definitely upset, and I had a hard job to persuade him to give me a pitchfork.

In the evening he is very tired. He sits in front of the fire with Mrs. Evans, who works diligently at a garment of black wool. Sometimes he takes the Bible and reads to her in Welsh, always turning to me if I am writing with:

'Please will I be disturbing you?'

I tell him that nothing disturbs me, which is not true, and I sit there, pretending to write, listening to the ancient tongue of Britain, rising and falling like a stream tumbling from the hills.

Probably the greatest moments of his life have been spent at prayer meetings. He sometimes talks about the great preachers he has heard. He talks about them as a Greek might have talked of Demosthenes. He describes how his father had once heard John Elias preach in Anglesey. He thinks that Elias was the greatest preacher the world has ever known.

'Mr. Evans,' I say, 'will you tell me the story about King Arthur?'

'Will you never be tired of hearing it?'

'Never . . .'

'Well, then, let me see . . . a shepherd from Dolwyddelan went to a fair in London, and it was a great fair with hundreds and thousands of people at it, yes, and when the shepherd was crossing London Bridge a man stopped him and he said to him: "Good evening, shepherd, may I look at the stick you are carrying? Where did you get it?" And the shepherd said: "I cut this stick with my own hands from a hazel tree that grew outside a cave in my own country, yes." Then the strange man told him that in the cave was a great treasure indeed. But if he wanted to carry away some of this treasure he must be very careful not to awaken King Arthur and his men who were asleep in this cave, you see. If he touched a bell that hung in this cave the warriors would awaken. "If you touch the bell," said the man, "King Arthur will say to you: 'Has the day come?' and you must say to him: 'No; the day has not come—sleep!'" And when the man had spoken like this to the shepherd he vanished, and the shepherd knew that he was some great wizard, yes. So the shepherd goes back to Wales and he finds the cave where he cut his stick and he goes into the cave. . . .'

At this point of the story Mr. Evans begins to resemble Mr. Lloyd George. His eyes shine. He is lost in oratory. He lifts his arms.

'And when he went into the cave he saw a great treasure of silver and gold piled to the roof of the cave, and he saw King Arthur and his men lying asleep with their swords beside them, and when he had taken some of the treasure and was going out of the cave he touched the bell that hung at the opening of it. . . . And there was a t-e-r-r-i-b-l-e noise, look you, of swords and armour and a g-r-e-a-t clashing in the cave as King Arthur and his men rose up from their sleep so that the shepherd trembled and could not move from the place. And he heard a voice say to him : " Has the day come ? " and the shepherd dropped all his treasure and said, " No, the day has not come—sleep ! " and ran out of the cave for his dear life. And for days and months and years he looked for the cave, but he could never find it again whatever. . . .'

I go up the flight of narrow stairs holding a candle in an enamelled stick. When I open the window I can hear the stream running in the darkness. The stars are bright and I can see the rounded forms of hills shouldering the sky.

§ 3

On the seventh day a hush falls over Wales.

It is a hush so deep and significant that you can feel it even in the country. As I lean out of the window it seems to me that the Sabbath hush has extended itself to cow sheds, hen coops and sheep folds. A figure crosses the farmyard. It is Mr. Evans. But what a changed person ! He looks like a stranger in his own home. Gone are his muddy workaday clothes and his great boots. His legs are encased in two baggy tubes of black cloth. He wears a white collar and a black tie, a cut-away coat of black, and on his head is a carefully brushed bowler hat. Even the hens and the ducks, I feel, regard him with changed expressions, and I am certain that the pigs, his more intimate companions, know that he is going to chapel.

Mrs. Evans is also a changed personality. She has put on a black coat and skirt of rather ancient design ; and she wears gloves ! The gravity of their clothes is reflected in their faces. They are a couple of perfect Puritans.

In silence we set out for the little Methodist chapel. We cross the farmyard in silence, in silence we unlatch the gate, in silence we walk slowly up the lane. As we pass a side road we meet Mr. and Mrs. Williams and their large cow-like son.

' Oh, it is very sat apout poor Mr. Edwards indeed.'

' It was only last week I did see him in Bala looking so well, you know.'

' And poor Mrs. Edwards—it is very sat indeed, dear me, yes . . .'

In this gloomy mood we progress slowly towards the chapel. I gather that Mr. Edwards was a deacon, or elder, who was discovered dead in his cow shed a few days previously. Mr. Williams is a more worldly individual than my dear old Mr. Evans. Although his clothes are black and his expression godly, his mind runs on material things. He wonders how much money Mr. Edwards has left whatever! But Mr. Evans declines to discuss the matter, indicating by his manner that it is not a fit and proper subject for the Lord's Day.

The chapel is a fairly large and hideous building that stands in open country. Welsh chapels belong to the Woolworth Georgian period of architecture: stern buildings that, unlike the English parish church, have never made friends with the landscape. The fact that they are not old and mellow has nothing to do with it. They are just the wrong kind of buildings to be planted in open country. They owe their architectural origin to that most debased period in church history when, during the classical revival of the eighteenth century, churches were built as much like town halls as possible.

We find ourselves in a plain, matter-of-fact hall. A gallery runs round it upheld by slender iron pillars. The ground floor is covered with pews of fumed and varnished oak. Each pew has a door to it, but some, grander than the rest, hold only one or two persons. These suggest that some members of the congregation are riding to heaven not in an omnibus but in a private car. The end of the chapel is occupied by a huge fumed-oak pulpit and a raised dais with a semi-circular rail round it and plush-cushioned seats for the elders.

Black cloth is draped over the rail, and little black bows of crepe have been tied to the shafts of the incandescent gas lamps that rise from it. This, I am told, is in respect for the memory of poor Mr. Edwards, the dead deacon.

The chapel is full of people who have walked or driven in from the surrounding country. They are a typical Welsh farming crowd: bent old women, big-boned farmers, thin, dark youths and, here and there, a surprisingly lovely girl.

Mr. Evans, grave as a living statue, leaves Mrs. Evans and myself to take a pew while he walks solemnly towards the deacons' bench. He mounts the steps, has a few words with a fellow deacon—I can hear him saying how sad it is, indeed, about poor Mr. Edwards—and then, taking a large handkerchief from his pocket, he blows his nose in a religious way and glances round the congregation. The service begins.

The deacons sit with their backs to the congregation as they face the pulpit. The precentor sits at a small harmonium set among the first row of pews. The minister mounts into the pulpit and begins to pray in Welsh. He is a man of middle age, rather plump and monkish-looking, and he has trained his voice so that it has become a perfect emotional instrument. It is good to hear words spoken with such pleasure and effect. As I listen to him, not understanding one word he says, it occurs to me that possibly the finest elocution in Great Britain is to be heard in Welsh chapels.

He announces a hymn. The precentor plays the air. We rise up and sing. Welsh hymns contain a beauty and a fervour unknown to us in England. Welsh hymn tunes are wonderfully melodious, quite unlike the dreary, elementary airs of *Hymns Ancient and Modern*. It is not necessary to understand Welsh to know that Welsh hymns with their passionate vitality must have played a tremendous part in the Nonconformist revival. And every one sings. There is no mumbling. It is whole-hearted singing. Men, women and children open their mouths and let it go.

The preacher prepares to deliver his sermon. The congregation settles down and prepares to listen to him, not with the bored expression common to all English congregations but with something of the alert expectancy seen in the stalls of a theatre. The Welsh love oratory. The event of the year in many a Welsh village is a preaching meeting. The eloquence of famous Welsh preachers is known to every one. For a hundred years the soul of Wales found its expression in sermons, and every child in Wales has heard stories of the great preachers of the past. There was John Elias, who, when preaching to a great gathering in the open air, described how God let fly an arrow from His bow. So great was his emotional power that as he spoke the gathering parted to allow passage for the shaft.

And as the minister speaks I, although I cannot grasp his meaning, appreciate the emotional quality of his sermon. He leans over the pulpit and preaches, not in the remote, impersonal tradition of the Church of England, but intimately, passionately, addressing his words to individual members of his congregation. He begins quietly, with many eloquent pauses. He then works up to a swifter space. The response from his listeners is like electricity in the air. He feels it. It is just the same thing that an actor feels coming to him from beyond the footlights: the sympathy, the appreciation, the sense of power. I admire the way he uses his voice and the way he works step by step towards a climax. He is a born orator. Then suddenly, as if carried away, as if drunk with the eloquence in him, he breaks into the *hwyl*, the famous intonation of the Welsh pulpit. His voice rises and falls in a measured manner that has an extraordinary hypnotic effect on the congregation. There is something about the *hwyl* like a war chant that grips the heart. He is like some prophet of old announcing the vengeance of the Lord. He is like some tribal chieftain stirring up his people to battle.

The effect on his audience is remarkable. The big farmers gaze at him with the faces of children. The women dab their eyes with handkerchiefs. Some one whispers something in Welsh. I feel that if he goes on much longer the congregation will break up in disorder. They sit spell-bound. Then, suddenly, his voice drops. He has finished.

It is with something like a sense of relief that I hear the next hymn. It brings us back from the perilous emotionalism of the past half hour. How strange to encounter such emotionalism in this bare Calvinistic hall.

'And did you enjoy yourself?' says Mr. Evans as we walk home.

'I did.'

'It is a great pity you could not understand the sermon, for Mr. Parry is a great preacher.'

As we walk home I realise, more than before, how vital a part the chapels have played in the development of the Welsh people. The service was exactly like family prayers on a large scale. The minister was the father of his family, the elders were his younger brothers.

We ate a cold meal and then waited until it should be time to attend Sunday School!

§ 4

The Sunday School in Wales is peculiar because grown-ups as well as children attend. In the old days age and youth went to school on Sunday in a very real sense because it was the Welsh Sunday School that taught the people to read their own tongue.

We found the chapel full of young and old. In an upstairs room was a class of infants. They were being taught the alphabet. In another class-room were children from the ages of ten to seventeen. They sat in little groups of five or six and each group had its own teacher. The grown-ups occupied the chapel.

The minister, who had noticed me at the morning service, hurried towards us and in the most affable and charming way took me from old Mr. Evans and, to my extreme discomfiture, gave me a place on the dais among the elders. I did not like this a bit because I could tell from the way the congregation looked at me that they expected a flood of oratory. Nothing startles me more than the fear of having to make a speech. I have made only two good speeches in my life : one happened and the other was carefully rehearsed for weeks beforehand. Every cow looking over gates between York and Beverley endured this speech of mine and found itself addressed as ' Mr. Chairman, ladies and gentlemen ', so that I was almost too word perfect. But the thought of speaking in this stern little chapel chilled my blood.

A deacon rose and delivered a long speech in Welsh about the Epistle to the Hebrews. The only words I understood were ' the apostle Paul '. The minister very kindly wrote on the back of an envelope the gist of the deacon's address. It appeared that the Sunday School was about to study the Epistle of Paul to the Hebrews. Every term, so to speak, one of the books of the Bible was chosen as a subject for study.

Young girls and boys in the twenties sat next to greybeards, listening with deep attention to the address. It was a remarkable sight and one that, I think, could not be paralleled outside Wales.

When the deacon had finished, the minister spoke. His manner was quite different from his preaching manner of the morning. He was amusing, friendly and informal. I had no idea what he was saying until, as a compliment to me, he dropped into English. I then realised with horror that, just as the school-master in Caernarvonshire had done, he had jumped to hasty and wrong conclusions about me. He knew I was a writer. He began to cover me with the most fulsome praise so that I felt myself getting hot and unhappy. Then he leapt to the conclusion that I was making an exhaustive inquiry into the Sunday School movement in Wales.

'It is a great compliment he has paid us coming here this afternoon to inspect our school,' he said, and I felt all the eyes of the congregation fixed on me. In a few vivid phrases he made me into a great expert. I was a man who was interested in all good movements. It was a fine thing that a man of such outstanding qualities should have decided to devote his abilities to a study of the Welsh Sunday School, and he felt sure that every one would welcome a few words from me on my discoveries and conclusions.

As this embarrassing half hour was the only occasion on which I had ever been inside a Sunday School, I felt in a position as false as that in which I was placed when the school-master described me to his choir as 'a great musician'. This jumping to conclusions is part of the quick, dramatic temperament of the Welsh. But what on earth could I say to them? One thing was obvious: I could not let down a minister in his own chapel. I would have to pretend to be an authority on good works.

I found myself suddenly talking about Italy! They gazed at me with alert and intelligent expressions. Sub-consciously, I suppose, the contrast between this bleak little Calvinist chapel on the edge of a Welsh moor and the rich, hot sunlight of Italy, the dim churches, the tapers and the haunting smell of incense, must have inspired my rambling remarks. I told them about St. Andrew, whose bones lie in a gold coffin in the cathedral of Amalfi; I told them about St. Paul and his wanderings; I even described Pontifical High Mass in St. Peter's and told them how the Pope rides in, to the sound of silver trumpets, high on the shoulders of men in the *Sadia Gestatoria* with the tall *flabella* waving beside him, like some Pharaoh entering the great hall of Karnak. In some desperate and clumsy way I contrived to link all this with Calvin and Methodism, and then, becoming aware of the little inward voice that always says to me when I try to make a speech, 'What an unutterable ass you are,' I instantly lost confidence in myself, ended and sat down.

For some obscure reason the speech was a success, or perhaps they were too polite to let me think otherwise. I left them—young and old—studying the *Epistle to the*

Hebrews, gathered into little groups, each one presided over by a teacher ; and I walked in the afternoon sunlight on the hills, swearing that I would never again be trapped like that.

Mr. Evans paid me the greatest of all his compliments over the nightly teapot :

'You would be a great preacher indeed,' he said.

But I think I ruined myself with Mrs. Evans. She was never the same again after my speech. I think she suspected that I was tainted with Popery.

§ 5

The stone soldier stands beneath a green hill with a rifle and a fixed bayonet. He gazes with a grim and threatening expression towards a fairy-like dell with a little waterfall in it. He wears much the same expression that he wore when as a little boy his mother told him stories of the *ladi wen*, or the dog of darkness, *gwyllgi*, or the *gŵyll*, which rides horses over the moors on wild nights. He wears the uniform of a Welsh infantry regiment.

Below him, carved in the stone of their native mountains, are the names of perhaps thirty men—Jones, Evans, Parry, Thomas—who left this little Welsh town never to return.

How true the Welsh have been to their military tradition. All over Wales these stone soldiers, or simple little Celtic crosses, perpetuate the memory of men who fought in the War. Wales has never ceased fighting. When we first see the Britons they are defying Caesar on the white cliffs of Dover. We see them fighting the Saxon. Later, we see them helping the Saxon earls to defy the Norman baron. Then for centuries Wales became the recruiting ground for the French Wars. The Welsh archers were the real victors of Cressy and Agincourt. They taught us how to draw the long-bow to the ear. 'In every English Civil War from Henry III to Charles I it was always found easier to recruit infantry among the poor of Wales than among the settled and peaceable English,' wrote Professor G. M. Trevelyan.

So the stone warriors of Wales stand in hill and valley, defying the little glens in which they played as children, linking Cressy with Ypres, linking Agincourt with Gallipoli.

An old and haughty Nation proud in Arms.

§ 6

I retraced my way to Dolgelly and took the road that skirts the vast shoulder of Cader Idris to Machynlleth. On this road is a still, dark tarn called Tal-y-llyn lying cupped between the hills. It is my idea of the lake from whose surface rose the white hand that drew Excalibur beneath the water.

Some miles onward towards Aberystwyth is a little village called Talybont. I can never resist a water-mill. I heard one thrashing and groaning like a sty full of pigs, and went to look at it. It was a big old one, green with weed. The stream that was turning it ran over clear stones, and was the sort of stream a fisherman dreams about in a bad season.

No one ever buys trout in Talybont, and sometimes an eighteen-pound salmon is grassed within sound of the wheel.

In this place I discovered the most idyllic factory in Wales. About ten people work a tweed factory as if the Industrial Revolution had never happened. The trout-stream gives them power and electric light, and about a century ago some one bought machinery which still works!

And there they are!

'The factory began in 1809,' I was told, 'when the farmers brought in their wool, which the cottagers used to make into flannels and blankets for them. It was a cottage industry. The women used to spin the wool at home and the men used to weave the cloth at home. Then the industry became prosperous and soon four mills were going. . . .'

The word 'mill' in Talybont means a rustic kind of barn with trees all round it, flowers up to the very door and the music of the trout-stream competing with the loom.

'Then the mills developed. They used to do a good trade in lead-mine hats—things like a shrapnel helmet and as hard as steel—but that trade died when the lead mines shut down. Then after the war we had a bad slump and took to making Welsh tweed. We are now doing a good trade. Our customers are largely recommended to us, but we send cloth to Italy and Germany and other foreign countries. Mr. Stanley Baldwin wears suits of Welsh tweed. Perhaps Mr. Lloyd George put him on to it, for we send lots of it to Criccieth. . . .'

I was shown the wool store. In the old days the farmers used to bring their wool to the mill; to-day the mill sends a man round the hills to collect fleeces from the farmers.

There are six qualities of wool in every fleece. This Welsh tweed is made of only first and second quality wool. That is why it is softer than Harris tweed. There is no 'kemp' in it. 'Kemp' is the wiry hair that sticks up out of Harris tweed and resists the dyeing vat.

'Everything is done here, from the selection of fleeces to the washing of the manufactured cloth. . . . Come and see the first process.'

Two men were working a combing machine. It was a very old machine, but it remembered how to comb. In an upper barn was a wonderful sight. Here were primitive twisting machines and spinning machines which have been at work for over eighty years! It was like going into a factory of the time of Arkwright.

'No; nothing ever goes wrong with them,' I was told.

The spinning machine, which runs the whole length of the shed, was made by Schofield, Kird and Marshall, of Huddersfield. You have probably seen things like it in a museum.

It has twelve reels with twenty threads on each reel working on 240 spindles. The moving carriage runs on ten iron wheels, and the old veteran can spin thread as well as any of the busy little upstart machines in Lancashire!

It has absolutely no temperament. It runs backwards and forwards on its iron rails cumbrously but efficiently and with a far-away expression as if it is still thinking about its old friend the 'Spinning Jenny'.

In another 'mill', beside another wheel, four hand-looms are generally at work making Welsh tweed. A good worker can turn out 85 to 100 yards a week and make anything from £3 to £4 10s. But there is nothing to spend money on in Talybont! And it is the most pleasant weaving-shed you can imagine. As you sit with the shuttle shooting across and the loom clacking like a hen-house you can shout through the window to Mr. Williams—look you—who has just landed a fine trout below the bridge.

The patterns of Welsh tweed are extraordinarily varied. The weavers make cloth in all the fashionable styles and in some which they regard with pride as their own speciality.

The cottage which serves as a showroom is piled with the

winter's work because it is mainly in the summer, when Wales is full of visitors, that the weavers make their profit.

'Are you going to extend the business or are you content with your present output?'

'We hope to extend and develop it. It is growing now. Welsh tweed is good right through, and we don't care who comes to see it. It is our ambition to make a golf suit for the Prince of Wales. . . .'

As we were talking I noticed a fishing-rod on a pile of cloth. The man who was showing me round cast such a look of longing towards it that I instinctively glanced down to the stream. It was just right! He was itching to get down to the trout; so I very thoughtfully said good-bye.

In a short time I was in Aberystwyth.

§ 7

Aberystwyth is leading a double life. It is not the simple seaside town praised on the railway posters. Behind its hotels and boarding-houses, its pretty hills, its inadequate pier and its half-moon of blue-grey shingle is something even more important than holidays: it is the oldest University town in Wales.

Every day the promenade is subject to attractive surges of scholarly maidens. They walk two by two, and sometimes three by four, hatless and with black gowns slipping from their shoulders. They carry books under their arms, and they talk incessantly! There is something that faintly suggests Gilbert and Sullivan in this chorus of scholarly maidens as they go arm in arm beside the sea, backed by the prim Victorianism of Aberystwyth's boarding-houses.

They walk from a severe-looking hostel at one end of the promenade to the University at the other end, a building whose general design (if you can call it that) suggests that it once bought a complete set of Sir Walter Scott's works on the instalment system and never really digested them.

The sons of Wales, unlike the daughters, are not kept under one roof. You can see them through the front windows of undergraduates' lodgings all over the town, bent over books, sometimes writing and sometimes gazing through the windows in the uncertain reverie of early manhood.

9a. BOATS IN FISHGUARD HARBOUR.

9b. WELSH PONIES ON THE GOWER PENINSULA.

10a. A CORACLE FISHERMAN ON THE RIVER TEIFI.

10b. THE COCKLE-WOMEN OF PENCLAWDD.

University towns always interest and depress me. I would not be twenty again for anything on earth.

Aberystwyth's intellectual activities, and also its reputation as a tourist centre and a holiday resort, make it obviously one of the most important towns in Wales.

It has more side-names than any other town in the Principality. The guide-books call it the 'Brighton of Wales'. The official corporation guide flies a bit higher and calls it the 'Biarritz of Wales'. People who are surprised and delighted, as I am, with its scholarship, have even christened it the 'Athens of Wales'. But a really good comparison would be the 'St. Andrews of Wales'.

It is, like the Scottish University town, famed outside the country, not for its national endeavours, but for its appeal to leisure moments.

Aberystwyth, to a Birmingham man, suggests bathing, boating, and a day out at the Devil's Bridge, but to a Welshman it is the town where Blodwen is trying to be a teacher and where David is climbing out of the agricultural into the professional classes.

The work of the University College of Wales is admired wherever academic honours are coveted.

And I could look at the architecture of the college for days and find something new to astonish me. It looks like an illegitimate child of the London Law Courts, that incredible and inconvenient fanfare of Gothicism. The architect was determined that nothing should be left out, that no period should be slighted, that the building should look like a text-book on architecture. My first impression was that here in Aberystwyth is the supreme example of that style, so well represented in England until a critical fire destroyed it, by the Shakespeare Memorial Theatre at Stratford-on-Avon, known as 'Early Marzipan'.

'Why did you build such a heroic building?' I asked a professor.

'We didn't,' he said. 'It had already happened! The story is interesting. In the middle of the last century the railway pioneer, Thomas Savin, evolved the surprising idea of offering a week's free board and lodging in a palatial hotel to any one who would take a return ticket from Euston to Aberystwyth. The promoters of the scheme believed that it would pack the town with visitors, and so great was their faith that they spent £80,000 on building what was then one of the most spectacular hotels in Great Britain. But the scheme fell through! The hotel became derelict! In 1870 the building was purchased for £10,000 and in it was housed the senior constituent college of the University of Wales. Of course, since the opening of the college in 1872 we have extended and spread out in all directions. Our Agricultural Departments and our Zoological Laboratories have other quarters, so has the Department of Music, the Department of International Politics, the Department of Geography and Anthropology and the Chemical Laboratories. The day may come when we shall leave the old building and house the bulk of our activities under one roof. The fine gift of 84 acres near the National Library by an old student, Mr. Joseph Davies Bryan, encourages this hope. . . .'

The foundation of the University of Wales by the gallant efforts of the Welsh people is, as I have already stated, one of the outstanding romances of modern Wales, and at the same time that men were dreaming of a University some one sent a copy of the first Welsh Bible to Aberystwyth. This Bible collected other books round it. It was a magnet that drew manuscripts and rare volumes to the town.

That was the beginning of the magnificent National Library—one of the finest libraries in the kingdom—which now contains over 200,000 books and 5,000 manuscripts. If a student would examine the ancient literature of Wales it is to Aberystwyth that he must go.

So this pleasant town beside the sea lives its double life: it welcomes the outside world with a smile, but it has a deeper significance: it is one of the corner-stones of the Welsh nation. Aberystwyth, no matter how proud it may be of its sea-breezes and its wide bay, must be prouder still of the part it has played in the national life of Wales.

§ 8

About ten years ago an unusual experiment was tried in a garden in Aberystwyth. A professor of University College decided to breed grass scientifically, with the idea of improving Welsh pasture-land.

He succeeded in creating from ordinary grass something that looked rather like asparagus!

That humble experiment has developed to-day into the Plant Breeding Station of the Agricultural Department of University College. Professor R. G. Stapledon's experiments are now known all over the world.

Visitors come to Wales from the ends of the earth to see them ; and an Imperial Conference recently established the Aberystwyth farm as the centre of grass and plant culture for the British Empire. When I went to the Plant Breeding Station I saw several hundreds of acres planted with various grasses. I saw sheep performing a protracted experiment which I will describe in a moment. I saw glass-houses of a peculiar design in which pedigree grass is ' married '.

This new grass bears no resemblance to ordinary meadow-grass. It looks more like a shrub. The most uncanny things have been done with grass. The professors take a certain type of grass and by mixing the strain produce from it grass that grows four feet high for hay, or grass that is low and luscious for cattle.

' We have applied science to the production of grass,' said one of the professors. ' You will see grass, only a generation or so removed from ordinary grass, being cultivated like wheat or oats. . . .'

We came to long glass-houses in which certain aristocratic strains were seeding. Girls were pinning paper-bags round them to protect them from having an affair with the wrong kind of bee.

There were houses full of incredible grasses, gigantic plants that looked more like river reeds than grass.

Then we came to clover.

The experiments made with clover are fascinating. There is clover from every part of the world. It is tested in Welsh soil.

If you are a Welsh farmer and you tell the Plant Breeding Station in what county in Wales your farm is situated, they can lead you to beds of Italian, Scandinavian, Russian, French and American clover and show you exactly what your field will look like if you decide to buy imported seed.

Should this depress you, they will compose a clover for you more or less as a doctor prescribes a medicine. They will consider the nature of your land, the character of your climate, the elevation of your farm, and they will say :

' This is the clover for you. Nothing else will give you the same return for your money.'

The precautions taken when pedigree clover is ready to breed are amusing. The glass-houses are shut tight. There is not a hole through which a fly could enter.

Then a professor goes forth to catch a bumble-bee. This unconscious ambassador of science is then given a bath to remove from it any alien pollen ! It is placed in a glass tube and disinfected.

Then the great moment arrives when it is allowed to fly into the pedigree clover and feed where it likes.

On meadowland in the Plant Breeding Station you will see groups of sheep tethered together feeding on certain prescribed patches of grass. They have the weary expressions of people condemned to live in first-class hotels.

'These sheep,' explained a professor, 'are the same type and were the same weight when the experiment started three years ago. They are feeding on different grasses.

'They are weighed periodically, and other data are noted. At the end of the experiment—in another year or so—we shall have new information on the feeding qualities of certain grasses. . . .'

Some sheep, however, are letting science down very badly ! Some of them, feeding on specially prepared grass, refuse to show any marked difference from those living on less exotic food. But that is merely one of the snags which plant-breeders like to encounter ! They will make careful notes of it, puzzle over it and—start again !

The interesting thing to a layman about this remarkable farm is that the study of such a common thing as grass has led a number of brilliant men into a world of mystery. They do not yet fully understand the laws which govern the production of grass. There is always a question mark round the corner !

'We have learnt a lot in ten years,' said one of them, 'but there are many years' hard work—many years of success and failure before we can say that we know everything about grass. What we have done is to produce better grass for agriculture.

'That is what we set out to do. The purely academic side of our work is secondary to the practical application of it on the farmlands of the British Empire.'

§ 9

Among the wise men of the Welsh University is the only Professor of Agricultural Economics in Great Britain. He is Professor A. W. Ashby, who knows most of the secrets of Welsh farming. I went to see him, partly because I heard that he is full of wisdom; partly because I had no idea what 'Professor of Agricultural Economics' means.

I found him surrounded by unreadable books and files, statistics and maps, a middle-aged man, the son of a farm-worker who went up to Oxford and carved his own career.

'What is your Department of Agricultural Economics?'

'It is the study of the financial side of farming,' said Professor Ashby. 'The plant-breeder is concerned with selecting and developing crops for better and heavier yield, the chemist with manuring them; but the agricultural economist asks what they cost to grow and what is their money value; why costs are high or low; what profits or wages result.

'He will ask also what is the most desirable type of farm, or does the landowner take too much rent, or is the industry paying sufficient wages to obtain efficiency and economy in work? And, not least important, is the middleman rendering good services, or is he too highly paid for them?'

'What problems are you trying to solve in Wales to-day?'

'We are trying to raise the incomes and the standards of living of small farmers and all agricultural workers. These incomes depend on some things which happen on the farm, in the markets, even in the homes of the consumer, some which happen when financiers meet and settle banking and credit policies, others when legislators make laws.

'The small farm of Wales is not an isolated industrial unit; it is subject to all the economic winds of the world. The hillside farm is just as much subject to the soft breezes or gales of finance as to the winds of heaven.

'When the unemployment rate rises in the coal-fields or the cities, the demand for butter weakens and the price falls, the children of the unemployed eat margarine and suffer from rickets, and the children of the small farmer go to school with poor shoes.

'When the New Zealand farmer raises the butter production of his cows, the Welshman is called on to follow in the process. Unfortunately, he rarely leads.

'While the cotton mills of Lancashire are closed they do not use sheep pelts on their rollers, and the Welsh butcher who goes to market pays less for his sheep because the value of skins is low. To put it briefly, our problems are those which effect an even distribution of wealth between agricultural classes.'

I asked the professor to tell me how many people are employed in Welsh agriculture to-day.

'There are,' he said, 'roughly 41,000 farmers in Wales, mostly cultivating small farms. These farmers employ about 37,000 farm servants or labourers. The number of farmers and relatives engaged in farm work is 56,000—greatly in excess of the number of wage-earners, for there are about three members of farmers' families to each pair of paid workers.

'In some counties, like Carmarthen, there are only about two wage-earners to five farmers and relatives. In England, on the other hand, there are about three employees to each farmer, in some counties even seven or eight. . . .

'In recent years about ten per cent of Welsh farm workers have reached the status of independent cultivators.'

I asked Professor Ashby to define the difference between Welsh and English farming.

'Farming in Wales is of predominantly a pastoral character,' he replied. 'There is little production of crops for sale and over 95 per cent of production consists of live-stock. The land in Wales is on the whole of lower quality and lower rental value than in England. But the Welsh farm labourer has a greater chance of rising in the industry and the social scale.'

'What,' I asked, 'is the future of Welsh agriculture?'

'An improvement generally in industry and trade would make a stronger demand for the produce of Welsh farms. But Welsh agriculture, like that of all other countries, has some changes to make, and much will depend on the initiative of the farmers and their ability to get capital and technical information. The best prices are obtained for the higher quality goods.

'On the whole, more knowledge and skill are necessary, and Wales will be called on to improve many of its farming processes in order to achieve this quality. I expect the farmers of Wales to rise to the occasion, but, of course, there will be many laggards who will refuse to believe that changes are necessary until they are compelled to make them.'

'What kind of changes are necessary?'

'Improvement in grassland, a search for the most economical method of feeding live-stock, the selection of the best types of live-stock for the production of first quality products, better marketing organization and a closer study of farm organization.'

We then discussed the problem of the unemployed industrialist in the South. Does the land offer him work?

'If we had the will and the policy to re-shape our agricultural system over large areas of Wales,' he said, 'we could employ more people on the land. Small attempts at settlement will not take us very far. It is preferable to set the existing farms on better lines than to make increases in the agricultural community. I would not, at the moment, expect any settlement which could affect conditions in South Wales.'

'What do you think of the Welsh farmer?'

The Professor thought carefully before he replied.

'That varies with my moods,' he said, 'and with the manifestations of his varied characteristics from day to day. At times it would not be fit for publication! But on the whole I have found him a wonderful man to work with. He is always cautious and, like all small farmers, tends to be conservative. What Welsh farmers need is good leadership from within their own class. One good technical and social leader who is a farmer will leaven a mass of rank and file farmers. There are many of this type but—more are needed.'

Somebody rang up to ask the Professor of Agricultural Economics to give a lecture on book-keeping in a village hall, so I left him.

§ 10

I was introduced to a young woman whose father is said to be a distinguished wizard. I asked what kind of wizard he was, because it is well known that there are three kinds: those who have sold themselves to the Devil in return for knowledge of the black art; those who have studied wizardry from books and those whose ancestors have handed down to them the gift of divination. I gathered that he belonged to the last class.

'Do people still believe in spells and witchcraft?' I asked.

'Yes, indeed,' I was told.

They mentioned the names of two wizards known to country-folk throughout Cardiganshire.

'And not only Cardiganshire,' put in some one anxious to bolster up the fame of the local magicians, 'but all over Wales.'

I learnt that these wizards are known by the word *consuriwr*.

'And do people go and consult them to-day?'

'Oh, yes,' I was told. 'Only the other day a woman went who had lost ten pounds in notes and the *consuriwr* told her to look for it in a certain place, where she found it.'

'And there was a man who came all the way from Cardiff to see the *consuriwr* about his young lady.'

'Really; and what did the *consuriwr* do about it?'

'He said, "Oh, don't marry her or you'll never have a day's happiness".'

I learnt that people consult the wizards if their cattle are ailing, if their children are ill, if anything sudden and unexpected happens, if money is lost, and in all the trials and uncertainties of love. The gifts of the Welsh *consuriwr* seem to me to resemble the Scottish 'second-sight', a disconcerting gift in the Western Isles where everybody has either heard or experienced it. It is white magic.

I got the address of the *consuriwr* and determined to set out on the following day and consult him in his lonely home in the hills. In the morning I discovered that a back spring was broken on my car. Was this, I wondered grimly, the result of playing with superstition! Had the car been bewitched? When no garage could replace the spring I began to fear the worst. There was nothing for it but to hire a car.

It arrived in charge of a friendly and voluble little Welshman. He had an earnest manner, a treble voice and a bowler hat. We set off at a snail's pace in the direction of Plynlimon. I soon discovered that my little friend knew everybody and everything. He was one of the most enthusiastic narrators I have ever encountered. As I sat behind him in the back of the car, he would half turn to see the effect of his conversation on me, lifting one hand from the wheel so that the car would slide a bit to the right in a horrible manner. I was ill at ease. He had another strange habit: a trick of interlarding his remarks with the words 'you know' or 'you know what I mean'. And there were no commas, semi-colons, colons or full stops in his conversation.

'Yes, indeed, I know the wizard you know,' he said; 'he is a great man you know I have driven many a man to see him you know from Cardiff you know and Bristol you know and Birmingham you know and in the summer young ladies go to see him you know to ask him questions about their young men you know but once in the winter time if you know what I mean a man came from London and he said to me you know can you drive me to see the wizard you know and the snow was falling and I said to him "Yes I can take you to see the wizard if I can get the car over Pont Mawr" you know and I did it although we had to get out twice you know and wipe the snow off the wind-screen and he told me as we went along that he had been to see all the great fortune-tellers in London if you know what I mean and not one of them could tell him what he wanted to know you know and I said to him . . .'

I interrupted this machine-gun fire by attracting his attention to something in the landscape, because during the recital he kept turning round towards me; and every time he turned he instinctively accelerated and made a graceful but unsafe gesture with his right hand.

'Yes you see that stone wall there you know that is where a coach and four horses went over in a mist if you know what I mean many years ago and nobody you know . . .'

I looked over a stone wall and saw a terrifying precipice falling away to distant fields.

'. . . was saved if you know what I mean which was a terrible accident you know . . .'

'But what did the man from London want to find out from the wizard?'

'I don't know you know because he never told me but he said as we went back that it was worth a thousand pounds you know what he had heard from the wizard.'

'I see.'

We then went through one of the bleakest mountain passes in Wales. It looked as though it had never seen a tourist. It was as God made it. The mists came down over it. The rain fell. Small white burns streaked in white lines from the hills. On each side of the road the wild, stark mountains fell away to a distant, shrouded earth. Now and then the mists blew away to show us for a moment the piled mass of Plynlimon on the left hand and to the right a hard, untracked wilderness of hills : a place in which a man might lose himself and die within a stone's throw of civilization.

We stopped under the shadow of a great hill. The driver, in whose manner I now seemed to detect a certain reverence, told me that the house of the *consuriwr* lay at the end of a downward path. I followed this path and came to a small farm. I knocked at the door. After a moment the door was opened, not as I had hoped by the wizard himself, but by a charming girl. I told her that I wished to consult the *consuriwr*. She was not surprised. She was sorry to say that her father had been called away and would not be back until night. I was disappointed and promised to call at some other time, a promise I intend to keep. . . .

On the road above, the little driver was full of interest. His sympathy was boundless when he learnt that the magician was abroad.

'Never mind,' I said, 'we will go on to Rhayader and Llandrindod Wells.'

The wilderness and the solitude continued mile after mile. We came to a stream that crossed the road.

'That is the river Wye you know,' cried my little friend.

'Not the Wye that runs through Herefordshire ? '

'Oh, yes, indeed, it is the same river you know. . . .'

I stopped him and got out to examine the beginning of that lovely lowland river that rises somewhere in Plynlimon. It was a mountain stream. It came rushing down from the uplands unconscious of its majestic destiny. My mind followed it through Wales into England. I saw it broadening on its course. I remembered how it looks at Ross-on-Wye on a summer afternoon, with cattle standing at the edge of it whipping the flies off with their tails.

We plunged again into the wilderness of hills. We sped round hairpin bends. We watched the clouds streaming over the shoulders of the hills and we travelled from rain into fine weather and into rain again. Gradually the country grew softer. We descended from the heights. We ran through the magnificent Wye Valley and came to a prim stone market town with a far-away look about it. This was Rhayader.

This little town with its nine hundred and fifty inhabitants is the capital of Radnorshire, one of the least-known counties in England or Wales. I have met people who have thought that Rutland was in Wales and Flintshire in England, and I suppose there are many who could not tell you where Radnorshire is to be found. Rhayader speaks with an English accent; in fact it reminded me of a market town on the Yorkshire moors.

'Radnorshire . . . is unique in having far and away the thinnest population per mile of any other [county] in England or Wales,' says Mr. A. G. Bradley in *The Romance of Wales*. For the total is under twenty thousand, though the area of the county is not especially small. Incidentally, this was about the average of England in the Tudor period—not a bad object-lesson to the historically-minded. And this paucity of inhabitants is not because its wild uplands form an especially large share of its area, but that it is just a county of farms like old England once was, with neither industries or towns worth mentioning. Radnor is also peculiar in being racially Welsh throughout, while at the same time no Welsh has been spoken within its bounds by natives for about a century. This, too, despite the fact that all along its westerly fringes the ancient tongue is still in use. Radnorshire English, again, is extraordinarily good, perhaps naturally, as a foreign tongue now the common speech for some generations. Towards Shropshire it has caught something of the Saxon 'burr', just as the West Salopians, probably from their mainly Welsh origin, combine the Border English with the Welsh intonation. This Border speech is, in fact, much the same on both sides, though its users admit no racial kinship. The small farmers' wives and daughters speak beautifully, and there are no dropped h's, though there are a few queer tricks, as, for instance, an apparent disinclination to commit themselves definitely, rather after the Scottish fashion. If, for example, you knock at the door of a farm-house and inquire politely if Mr. Jones lives there, even should he open it himself he will answer with equal civility that he 'expects so'. Should you chance to ask if Mr. Pryce is his landlord, you will be told he is 'sure to be'. This fancy for indirect expression takes whimsical shape in the universal terminal to most Radnorian sentences of 'or something'. 'I am going to Knighton Fair to-morrow to buy a horse'—and then after just a perceptible pause—' or something'; the speaker, of course, not having the faintest designs on anything but a horse! . . . But if people in Sussex and London and Norfolk never heard of Radnorshire, Salopians know it well. Having no towns, Shrewsbury is virtually its capital. Sometimes it is called the capital of North Wales, though, of course, no true North Walian would admit the claim!'

The first thing I noticed about Rhayader was a stray foxhound. The next thing was a second stray foxhound. He was behaving in a manner unusual to foxhounds. He was standing on his hind legs in an hotel yard, trying to push the lid from a dust-bin. The lid fell with a clatter. The hound seized a scrap of food. A maidservant, roused by the noise, rushed out into the yard and shooed the poor hound away.

'Only the other day, sir, one of those hounds got into the kitchen and ran off with a whole leg of lamb,' she explained.

'But why do foxhounds steal lamb in Rhayader?' I asked.

'Because the poor things are hungry, sir,' she said rather obviously.

I learnt afterwards that certain local farmers keep a pack of hounds and turn them loose on Rhayader to fend for themselves when the hunting season ends. The unfortunate creatures are forced to haunt the streets for any scrap of food they can pick up. I suggest that if the farmers of Rhayader cannot afford to keep a pack decently they had better give up hunting. . . .

I went a few miles out of Rhayader to see the Birmingham Water Works, one of the latter-day wonders of Wales.

§ II

Birmingham's water supply is famous. It travels by pipe lines for 73½ miles across England. The three reservoirs, Caban Coch, Pen-y-Gareg and Craig Goch, lie among exquisite, gentle mountain scenery which reminds me of Loch Lomond more than anything I have seen in Wales. The Elan Valley is, to my mind, more beautiful than any lake scenery in the Principality.

You might think that the business of providing a great modern city with about twenty-seven million gallons of water every day would require a small town of workers. It seems to me that these immense lakes are sent on their journey to Birmingham by a mere handful of men who just turn handles, levers or watch power-house dials.

The reservoirs have been made by damming the valleys through which the rivers Elan and Claerwen flow into the Wye. The four reservoirs, or lakes, lie in steps, each one higher than the first, and their water thunders down over high dams from lake to lake in magnificent artificial Niagaras.

I was interested in the lake formed by flooding a portion of the Elan valley in which stood two houses associated with Shelley, Cwm Elan and Nant Gwyllt. Many books on Wales state that these two houses are submerged beneath the waters; but this is not true.

'We pulled them down stone by stone,' I was told. 'There was also a church. We had to build another one to take its place. It is built on what was once a hill but is now the shore of the reservoir.'

It was to the house, Nant Gwyllt, that Shelley came soon after his unfortunate marriage with young Harriet Westbrook. He is, perhaps, the only great English poet who ever made Wales his home. The Welsh considered him to be a lunatic. It was in Tremadoc, at the house called Tan-yr-Allt, now demolished, that Shelley had his mysterious encounter with the would-be assassins. Many people have been puzzled by this episode in his nervous life and have attributed it to his inflamed imagination. He rushed into the house one night, bleeding and holding a pistol, saying that he had fought in the shrubbery with armed men who attempted to kill him. It seems to be generally admitted now that his assailant may have been a farmer named Evans who was enraged by the poet's habit of wandering about the hills with a loaded pistol and shooting, from humanitarian motives, any sheep that was suffering from the scab! If Evans meant to frighten Shelley away he succeeded. The very next day Shelley and his small household disappeared from Tremadoc!

Midway in the Elan Valley is a control tower which draws off water from the reservoirs and pumps it to the filter beds on the first stage of its journey to the Midlands. I was taken down a winding iron staircase below the surface level of the lake to see this water. The thunder of it far below rose up to us as we descended into the dark iron tube.

'A lot of people turn back,' yelled the official. 'They can't stand the noise.'

And we came to a queer grotto under the earth where the mad, dark-looking waters were raging in a tunnel. It was not a pleasant sight. If something went wrong I felt that we might have been drowned like rats.

And when we emerged I looked out at the placid lake where a man in a boat was trying to catch trout in the bath water of Birmingham.

§ 12

Llandrindod Wells is the best known spa in Wales. There are Builth Wells, Llangammarch Wells, Llanwrtyd Wells, Trefriw, in Caernarvonshire ; but Llandrindod has more than a local fame.

I liked the look of it so much that I determined to go there some day and sample its waters. It is a spa set in a garden. Nature has obligingly shot up its medicinal waters in a rustic glen, and the municipality has, with more than municipal wisdom, improved and cultivated the surroundings. All round Llandrindod is magnificent open country.

I was surprised to learn that Pliny, writing in the first century, mentions only two spas, Bath and Llandrindod—Balnea Siluria.

Like Harrogate, Llandrindod Wells is lucky in the variety of waters which it possesses. There are about twelve kinds, which can be divided into three groups : mild salt springs ; mild salt springs containing sulphuretted hydrogen and, thirdly, chalybeate waters.

I went into the pump-room in the park and tried a glass of saline, which I thought pleasant and innocuous—just the sort of thing a doctor would order when there is nothing seriously the matter with you.

I was interested in the spa's most recent treasure : one of the latest and most expensive X-ray outfits in the country. You stand behind a kind of screen, there is a flare of light and those on the other side of the screen can see through your head or any other part of you.

Although the spa prides itself on the belief that the Romans used the waters for rheumatism, there is no definite proof that they did so. The real history of Llandrindod Wells begins about two centuries ago in the reign of Charles II when the royal physician advised the Merry Monarch to take the waters. I wonder if this happened during the mysterious visit of Charles II to the Vaughans of Cors-y-gedol? The exploitation of the spa dates from more recent times, when the first hotel was erected.

On the way back my little driver treated me to another torrent of talk. I gathered that he was a Welsh home ruler: 'The world has changed you know,' he said, 'and the Great War changed it you know and here in Wales we have never liked servility if you know what I mean while in England in which I have been more than once there is too much servility you know which I think is all wrong for we were all made equal you know and a man can respect another man without taking his hat off to him every minute of the day if you know what I mean and if the people of Wales could rule our country for themselves instead of being ruled by Englishmen from London you know it would be better for everybody you know . . .'

We swung on over the now darkening moors. A drizzle of rain developed into a deep mist in which our headlights lost themselves. Corners rushed madly at us. Stone walls sprang out of the emptiness, giving a view of swirling mist as the tattered edges of cloud were blown earthwards. And the wind grew cold and whistled icily. I was aching to probe my little friend's nationalism, but I did not dare to lead him into any more rapid and unpunctuated conversations which involved a hand lifted from the wheel and a backward turn of the head.

So for hours, blinded with mist and cold with the mountain wind, we sped over the highlands until we saw the lights of Aberystwyth lying before us at the bottom of a hill.

CHAPTER TEN

WELSH RAIN ALL THE WAY TO CARDIGAN, I LOOK AT FISHGUARD AND REMEMBER THE LAST FRENCH INVASION, I VISIT THE TOWN OF ST. DAVID'S AND SOON FIND MYSELF IN 'LITTLE ENGLAND BEYOND WALES'

§ I

WELSH rain. . . . It descends with the enthusiasm of some one breaking bad news. It comes down in a constant cataract. It blots out sea, sky and mountain. Vast shapes from the beginning of the world that tower to the clouds are as if they had never been. The rain is like a separate element. A man can lose himself in it as if lost in fog. It flies, abetted by its companion the wind, to the left and to the right. It even blows upward over the edge of high places. It runs round corners with the wind. It finds its way up your sleeves and down your neck. It sings a song on the roads as it runs, a miniature stream, to join other rivulets until it forms a little mountain torrent. In the hills it comes rushing through the heather-stems to fall in hundreds of tiny waterfalls—hundreds of Lilliputian Bettws-y-Coeds—over stone walls upon the mountain passes. And a man looks at it in amazement and thinks that Owen Glendower must have been at his tricks again. In such wind and rain was the tent of King Henry IV blown down when the English armies were seeking the Welshman. And no wonder the whisper went round that he could control the elements; for rain in Wales can seem directed by some malignant producer, some one bent on drowning the earth and wiping from the mind of man all memory of dry places.

In such a determined storm I left Aberystwyth and took the coast road to the south. I knew that it was the coast road because the map said so. But when I looked to the right, where the waters of Cardigan Bay should have been, I saw only a ghostly greyness like a veil, a melancholy curtain of falling water.

There was a sea-mist. Now and then I would look down towards the right and see the shadow of a little coaster tossing on water the colour of lead, or I would see a cliff shining in the rain. Gulls driven inland by the wind perched on the stone walls and flew over the fields.

In a few miles I came to a wet little place called Aberayron. There was not a soul to be seen. I went into an inn, more for shelter than anything else, and there I met a depressing old man glooming over a pint of ale. He said that times were bad and would never get any better. He had a strange habit of saying 'Oh dear' to any remark made to him. If you said that it was a foul and ghastly day he would reply, 'Oh dear, yes.' But he could vary the meaning of his 'Oh dears.' He could make them sound pathetic, indignant, querulous, lachrymatory, confirmatory, shocked, incredulous and affirmative. He told me that Aberayron used to be a fishing-port, but now the inhabitants fish instead for summer visitors. They made Welsh tweed in the village.

I decided, for no reason except that I was bored to tears, to buy myself some Welsh tweed, and my morose friend very kindly offered to take me to the shop. Was it hand-loom tweed?

'Oh, dear, yes indeed. . . .'

So off we went. I picked a length of rather loud brown tweed, thick stuff like Harris but without the long hairs. It was the sort of tweed you would choose only on a wet day. The Aberayron tweed is cheaper than the tweed of Talybont. I paid four and sixpence a yard for it, which is the same price you pay in Kenmare, in Kerry, and in parts of Donegal.

When I offered to buy my sad friend another drink in slight recognition of his courtesy, a shocked expression came over him, he lifted one hand and in a tone of voice which he might have employed had I suggested that he might help me to bury a murdered body, said:

" Oh *dear*, no. . . .'

I went on in the pelting rain thinking what a funny trick was that 'Oh dear' of his, as monotonous as the 'you know what I mean' of the Aberystwyth motor-car driver. But the old man put a wealth of meaning into his 'Oh dears', sometimes drawing out the 'Oh' and sometimes the 'dear'.

The amount of surprise which a Welshman can express in the word 'Oh' is astonishing. Some of them draw it out for seconds:

'O-o-o-o-o-o-o-o-h-h-h-h-h-h-H-H-H! That is *t-t-terrible*!'

they will say about something that is neither terrible nor surprising, and the 'Oh' comes in a hushed, shocked way from the back of the throat, but rising in tone as it expresses amazement and incredulity.

I began to wonder what word is capable of the most subtle inflexions, and came to the conclusion that it is the word 'darling' as used by women. There is the plain ordinary 'darling' and the 'dar-*ling*' which denotes assumed disapproval. There is the dar-LING (always sung on a rising scale) which summons the beloved from a distant place. There is the 'Oh DAR-ling' which expresses real concern and the 'D-a-arling' which is always said to an accompaniment of tears. There is the sudden suspicious 'Darling?'—a question—that flings a man off his balance and the sharp, sudden 'DARLING!'—an exclamation—which precedes a stern rebuke. There is the dangerous 'darl-i-n-g' which is a cloying, clinging word and always means trouble, and the various assortment of almost unrecognizable, but passionate, 'darlings' which range in sound from the Old English 'deorling' to words which might be the effort of a person without teeth trying to say 'Durham'.

With such silly thoughts for company, I splashed and skidded over a bleak road that left the sea and ran inland, the rain still pelting down, the hills covered with low clouds, and at length I ran over a bridge into the little town of Cardigan.

It is surprising to discover, as you so often do in Wales, that a town with a name known all over the world is little more than a village. Cardigan is a small place on the Teifi with one street of shops and a general air of having retired from business. I was stopped in the main street by a great herd of parsons. They came pouring out of a public building on the right of the main street and stood in the road under hundreds of umbrellas. There were deacons with them and the sombre wives of deacons. This was an annual religious conference. It was so important that even the London newspapers published in Manchester had invoked the aid of some Welsh sub-editor and had printed their contents bills in Welsh. This was annoying. If they had only done the usual thing:

MINISTER

ATTACKS

MODERN YOUTH

I would not have bothered to buy a paper. But the thought of two London papers notorious for their ignorance of Scotland, Wales and Ireland seeking to compliment Cardigan with a display of Welsh was so affecting that I bought copies, and took them into an inn that might have been transplanted from Salisbury. Here I opened them with a certain anticipation and read in the news columns: 'Minister Attacks Modern Youth.'

The inn was full of large and comfortable-looking farmers. They seemed to me a different type from the farmers of the north, not perhaps so morose and introspective. They were speaking in Welsh and appeared to be a hearty, jolly crowd.

I went into the dining-room, but it was in an ecclesiastical panic. Three or four startled-looking maids were trying to marshal a great crowd of ministers and other religious-seeming people. I could smell the roasting mutton which was to give them strength to deliver another savage attack on youth. And, becoming suddenly consumed by a violent passion for a pork pie, I left them and went out into the streets of Cardigan.

The shops close in Cardigan sharp at one and a calm as deep and important as the siesta in a Spanish town lies over the place. I found a shop where a pretty Welsh maiden sold me not only a pie but several of those currant sandwiches beloved by youth, ancient and modern.

The rain surprisingly stopped; and I was soon on my way south.

§ 2

The small town of Fishguard occupies the cliff-top while the harbour lies at the bottom of a terrifying hill.

If the sun is shining Fishguard is one of the most beautiful harbours you have ever seen. The deep blue water lies securely shielded by two great headlands that thrust themselves into the Atlantic. The bay is deep enough to give anchorage to the largest of liners. The red-funnelled boats that go over to Rosslare in Ireland are generally to be seen, getting up steam for the night passage; and sometimes, I am told, a big liner comes in from New York with the mail-bags.

But when you look at Fishguard Bay you must remember the last hostile invasion of British soil. There is a strong flavour of musical comedy about it, although it caused a deal of excitement at the time.

It was on February 22nd 1797 at ten o'clock in the morning that three men-o'-war and a lugger were seen coming towards the bay from the direction of St. David's Head. The people of St. David's, considering them to be British ships because they flew the British flag, cheered them heartily until a retired seaman recognized them as French warships. A panic spread through Pembrokeshire. Men and women fled inland with their valuables.

The French ships dropped anchor and landed a force of six hundred French infantry and eight hundred French convicts in a little cove at Carreg Gwastad Point, about two and a half miles west of Fishguard. The troops were under the command of an Irish American, General Tate. We can imagine the alarm in Pembrokeshire, which had known no fighting since the Civil War, with the enemy on its doorstep and no local troops within many miles of Fishguard! Messengers rode north and south. Lord Cawdor, who was the acting Lieutenant of the county, lived thirty-five miles away. He was awakened in the middle of the night with a no doubt highly coloured account of the invasion. He jumped out of bed to take command of the defence force. Meanwhile the 'fiery cross' had been sent round to the local yeomanry and militia. There must have been many dramatic farewells and many heroic moments that night as squire and farmer said good-bye to their womenfolk, buckled on swords or grasped muskets and set off to fight the bloodless battle of Fishguard Bay.

Lord Cawdor arrived at noon on the following day with a mixed force of yeomanry and militia. His total force was about seven hundred and fifty, but his 'army' was followed by a great rabble armed with mattocks, spades, scythes, and reaping-hooks. A Captain Davies, who had seen active service, was entrusted with the responsibility of placing the British force in the most imposing formation. He very wisely dotted it about the hills.

The French meantime were not happy. For some reason, which, I think, has never been explained, their fleet suddenly hoisted sail and deserted them! They were left on the rugged shore watching the mysterious preparations of the defenders. They saw gorgeously dressed and splendidly mounted men cantering about, and these—the Castle Martin Yeomanry—they mistook for the staff officers of a very imposing army. The wind that blew away the warships began to blow in the French camp! But—says legend—the Frenchmen's terror was increased when on the distant hills they saw the marching and counter-marching of red-coats. They did not know that cunning Captain Davies was using the Welsh women in their red cloaks and their tall beaver hats to impress them! It is even said that this Welsh Ulysses marched a file of women up and down a hill in the approved operatic manner in order to cause the enemy to believe that a huge army was marching to the support. For two hours the gallant 'red cloaks' are said to have impersonated the British Grenadiers!

That night at ten p.m. two French officers came up under a flag of truce. They were summoned to a council of war held in the old Royal Oak Inn, where they delivered the following letter from General Tate:

CARDIGAN BAY
5th Ventose
5th year of the Republic

SIR,

The circumstances under which the body of troops under my command were landed at this place render it unnecessary to attempt any military operations, as they would only lead to bloodshed and pillage. The officers of the whole corps have, therefore, intimated their desire of entering into a negotiation upon principles of humanity for a surrender. If you are influenced by a similar consideration you may signify the same to the bearer, and, in the meantime, hostilities shall cease.

Health and respect
TATE, *Chef de Brigade*

The British force had by this time acquired a terrific superiority complex. The wretched Frenchmen were told that unless they would surrender unconditionally they would be attacked by twenty thousand men! They were then blindfolded and led back to their cove.

Early on the following morning Major Ackland, a Devonian who had recently settled in Pembrokeshire, rode over to the French with an ultimatum, written in not quite such good English as that of the French *Chef de Brigade*, and signed by Lord Cawdor:

> SIR,
>
> The superiority of the force under my command, which is hourly increasing, must prevent my treating on any other terms short of your surrendering your whole force prisoners of war. I enter fully into your wish of preventing an unnecessary effusion of blood, which your speedy surrender can alone prevent, and which will entitle you to that consideration which is ever the wish of British troops to show an enemy whose numbers are inferior. The major will deliver you this letter, and I shall expect your determination by ten o'clock.
>
> I am, etc.
>
> CAWDOR

The end of it was, of course, the unconditional surrender of the French. They first opened the pans of their muskets and shed the powder, then, with drums playing, were marched without arms or colours to the junction of the Fishguard-Goodwick road.

The prisoners were split up among the local gaols, and, if I know anything about yeomanry and militiamen, the British forces indulged in a series of congratulatory dinners! But the story was not quite over. Two Welsh girls who were employed at one of the prisons fell in love with two of the French soldiers. They smuggled a shin-bone of beef into the prison with which the Frenchmen painfully excavated a hole in the prison wall big enough to take a man. A number of Frenchmen wriggled through this hole one night and were guided by the girls to a cargo-boat in the harbour. They boarded it, but did not get it off owing to the lowness of the tide. They then seized Lord Cawdor's yacht and got clear away!

The two Frenchmen married their Welsh lovers, and the story goes that when the Peace of Amiens was signed the girls revisited Pembrokeshire, where they received a great welcome!

So ended the invasion of Fishguard Bay.

§ 3

The road runs on up hill and down again through a bleak land swept by salt winds from the sea. As you go over this road you feel that there is something great and unforgettable at the end of it, for it is a lonely road and an old road. It is also a melancholy road on a grey afternoon with a grey Atlantic beating against the green lowlands, for the great mountains of Wales lie back to the eastward.

The road takes you to a village which has three streets. It is a hushed little village and in the middle of it, looking as if it has been blown from a great church, is a grey tower. You discover, when you approach this tower, that it belongs to a splendid church that hides itself in a hollow. Whether its far-off builders placed it there to safeguard it from the Atlantic winds or to hide it from pirates in war-boats we do not know, but no other great church hides itself so securely from the winds of God and the eyes of men. This is the Cathedral of St. David.

It is the most historic and the most significant building in Wales. I went down thirty-nine steps to it, and before I entered I sat for a time looking at it, thinking that from the outside there is nothing to admire. You must admire it with your imagination.

This is the oldest cathedral in Great Britain. In its foundations Roman Britain and Wales meet. It was founded by St. David about the year A.D. 550—or forty-seven years before Pope Gregory sent St. Augustine to convert England! When the first Christian church was built on this site it is probable that the only other Christian churches in Britain were St. Ninian's white chapel at Whithorn and an anchorite's little cell at Glastonbury.

St. Columba had just planted his first monastery in the oak grove at Derry, but he had not yet deserted Ireland to found Iona. It is an astonishing experience to look at a church with a history that goes back beyond Iona, beyond Canterbury Cathedral, beyond Lindisfarne.

I looked at St. David's and tried to imagine what these islands were like when the saint came to this bleak place to plant his church. The whole of England was scattered with Roman ruins and with Roman towns like London, with grass in their streets and weeds on their walls; for the Saxon feared those ghostly old cities: he thought they were haunted, as, no doubt, they were. The Britons had been pressed back towards the mountains of Wales, taking Roman Christianity with them.

An old man would, as a boy, remember talking to old people who had lived on in the terrible chaos that followed the withdrawal of the Roman legions after four centuries of colonization in this country. He would have heard stories of Britain in the good, safe Roman days. To him and to his generation they would be 'the good old days'. He would have been told many a story of the ruins that still scattered the land, of the temples and the theatres and the stately villas with their pavements and their mosaic work, their gardens, their orchards and their fish ponds.

This Welshman, or Briton, would look back over a lifetime of horror; a lifetime of slaughter and raiding; a lifetime of battle and flight against the heathen Angles and Saxons from over the sea. He might tell his children, as they huddled together over a wood fire in a hut made of wattle and mud, how few were the years that separated them from that splendid time when Britain was safe behind the shield of Rome.

St. David was born in this age. It is said that he was born in A.D. 530, just 140 years after Honorius withdrew the legions from Britain. He would be born into a Britain that was still Roman in thought and speech. We know little of him. He belongs to an age which is like a mist on a mountain, that blows aside for a moment to show a half-revealed thing before closing down again in impenetrable mystery. Dewi Sant was a great man and a good man. All we know about him historically is that he was a great theologian, an enemy of Pelagianism and that he died at the age of seventy.

'The Cymric attempt at continuing the political unity bequeathed by Rome to the west,' wrote Sir O. M. Edwards, 'found expression in the romances of Arthur, whose dim and majestic presence gradually dominates Welsh political thought. A Welsh poet wandered from grave to grave, asking the same simple question over each grave on which the rain fell: "Whose grave is this?" One slept under the mighty oak, another where the surf beat on the shore; one on the crest of the hill, another in the lowly dale. One grave was long and narrow ; another was covered with dead grass and sere leaves. It was not known who lay in one grave ; in another it was well known that Cynddylan slept—he of the ruddy sword and the white steeds. Among the graves on hill and dale and sea-shore there was no grave for Arthur. He had become the spirit of unity, of independence, of stately wisdom ; " folly it would be to think that Arthur has a grave."

'The period which bequeathed to Wales the mythical champion of its traditional unity, also gave it a patron saint. St. David represents the final victory of Christ over a host of deities—Lud of the Silver Hand, patron of flocks and ships ; Merlin imprisoned in an enchanted palace ; Lear and Old King Cole ; Gwydion ap Don, who created the maiden Flower-aspect from rose and broom and anemone ; Elen, goddess of marching armies, and Ceridwen, goddess of wisdom and knowledge ; and a host of others, some mighty and some maimed, some possessed of wonderful power, others known for the good they did. The disappearance of the motley throng was not final ; many of them, especially well deities, reappeared disguised as the saints of the new religion—some have remained in popular superstition to this day.'

And in this quiet place, where the cliffs of western Wales look over the sea to Holy Ireland, St. David of Wales built a little Church to the Glory of God nearly half a century before Pope Gregory ordered the timid and unwilling Augustine to convert Angle-land that had once been Britain.

I entered the cathedral and found myself in a building that impressed me at once, partly because of the tone of the purple and reddish stone with which it is built, partly because of the rich transitional-Norman arches, partly because of the magnificent but totally out-of-place oak roof, and also because of the sharp contrast of the stern exterior.

Wales possesses more Norman castles in a small area than any country in Europe, but this was the first great Norman building I had seen which was dedicated to God. The small British churches on this site were burnt and pillaged by the Danes, and it was not until the time of the third Norman bishop, Peter de Leia, that the present St. David's sprang up in the hollow. Like all ancient churches, it has been rebuilt and restored from age to age.

The most perfect portion of St. David's is, in my opinion, the Sanctuary. Here is an exquisite and perfectly balanced exercise in stone, much as it left the builders in the time of Peter de Leia. Nearly every feature of St. David's can be surpassed by cathedrals in England, but this Sanctuary is, in its way, unique and perfect.

Behind the altar is Bishop Vaughan's chapel, with its delicate fan-traceried roof and its alcove in which, during the nineteenth century, Sir Gilbert Scott, when restoring the building, discovered an ancient chest containing the bones of two men. They were preserved and re-interred. In 1921 they were again seen during alterations to the building, and this time they were scientifically examined. They were said to be those of an unusually tall man and a short man. One of the skulls was said to be of remarkable mental capacity. It was concluded that the bones were those of St. David—who is known to have been a tall man—and of a contemporary holy man, possibly St. David's legendary teacher and relative, Guistilianus, or Justinianus.

East of the choir is a plain arcaded shrine known as the Shrine of St. David, although it is obviously merely the place on which rested the movable casket containing the relics of the saint. A few yards away is a plain sarcophagus of Purbeck marble, the most interesting tomb in St. David's: the tomb of Edmund Tudor, Earl of Richmond, father of King Henry VII.

It is strange to stand in this church on the wild, western limits of the Principality above the father of the great Tudor and Elizabethan age. This tomb stood originally in the church of the Grey Friars in Carmarthen and was brought to St. David's during the Dissolution by the order of Edmund's grandson, Henry VIII.

Edmund was the eldest son of the handsome Anglesey squire Owen Tudor, whose secret love-affair with Henry V's widow, Katherine de Valois, caused a deal of scandal at the time. Edmund's only claim to fame is that he married and became the father of a son called Henry. He was never to see the 'lad who was born to be king'. Edmund's married life lasted barely a year, and the child was born after his death.

So rests the grandfather of Henry VIII and the great-grandfather of Elizabeth: a Welshman who was never to know that he had founded a new dynasty and had reconciled his country to her ancient foe.

When the evening sun falls over St. David's Cathedral, gilding the old stone, shining on the gentle green hills, the white twisting roads and the little farms, the smallest ' city ' in the kingdom lies lost in its mighty memories. The sea wind drops, the smoke rises upward from the chimneys, and a man looking at the church in the hollow knows it to possess the longest memory in Britain.

§ 4

Sixteen miles and seventeen hills separate the City of St. David's from the town with the English name—Haverfordwest. . . .

I am writing on a green hill in Pembrokeshire.

Something uncanny has happened to Wales! This is not Wales—it is England.

It is impossible to believe that this green hill is a Welsh hill; it is impossible to believe that the wood below is a Welsh wood; that the whitewashed farm in the hollow is Welsh, and that the gates with their heavy stone lintels are Welsh gates. As soon as you cross the boundary from Cardiganshire into Pembrokeshire you seem to leave Wales behind. You might be in Cornwall, in Devon, or, most likely of all, in Somerset.

Pembrokeshire is that strangely-shaped, thrust-forward portion of Wales on the extreme south-west, and if you look at a map you will see that the very names of the towns and villages in Pembrokeshire are English names.

You might draw a line through this country—to the north are the difficult Welsh names; to the south are the easy, homely, English ones.

You have hundreds of places ending in the English ' ton '—Puncheston, Rudbaxton, Lambston, Haroldston, and lovely English names like Tavernspite and Spittal and New Hedges. And this—the Ordnance Survey map expects me to believe—is Wales!

Pembrokeshire racially is to Wales rather as Ulster is to Ireland. It is a much older example of colonization. And it is the only attempt to anglicize Wales which has stood the test of time.

All the old English stronghold towns in the North are now Welsh. Could you find a more Welsh town than Caernarvon or Conway? But here in the West is a little survival of the Flemish colony planted in Wales 830 years ago during the reigns of Henry I and Stephen. It is one of the most interesting examples in the British Isles of a racial difference that has persisted through the centuries.

In Ulster, of course, you can spot the sturdy descendants of the Scots who were planted there in the reign of James I; in Norfolk, notably in Norwich, you can see men and women who are obviously descendants of the Flemish weavers of Plantagenet times. The town and some of the inhabitants of Boston, in Lincolnshire, might be transported to Holland without appearing in any way alien; but nowhere in England is anything quite like this county with a dual personality, where two races, their old feuds forgotten, live side by side, the boundaries of their territory clearly marked by language, architecture and place-names.

This county, half English, half Welsh, is one of the curiosities of the British Isles.

'English, I am told, has been pushing into the Welsh country for the last generation," wrote Mr. A. G. Bradley in *The Romance of Wales*. 'It used to be said that the line of cleavage at one point ran down the middle of a village street! That the one side of it remained for life ignorant of their opposite neighbours' speech and resisted the villagers' passion for gossip would be a strain on the reader's credulity. But on one of my visits to Pembrokeshire I remember there was quite a commotion because a Welshman had been appointed Relieving Officer in a parish just south of the line. He was fully qualified, bi-lingual and not unpopular, but he found himself politely refused at every attempt to get quarters. Finally the policeman as an independent member of society accommodated him. But then there was his horse, an official necessity. In the matter of provender and standing room he found every stable door closed against him. In the end the poor man had to be removed to some more congenial area in the Welsh division.'

Haverfordwest, wearing an English expression, sits on a fine hill. You could plant it anywhere in Devon or Somerset and it would look right. There is nothing of Wales about it: even the voice of Haverfordwest is the voice of England.

§ 5

I suppose if you set an examination paper in geography most people would tell you that Milford Haven is in Devon. There is a kinship between it and Plymouth Hoe. It suggests Francis Drake and the Armada. It is something of a shock to discover Milford Haven in South Wales—the only great fishing-port in the Principality.

Milford Haven has, industrially speaking, had bad luck. During the Middle Ages it was the port of departure for Ireland. It was from Milford Haven that Henry II set out to conquer Ireland in 1172. For several centuries it enjoyed the distinction of being a national port until Telford drove his great road from Shrewsbury to the Menai Straits, when the Government transferred the Irish mail traffic to Holyhead. Milford's next blow was the closing of the naval dockyard in 1814.

But Milford, like Norwich, managed to survive adversity and even, as is often the way with towns as with individuals, to profit by it. On the ruin of its past hopes grew up a great fishing industry—the only great one of its kind in Wales—and the docks, which were opened in 1888, now give shelter to one of the finest trawler fleets in the kingdom.

It is a great sight to see the trawlers come in heavy with their catch. There are about 120, some of them the largest and most modern fishing-vessels in Great Britain. They come steaming up the magnificent harbour, sometimes in small companies. They have been out, perhaps, a week or a fortnight. Their crews have not had time to shave. They climb about the decks in great sea-boots. They prepare to unload their catches.

Hundreds of men on the dockside are waiting for them. Tons of fish lying in crushed ice are dumped on the quayside. The largest number of sea-gulls I have seen in any fishing-port waits philosophically for the scraps, whitening the galvanized iron roofs with their wings.

The sight of a catch laid out on the dockside of Milford Haven is as spectacular as anything of the kind I have seen. The men work all night sorting and washing the fish. By dawn about 60,000 square feet of fish are dressed by the right, looking like some weird army kit-inspection. The buyers come at 8 a.m. The sales are over at 10 a.m. Shortly afterwards the special trains steam out of Milford Haven, taking fish to the ever-open mouths of London, Manchester and Cardiff.

There is great excitement when a trawler runs into a shoal of herring. No fishing-port in the country can turn a herring into a kipper quicker than Milford Haven. I read a signal asking the smoke-houses to get ready because herring were arriving. I saw the ship arrive. I saw the piles of silver, red-eyed fish hauled ashore. In a few minutes, girls with sturdy, bare arms were slitting and gutting them in three decisive movements; a few minutes more and they were hanging in the smoke of oak chips.

'And,' said the man in charge of the kiln, 'these fish, which were swimming in the Atlantic a few hours ago, will be on London's breakfast-table to-morrow.'

If you get tired of looking at fish and ships in Milford Haven you can chase the ghost of Nelson's Lady Hamilton. Her husband, Sir William Hamilton, lies buried in the churchyard. He was a large landowner in this part of Wales.

Nelson's memory is kept green in Milford by the rather strange relic, the truck of the French battleship *L'Orient*, which blew up at the Battle of the Nile. This was the ship, immortalized by Mrs. Hemans, on whose 'burning deck' the boy stood 'whence all but he had fled'!

But Milford, generally speaking, cares less for this than for getting the kippers to London in time for breakfast!

Just east of the Headland, in Mill Bay, you can see the spot where Henry Tudor, Earl of Richmond, landed on one of those rash adventures which sometimes come true. It was one of the most important moments in the history not only of Wales but also, as time proved, of Europe. The world said good-bye to the Middle Ages when Henry Tudor stepped ashore at Milford Haven.

His life in exile, his adventures and escapes, his bid for a crown and a wife are among the most romantic episodes in history. Perhaps only his forbidding and cautious personality and his success in later life have prevented him from becoming the hero of ballads. This first Tudor, whose Welsh blood linked Wales with England and whose stern hand was fated to lead both countries back to the paths of order and sanity, spent a youth as romantic as that of Bonnie Prince Charlie.

He was born at Pembroke Castle when his mother, Margaret Beaufort, was barely fourteen years of age. It was through her and her descent from John of Gaunt and not through his father, Edmund Tudor, that in later years he claimed the throne of England. His father died in the year of his birth and he was placed under the protection of his uncle, Jasper Tudor. When he was five years of age his grandfather, Owen Tudor, the gallant old Anglesey squire, then a man of seventy-six, together with Jasper Tudor, fought at Mortimer's Cross. Owen was captured and executed; Jasper escaped. The infant Henry was left unprotected in Pembroke Castle. His adventures had begun!

When a lad of fourteen, having survived many dangers, Henry found himself exiled in France with his uncle, Jasper. The Wars of the Roses ploughed their protracted way from battle to battle. The English nobility was bleeding itself to death; and with every death, the young Welshman, Henry Tudor, found himself a little nearer to the throne. This alarmed Edward IV, who plotted to seize the exiled Tudors. For years they lived abroad, watched and suspected.

Edward IV died. Richard, Duke of Gloucester, after murdering the boy king, Edward V, and his brother in the Tower of London, seized the crown. Wales and England now looked over the Channel towards Henry Tudor, Earl of Richmond. Spies and messengers were frequent visitors. One of these, sent by Henry's mother, who was now married to Lord Stanley, suggested that Henry should marry the rightful heiress to the realm, the Princess Elizabeth, eldest daughter of the dead king, Edward IV. Such a marriage would unite the houses of York and Lancaster—Henry Tudor, through his mother, was the great-grandson of John of Gaunt, while Elizabeth represented the House of York.

Henry decided to put his fate to the test. He sailed with a fleet of forty ships furnished by the Duke of Bretagne. One story is that he heard of the failure of a rising in his favour and put back to France, another is that he was beaten from the coasts of Devon by a great storm, and a third story, that persists in Wales, is that he landed and lay hidden for several months at Mostyn in Flintshire. There is a story that a party of Richard's troops searched Mostyn Hall one night when Henry was about to dine, and that the young earl escaped by leaping through a window.

However that may be, this first attempt of his to win a bride and a crown was a failure. He returned sadly to France. But in England men were thinking of him ; and even Nature, if legend speaks the truth, was on his side. Huge crowds went to see a remarkable rose-bush that bore on its stems both red and white roses !

About this time a messenger arrived in France bringing to Henry Tudor a letter and a ring from the Princess Elizabeth. The messenger found Henry at a monastery near Rennes, dressed in a black velvet surcoat that reached to his knees. Henry kissed the ring and read the letter. He then, with typical Tudor caution, remained silent for three weeks, at the end of which time he went to Paris and took an oath to marry Elizabeth of York if first he could vanquish the usurper, Richard III.

When he had taken this oath the English students of the University of Paris did homage to him as King of England. The Queen Regent of France advanced him a large sum of money, and when she demanded hostages for its repayment Henry, with grim Tudor wit, left her his intended brother-in-law, the Marquis of Dorset, of whom he was rather suspicious !

Now Richard III had his spies, and news travelled fairly quickly in England. Horsemen were posted twenty miles apart and could carry despatches a distance of a hundred miles a day. Richard knew of Henry's projected landing and published a proclamation, pouring scorn on his Welsh and Lancastrian descent :

> Forasmuch as the King, our Sovereign Lord, hath certain knowledge that Piers (Courtney), Bishop of Exeter, Jasper Tydder (*Tudor*), Son of Owen Tydder, calling himself Earl of Pembroke, John, late Earl of Oxford, and Sir Edward Wodevile, with others diverse, his Rebels and Traytors, disabled and attainted by the authority of the High Court of Parliament, of whom many be known for open Murderers, advowterers (*adulterers*) and Extortioners, contrary to the pleasure of God, and against all truth,

11. WOMEN IN TRADITIONAL WELSH DRESS.

12a. A PIT BOY
IN THE 1930s.

12b. MINERS AT WORK
ON THE COAL FACE
IN HEARTBREAK
VALLEY
IN THE 1930s.

honour and nature, have forsaken their natural country, taking them first to be under the obeysance of the Duke of Bretagne, and to him promised certain things. . . .

The said Traitors have chosen to be their Captain one Henry Tydder, son of Edmund Tydder, son of Owen Tydder, whom of his ambitious and insatiable covetise encroacheth and usurpeth upon him, the name and title of Royal Estate of this realm of England; whereunto he hath no manner of interest, right, title or colour, as every man knoweth; for he is descended of bastard blood, both of his father's side and of mother's side; for the said Owen the grandfather, was bastard born; and his mother was daughter unto John, Duke of Somerset, son unto Dame Catherine Swynford, and of their indubitable Advoutry gotten; whereby it evidently appeareth, that no title can or may in him, who fully intended to enter this realm, proposing a conquest, and if he should achieve his false intent and purpose, every man's life, livelihood and goods shall be in his hands, liberty and disposition; whereby should ensue the disheriting and destruction of all the noble and worshipful blood of this realm for ever.

Our said Sovereign Lord willeth and commandeth all his Subjects, to be ready in their most defensible array, to do his Highness service of war, when they by open proclamations, or otherwise, shall be commanded to do so, for resistence of the Kings said Rebels, Traitors and enemies.

Witness myself at Westminster, the 23rd day of July, in the second year of our Reign.

§ 6

It is a day in the beginning of August in the year 1485.

Watchers on the cliffs of Pembrokeshire see the combined fleets of France and Bretagne cast anchor off Milford Haven. A young man of twenty-eight steps ashore. He is long-faced, pale, reserved. With him is his uncle, Jasper Tudor.

'Welcome, for *thou* hast taken good care of thy nephew,' is the greeting as Jasper steps ashore, a grim reference to the princes murdered in the Tower by their uncle, Richard III.

Henry Tudor has with him a small French force. The whole of Wales is on fire with the enterprise, but many of the great lords hold back, just as many of the Highland chiefs held back when Charles Edward landed in Scotland. But the hesitation is only momentary. England may see in this pale young man a descendant of John of Gaunt, but Wales sees in him an older face: the face of Cadwaladr. They see in him a Welshman, a man of their ancient blood who comes, fulfilling the prophesies of Merlin, to sit upon the throne of England. Englishmen may see in his projected marriage with Elizabeth of York the union of the Roses; but Welshmen see in it the union of the descendant of Rhys of Dinevor with a woman in whose veins runs the blood of Llewelyn the Great.

So, as Henry, Earl of Richmond, marches through Wales he gathers an army as he goes. He marches to Cardigan. Richard Griffith and a small force join him. The ruler of South Wales, Rhys ap Thomas, brings in his men. Henry marches to Machynlleth, crosses into the valley of the Severn, passes through Newtown and Welshpool and enters Shrewsbury. Other forces, learning of the Welsh march over the Border, set forth: Richard ap Howell leads a force of one thousand six hundred miners and colliers from Flintshire. And at Newport Henry gathers his first English supporters: five hundred men under Sir Gilbert Talbot.

For a fortnight he marches with his increasing army, wondering whether Lord Stanley, who is married to his mother, will support him or not. The Stanleys hold North Wales as Rhys ap Thomas holds South. Lord Stanley and his brother, Sir William Stanley, give no sign. They march in two divisions with their armies, watching, taking neither side. So Henry Tudor enters England.

King Richard III comes to Leicester at sunset. He rides a splendid white war-horse and wears the same suit of burnished steel armour which he wore at Tewkesbury. His helmet is surmounted by a gilt crown. Behind him rides one of the finest cavalry forces in Europe. His total army is about thirteen thousand men; Henry Tudor commands about five thousand. Richard sleeps that night, not in Leicester Castle, which is uninhabitable, but in the Blue Boar Inn.

Early in the morning Richard and his army leave by the south gate of Leicester. As he crosses the bridge, his foot strikes a projecting piece of wood and a blind beggar cries out:

'His head shall strike that very pile as he returns!'

The army of Richard and the small Welsh army of Henry lie that night opposite to one another on the heath of Redmore, near Bosworth.

Early in the morning, the Welsh army advances up a gentle slope in the face of the sun. The light shines on three standards. One is the figure of St. George ; the second is the Red Dragon of Cadwaladr ; the third is the Dun Cow of the Tudors. John de Vere, Earl of Oxford leads the right ; Sir William Stanley, who at the last moment shows his hand, leads the left ; and Henry himself leads the centre. King Richard hopes to overwhelm the Welsh army with one great charge of cavalry. Charge after charge is made. But the fortune of the day is turned when Sir William Stanley, Chamberlain of North Wales, comes over to the Tudor side with the strength of the men of the North. So North Wales links hands with South Wales on Bosworth Field.

Two hours of fighting, and the battle is over. Richard, who, no matter what men may say about him, was a fearless and gallant soldier, leads three charges against Henry and three times is beaten back. Then, spurring out alone, he seeks a personal encounter with the Tudor. He rides madly towards the standards of England and Wales. They cut him down and his blood runs into a brooklet. In a few moments his body is plundered of its armour. The crown from his helmet is found on a thorn bush. Lord Stanley, his convictions now made up, places it on the head of Henry Tudor, calling him—King Henry VII of England—and Wales.

And on the evening of that day the body of King Richard III, naked and bleeding, hanging head down from the saddle-bow of a horse, came back over Leicester Bridge. The head hung like a thrum-mop, and as it passed the projecting post it struck the wood, fulfilling the prophecy of the blind man.

The Middle Ages were over : the modern world was ready to begin. Henry VIII and Queen Elizabeth, Shakespeare, the American Continent, Commerce, Industry, Imperialism, and all the doubtful blessings they have brought us, were in the Eye of Time when a pale, crafty and victorious young Welshman took the road to London on an August day of 1485.

§ 7

In order to understand Wales, and her place in the Anglo-Celtic community within Great Britain, it is necessary to realize that when Henry VII was crowned King of England the Principality considered that it had revenged itself for the Norman invasion. The Tudor Age was a time when Welshmen were as much in favour at Westminster as Scotsmen were to be during the Stuart Period. (Elizabeth's great councillor, Seisyll, which, anglicized, is Cecil, was of Welsh origin.)

Henry entered London surrounded by Welshmen. The Red Dragon of Wales flew above him. Few people realize that the official known as Rouge Dragon Pursuivant, who still has an office in Queen Victoria Street, was created by Henry VII to signal the triumph of the Red Dragon of Cadwaladr. The Tudor conqueror entered London not on a war-horse, as every other conqueror had done, but sitting strangely in a clumsy coach of a kind used by women. It was a queer entry and astounded the Londoners. Perhaps it was prophetic of the new age: an age which was to reach its climax in the personality of a woman, Henry's grand-daughter Elizabeth.

His first act on reaching London was to go to the Church of St. Paul, and there, during the singing of a *Te Deum*, to offer up his standards.

Within a year he had married Elizabeth of York. Their wedding day was celebrated 'with all religious and glorious magnificence at court, and by their people with bonfires, dancing, songs and banquets throughout all London'. The officiating prelate was Cardinal Bouchier and, as a writer of the time prettily expressed it, 'his hand held that sweet posie, wherein the white and red roses were first tied together'.

In the same year Elizabeth gave birth to a boy child, and Henry, who knew the Welsh legends of King Arthur and the bardic songs which for centuries proclaimed the fact that a British prince would some day sit upon the English throne, gave his first-born the name of Arthur. So the legends of the prince who waited for the hour to strike as he slept in a cave on Snowdon seemed to have come true at last.

Although the high honour in which Welshmen were held during the Tudor Age is a commonplace of history and is clearly reflected in the plays of Shakespeare, it was not Henry Tudor but his mighty son, Henry VIII, who directed his attention to the affairs of the Principality.

He framed the Act of Union, and under his strong hand the Marcher Lords of the South were dispossessed and their wide territories shorn off into 'shires'. It was a good time for Welshmen of blood and money. They were sure of a welcome in London; but the days that followed under the Welsh House of Tudor were black times for the common people of Wales.

The romantic triumph of the Tudors has been finely summed up by Professor G. M. Trevelyan in his *History of England*:

'The racial enthusiasm of the Welsh for a descendant of their ancient British princes—marching, as Henry was careful to march, under the red-dragon standard of Cadwallader—broke out into prophesy and song, and enabled him to raise in little more than a week a small army of zealous supporters as he traversed that ever-warlike land. They, with the help of a few French and English adventurers, won Bosworth Field against a King for whom the mass of his English subjects were ashamed to fight. Here, indeed, was one of fortune's freaks: on a bare Leicestershire upland, a few thousand men in close conflict foot to foot, while a few thousand more stood aside to watch the issue, sufficed to set upon the throne of England the greatest of all her royal lines, that should guide her through a century of change, down new and larger streams of destiny, undreamt of by any man who plied bow and bill that day in the old-world quarrel of York and Lancaster.'

§ 8

In a few miles I came to the ancient town of Carmarthen. The streets were packed with country people who had come in to market. I was back in Wales again!

Carmarthen is full of character. There are narrow little old streets and wide modern ones, and what is left of the castle, now a county gaol, stands on a ridge and gazes down on the slow, narrow Towy. Perhaps because it was market day I thought that Carmarthen was the most vivacious market town I had seen in Wales. I heard more laughter and saw more smiles in the streets of Carmarthen than I had seen in any town in the Principality. There is no finer sight, for my eyes at least, than a market town full of prosperous-looking farmers, their wives, their sturdy sons and their clear-eyed daughters. The green Vale of Towy was smiling in the streets of Carmarthen, and, as I saw it, it occurred to me how different is the expression of people who live in fertile valleys from that of men and women who live in the hills. Something of the coldness and the bleakness and the silence of Snowdon comes into Caernarvon on a market day, but Carmarthen has the expression of a fat harvest-field on a sunny afternoon. I went to the old church of St. Peter to stand beside the stiff effigy of Sir Rhys ap Thomas and his lady ; that great chieftain of South Wales who helped to place Henry VII on the throne. . . .

I was standing on the bridge above the Towy when I saw a gigantic beetle walking on his hind legs, or it might have been a huge, performing turtle. Had Julius Caesar been with me he would have recognized it at once as the 'coracle' of the Ancient Britons. There is surely no more interesting survival of the kind in the kingdom than the primitive coracles which still navigate the Dee at Llangollen and the Towy at Carmarthen. In the remote parts of Connemara in Ireland I have seen the canoes called *curraghs* which are made of skins or canvas stretched over a wooden frame, but these are not so true to type as the Welsh coracle, which is merely an almost round basket that floats lightly on the water.

The fisherman was carrying the coracle on his back. These men tramp to and from the river during the salmon-fishing season, which lasts from April to August, with their historic craft attached to them by a strap that runs from the seat of the coracle across their chests. They look most amusing when they are moving away from you—just a huge, clumsy-looking shell and two grotesque legs.

I went down from the bridge and talked to the man. He told me that there are perhaps a dozen coracle fishermen on the Towy. It is an hereditary occupation, son succeeding father ; and no interlopers are admitted. The fishers pay a tax of £3 4*s*. a year for their licences and are permitted to net salmon during the season. Two coracles paddle along with a net, about ten feet wide, stretched between them. These nets must be so constructed that all fish under a pound in weight pass through them.

'Will you let me sit in your coracle ?' I asked the man.

He smiled and, turning back to the river, obligingly launched his clumsy basket on the calm water. It lay there like an eggshell. After a moment's hesitation I stepped in gingerly. I have rarely felt so unsafe. The fisherman prevented the craft from turning turtle and stepped in after me. He took the single paddle with which these boats are propelled and we moved out into the river. As I sat there with my feet timidly placed on the exposed wicker-work skeleton of the coracle, I could actually feel the water beneath me! It was unpleasant. My friend worked his paddle with one hand. He held the end of it under his arm-pit and moved the blade with a curious movement in the water. Steering a coracle is a work of art; sitting in one is also a work of art and faith. It is exactly as though one were venturing out in a canvas camp bath!

The man told me that many of the Towy coracle fishermen make their own coracles.

'What is the hammer for?' I asked, noticing a wooden mallet strapped to the seat.

'To kill the salmon,' he said.

I was not sorry when my Ancient Briton steered his walnut shell to the river-bank.

CHAPTER ELEVEN

IN WHICH I ENTER BLACK WALES AT LLANELLY, WATCH MEN TAP A FURNACE OF LIQUID STEEL, AND AT SWANSEA SEE THE SMELTING OF COPPER AND SPELTER, ENDING WITH A DONKEY RACE BETWEEN THE COCKLE-WOMEN OF GOWER

§ 1

I HAD been travelling for some miles through the soft Carmarthenshire country when, topping a hill, I saw lying before me a black town with smoke over it and chimneys rising above long streets of grim, slate-roofed houses.

Wales is so beautiful and so unspoilt that one's first industrial town is rather a shock. This town looked like a crazy intrusion. It stood up, rather horrible and gaunt, but all round it was open country. I passed groups of men in blue suits with cloth caps on their heads and neck-cloths round their throats. The mark of the town was on them. The stamp of the machine was on them. I stopped one group and, in order to hear their accent, asked :

'Is that Llanelly ?'

'Yess, that iss Thlan-ethly,' they replied.

We talked about weather, work and industrial depression ; and I was impressed, as I was to be impressed so often in South Wales, by the gentle manners and the air of good-breeding which distinguished these men. Certain industrial areas in England which have shut out all beauty from the lives of men have, not surprisingly, bred a sullen and unpleasant type of worker, but these Welshmen were quick, intelligent, well-spoken, humorous and kindly. So much I could tell in five minutes. And looking back on this, my first meeting with the South Wales worker, I realize that my first impression was accurate.

In Llanelly I met the kind of men you meet in any industrial town : commercial travellers, managers of tin-plate works, steel foundries, young metallurgical chemists, and so forth.

One man invited me to see the most spectacular and typical

sight in Llanelly, the tapping of a steel furnace. I promised to meet him at the foundry later that night.

§ 2

It is about 10 p.m. The town of Llanelly is going to bed, but the Steel Works which feed the Tin-plate Works are well on into the night shift. You can see the glow of its furnaces for miles. There are four furnaces in a row. When their doors are lifted for six inches you back away and hide your eyes from the white heat of the liquid steel.

The men who tend the furnaces look like devils as, grasping long shovels, they move about, pitch-black against the orange glow. A queer thing that might have flown in the darkness straight from hell glides and twists about like some immense bat. It is an electric furnace feeder. It runs on overhead rails, and is driven by a man who guides it among the assembled devils with the skill of a taxi-cab driver in Piccadilly.

At the end of the feeder is an object rather like one of the big hydraulic buffers from Euston Station. The feeder swings round to where a line of railway wagons has deposited a pile of scrap metal—bits of battleships, perambulators, iron bedsteads, and all manner of worn-out things. The buffer picks up an iron cage full of metal, the feeder swings round and glides to a furnace, the door opens, the heat comes leaping out, the battering ram slowly enters the inferno and gently tilts the metal into the seething horror of white-hot steel.

For one moment you see a slab of armoured plate, a bit of bedstead and a bicycle wheel trying hard to maintain their identities in the heat ; then slowly they lose colour, sink, and are lost in the bubbling steel. . . . So a furnace accepts a mouthful of food.

'We're going to tap No. 1 Furnace. . . . Come along and see it !'

At the end of the line No. 1 Furnace is ready and waiting. I am given a pair of blue glasses. The devils who creep cautiously up to within twelve yards of No. 1 Furnace also wear blue glasses. No man could face the open door and gaze with unprotected eyes on a bath of sixty-five tons of molten steel.

Through the glasses I see a moving, bubbling cauldron of white-hot soup. The steel is boiling. Sometimes great chunks like pink icebergs fling themselves out of it for a second and sink again. The thing is like a star in flux, like matter being forged in heat, like the beginning of a world. When the surface of the steel is even it ripples like a pond. Breaths of something hotter than heat seem to pass trembling and shuddering over it. Now and again horrid, obscene eyes open and shut on the steel pond, winking terribly, soundlessly.

A devil in goggles creeps to the furnace with a twelve-foot pole. He thrusts it into the steel. He moves it about. He withdraws it. A sample of the steel is taken and examined. Yes ; the furnace is ready to be tapped.

At the back of the furnace men are working in terrible heat to release the sixty-five tons of steel. It will run down an inclined way into a huge cauldron. Through the darkness of the immense steel works glowing red-hot ingots, weighing twenty-four hundredweight, go swinging through the air. Over to the right you can see a red-hot rail shooting backwards and forwards under the rollers.

'Stand back, there !'

Suddenly the darkness is lit by a brilliant light, showers of sparks arch themselves, and a hissing stream of liquid steel comes gushing from the furnace to fall into the cauldron. As it spills over the iron rim of the cauldron it looks like pinkish milk ; as it settles it is a beautiful incandescent tangerine colour. The power locked up in it is terrible. If it disobeyed the devils in goggles and burst its red-hot banks, we should be dead or maimed for life in two seconds. The heat of it as we stand twenty yards away is almost unbearable.

The molten steel rises slowly in its giant pot. A scum forms on it. Sparks skate over it. Bubbles of steel open and shut their eyes. The stream of red-hot metal ceases. The sparks give one last firework display and sixty-five tons of steel for salmon tins have been safely decanted. . . .

Through the darkness fly the cranes bearing red-hot obelisks. At any moment something molten may fly out of the night and miss you by yards. Now and then, just as you are about to put your foot on something, you recoil, feeling a breath of heat on your face.

That is a steel works at night.

A few yards away a young chemist is working. He stands in a little shed full of bottles. The door is open to the night. As he works, he can hear the thud of the rolling machines and the scream of the white-hot metal pouring from the fire.

Before the sixty-five tons of steel are cold—in fact, before they have changed from the pale pink of incandescence to the dark red of cooling metal—this young man has received a sample and has split it up chemically into its primitive constituents.

He sits at a pair of scales and weighs an ounce of hot steel filings! He takes this sample and tests it for carbon, sulphur, phosphorus, manganese, tin and nickel. He moves swiftly among his retorts and test-tubes. He boils up the steel with chemicals. He melts it. Then he makes a sum on a piece of paper and fills in a report stating that sixty-five tons from No. 1 Furnace contain this proportion of carbon and that proportion of nickel. . . .

'Could you condemn all those tons of steel?'

'If I found a serious fault.'

'Does that often happen?'

He smiled in a superior way.

'Not in these steel works. . . .'

The manager comes in, glances at the report. The young chemist turns down his bunsen burners and washes his test-tubes and his bottles.

Away at No. 2 Furnace the devils in blue goggles are stoking the gates of hell. In an hour or so No. 2 will be ready to loose a stream of white-hot hissing metal into the night. . . .

And that is the first chapter in the life of a salmon tin.

It is astonishing to see how much punishment steel endures before it can become a tin can. Long rails are chopped into lengths as a grocer cuts cheese. These lengths go again into the furnace. They are picked out red-hot. They are passed through rollers until they are as thin as cardboard and as large as a bath mat. They then pass to teams of six men, who seem to be playing some queer, unknown game.

The red-hot plates come from the furnace and are pressed out through rollers. A man seizes them with tongs, bends them double, stamps on them, and flings them to one of his mates. The plates go through the rollers and in a second are doubled again and stamped on and flung back. The operation is repeated. Now each plate is in eight thicknesses.

The team work so quickly, tossing the red-hot metal to one another, that the plate is never still. The men work like athletes.

If you asked me to show you a man who does a hard day's work I would point to a tin-plate millman.

The plates, tightly pressed together in their eight thicknesses, then come into the hands of girls. It is a tradition of long standing in Wales that women pull apart the pieces of metal. They stand in a line with their hands bound in rags and in coverings which once were gloves. In the palm of each hand is a piece of metal. The girls take the plates, and in one swift movement strip plate after plate from the pack.

'How many plates do you strip in a day ?'

'Eighty boxes,' said a girl.

Now, eighty boxes of steel plates, twenty-eight by twenty inches, contain 4,480 plates ! That, I think, is a day's work !

The sight of these girls swiftly tearing steel apart is as fascinating as the work of the millmen. They seldom make a mistake. If now and again a strip of steel refuses to leave the pack the fault is rarely that of the girl : it is due to some change in the metal during its fierce encounter with Fire and Force.

After a long walk through furnace rooms and through sheds which smell of sulphuric acid you actually see the machine which makes steel into tin-plate ! The word tin-plate is misleading. The tins in which you buy salmon, milk, apricots and such-like things are really thin steel covered with the minimum amount of tin. There is one pound of tin to fifty-six steel sheets.

The machine which spreads the tin on the steel is rather like a printing press. It is uncannily intelligent. The plates go in at one end dull and steel-like ; they come out at the other shining and tinned.

It is, like most complicated machines, unpleasant to watch because it is so terribly efficient. You long for it to make a mistake. But it never does ! It takes each steel strip almost tenderly. It passes it on through rollers until it encounters a shining bath of molten tin. It hands on the tinned plate to a tank of palm oil, which distributes the tin evenly over it, and then, with maternal care, it rubs the finished plate with a series of cotton rollers, and, behold, the long journey from steel furnace to canning factory is almost ended.

§ 3

The town of Swansea would never win a beauty competition, but its people are fortunate because they live within a stone's throw of a perfect paradise—the Gower Peninsula.

Swansea interested me. It is an ancient town that destroyed all evidence of its past during the gold rush which began with the Industrial Revolution. I was surprised to learn from a tablet on a house in Upper Goat Street that the incredible Beau Nash was born there. Swansea is one of the last places on earth which one would associate with England's first 'gentleman'.

I had not been in Swansea long before I was told about copper and anthracite.

'The first thing you must do,' said a Swansea man, 'is to visit a copper works. Our fortunes were built on the copper trade. It was our first adventure in industry. Centuries ago the Cornish copper ore was shipped to the coal of Swansea to be smelted; then later we had a fleet of wooden ships which ventured over the world in search of copper ore. They sometimes took two weeks to round Cape Horn with their cargoes. . . .

'We have to thank copper not only for our first industry but for developing our coal trade and our shipping. Now, although steel, tin-plate and other allied trades have overshadowed copper, that historic industry changed us from a small seaside place into one of the greatest industrial towns in Wales. . . .'

Obediently, I explored a grim and terrible valley. A century, or a century and a half ago, it was, like all South Wales, a pretty, peaceful spot. Then the Industrial Revolution changed it. The most hideous creation of man, the foundry, with its bleak chimney-stack, took possession of it. They now stand the length of it, frightful and ogreish. The smoke drifts before the wind. In works and factories Fire and Force are torturing the intractable, transforming it and sending it out into the world in a thousand shapes. That is the drama of Swansea. And to Fire and Force—those primitive begetters of metal—has been added Science. Behind the smith with his hammer is now a chemist in spectacles.

I discovered that all the copper works of Swansea have closed down, with the exception of the two immense and adjacent works now controlled by Imperial Chemical Industries Ltd., and known as I.C.I. Metals. These works are a kind of blackened township at Landore. They have a railway system of their own. They are so ancient that a pre-railway canal runs through them. They are so modern that every brew of copper is tested and analysed in laboratories.

I walked for half a mile or so before I saw any copper. It was in the raw state. It was ore from Chile. It was in large rough cakes and possessed that lovely turquoise patina which collectors of ancient bronzes prize so highly.

'To-day,' I was told, 'the ore is smelted at the mines and comes to us to be refined. It contains 95 per cent copper and 5 per cent of iron, sulphur and other impurities. Our first job is to remove these impurities and cast the refined copper into suitable shapes for working.'

I entered a furnace-room which might have existed in Ancient Egypt.

The method of working copper has not really changed since the metal was discovered. (The chemists of I.C.I. Metals, Ltd., may fling up their microscopes in horror ; but this is true !) The coppersmiths who were ladling out the refined copper have their prototypes in the bas-reliefs of Egypt.

The glow from the furnaces silhouetted them as they thrust long-handled ladles into the incandescent metal. The copper bubbled like boiling soup. Air had been blown into it. This had oxidized the impurities and caused them to form a scum that had been skimmed off.

Then young saplings had been thrust through the furnace doors under the surface of the molten metal. These saplings had generated hydrogen and carbon monoxide, which expelled impurities from the metal.

How primitive and yet how scientifically right ! As a chemist described the process in technical terms, I could not help thinking that thousands of years ago some man who had never heard of carbon monoxide discovered that a nice, juicy young tree had a wonderful effect on boiling copper !

The furnace-men ladled out the white-hot copper like cooks in a soup-kitchen. They poured it into moulds. They tipped up the moulds into a water-trough. There was a hiss of steam and a shower of sparks, and, behold, a great cake of copper, ready to be beaten into an engine plate, a geyser, a boiler, a brewery cauldron, or one of those large and unnecessary trays, complete with coffee-cups and finger-bowls, which tourists in the East buy from some old villain of a coppersmith.

The cast cakes of copper then go into the torture chamber. They are again heated. They are passed back and forth in rolling mills, becoming thinner every second. An overhead crane comes sliding the length of the shed. It thrusts a hand into a furnace. It picks out a sheet of red-hot copper as big as a carpet. It lifts it to the bed of a rolling machine. The rollers press it out.

The crane glides away with it to a machine that shears the metal as if it were cardboard. It sweeps on in mid-air to a great hydraulic hammer that beats and pounds it. Men attack it with pneumatic chisels, and at the end of its adventures some one writes on it in white chalk :

'L.M.S.'

'Locomotive fire-boxes !' says the chemist, pointing to a shed full of red-gold copper. 'We made the fire-boxes for the Royal Scot and the King George V.'

The stock rooms of I.C.I. Metals, Ltd., are remarkable. Tons of copper sheets, tons of copper discs, tons of burnished copper are waiting to be sent to every part of the world.

I saw copper that will in some months' time be beaten into shape in the bazaars of Calcutta, Cairo, Jerusalem. I saw copper consigned to Norway and Sweden. I saw copper in polished piles which some day will enter a thousand bathrooms as 'the geyser'.

As we were route-marching again through the works I encountered a distressing pile of worn-out relics. It was the sort of thing that is often shamefully hidden behind a hoarding. It was a strange thing to see in this town of bright metal. There were horribly crushed coffee-pots, copper pans with holes in them, dissipated-looking copper cups and other objects whose original shape and intention had been lost in decay. It had been raining and the junk-heap had—oxidized is, I think, the right term.

'Oh, that !' said my guide. 'Some blighter in the Near East couldn't pay his account so he sent us his scrap-heap !'

'What will you do with it ?'

'Boil it down. . . . We also have another bad debt—a fig farm somewhere in the East.'

Even more interesting than the refining, the rolling, or the annealing of copper, is the chemical laboratory. Every brew of copper is tested by experts. They analyse it. They examine it microscopically. They test its tensile strength. They do more: they compose copper as a woman might compose a soup. If you go to these chemists and tell them that you want copper for a particular purpose, they will make a few experiments and recommend a metal to you. The rough-and-ready rule-of-thumb method which inspired the old coppersmiths has gone for ever. The making of copper is a science.

'If you tell us to what use you intend to put copper,' said a metallurgist, 'we will give you the right thing. We are always experimenting. We are always examining difficulties. We are always applying modern science to the manufacture of copper. . . .'

On my way back from Landore I saw the tombstones of the industry: the great heaps of Chilean slag which wooden ships brought to Swansea in those old days when every other chimney was dedicated to copper.

§ 4

Mr. Bateman might draw a comic picture of the visitor who lit a cigarette in the Anglo-Persian Oil Refinery at Llandarcy, near Swansea, for I can imagine no greater lapse in conduct. I think the men who preside over millions of tons of petrol would die of horror, and it is certain that fire brigades would converge on the criminal from every point of the compass!

When they had examined me for patent lighters and matches, they allowed me to enter this town of petrol. It is one of the sights of South Wales and the largest oil refinery in Europe. It looks rather like an ambitious township in Canada. There are some 650 acres covered with buildings which are as spotless as the engine-room of a battleship.

From the top of the water tower you can look towards Swansea Docks, where the Anglo-Persian's fleet of oil tankers comes in with the crude oil from Persia. Not far from the docks is a tank farm. There are sixty tanks, which can store 160,000,000 gallons of oil. The water tower holds 250,000 gallons, and at the top is a room with a searchlight in it.

'If we had a fire,' said my guide, looking round vainly for a piece of wood to touch, 'we would play the light on it and control operations from this tower. . . .'

'If we had a fire!'

No wonder the men who guard millions of gallons of petrol touch wood at the thought of it!

Through this town of petrol runs a railway line worked by fireless locomotives. These strange little engines have no chimneys. They are worked by compressed steam. Every now and then they puff their way to a shed where men are waiting to charge them with sufficient energy to keep them going for four hours.

The first impression is that the oil refinery requires a minimum of human effort. It is a triumph in organization and machinery. Vast machines appear to be quietly working on their own. In great sheds and in huge steel and concrete rooms one man in spectacles gives a slight turn to a wheel or bends over a mathematical calculation.

'Over seventy miles of pipe lines,' I was told, 'bring the crude oil from the tank farm. It is travelling under our feet now on its way to a series of stills. The oil is heated, and gives off vapours, which are split up into different products such as aviation spirit, petrol, white spirit, and kerosene. . . .'

After I had been walking for about two hours it occurred to me that I had not seen, or smelt, one drop of petrol!

'Petrol?' said my guide. 'If you are very anxious I might try and show you some!'

We went up into a place where several stills were under the watchful eye of a man with a safety lamp. He unclamped one of them, thrust the safety lamp into the darkness, and I saw a river of petrol flowing steadily past.

The surprising thing about crude oil is the almost miraculous way in which it is split up into various products.

'We distil seven spirits, four lubricating oils and two fuel oils,' I was told, 'and scientific investigation is going on. Our chemists are always experimenting.'

I was taken to a still where the oil is subjected to great heat; I was then taken to an ice house. The pipes were thick with frost. Here, in an atmosphere which is that of an Arctic winter, the chemists of Llandarcy draw wax from the oil. And the process of distillation goes on. The dewaxed oil, when redistilled, rewards the chemists with three types of lubricating oil!

And when they have done everything that science can do to crude oil the final residue is pitch!

Chemists bend over their little flames in one of the most up-to-date laboratories of the kind in the country.

Over a thousand routine tests of oil are made every day in order to ensure uniformity of product. These tests cover every stage of its progress through the refinery. You see samples of crude oil—a thick, brownish fluid—and you are also shown the surprising variety of distillates which modern science derives from it.

'We do not yet know all there is to be known about oil,' said a chemist. 'Our research work is tireless. . . .'

As you leave the town of petrol, rather awed by its silent efficiency, the commissionaire restores to you a box of matches. . . .

You may smoke.

§ 5

Metal-minded Swansea talks to you about more things you do not understand than any other town in Great Britain. Metallurgists are essentially technical. They love to talk in algebraic formulae, and the only thing to do is to look intelligent and to nod occasionally.

Spelter is one of the mysteries. I defy the average simple-minded man to understand one word when a Spelter man tries to describe this metal. In time it may dawn on the listener that Spelter is the expert's name for Zinc.

The biggest Spelter, or Zinc, works in Great Britain is to be found just outside Swansea at Llansamlet. It looks like a huge liner with more than its allowance of funnels.

Outside in deep pits they show you tons of what appears to be brown dust. This is Spelter Ore from Australia. But it is not yet Spelter!

I believe the right word for it is 'Concentrates'!

I would like to take a band of mediaeval alchemists through a Spelter works.

In ancient times magicians and men who searched for the Philosopher's Stone were deeply puzzled by Spelter. In 1597 they got as far as calling it 'a peculiar kind of tin'; which was, after all, not such a bad guess. The white powdery oxide into which it burns when it catches fire was in the old days known as 'philosopher's wool'.

But nothing that Spelter did to pull wool over the eyes of the Middle Ages could compare with the utter intellectual confusion caused by a great modern Spelter works. In the first place the huge work seems filled by an uncanny intelligence. You go through enormous sheds where machinery is quietly doing its job without any human supervision. Now and then some one more like a chemist than a mechanic will come in, look round and go out.

And the work goes on.

First of all you see Spelter Ore spread out like some regrettable pudding on a long travelling bed.

It is red hot. It is, in fact, a red-hot cake. The dust has been made into lumps!

'Now this Spelter . . . ?' I asked.

'It is not yet Spelter,' I was told sternly. 'It is now Sinter.'

'Well, what is Sinter?'

'It is desulphurized Spelter Ore. Here we draw off the sulphur. We make tons of concentrated sulphuric acid every day.'

I was taken to giant stills where the fumes of the sulphur are converted into an acid so strong that the faintest whiff of it would send you out gasping for air.

The ore then continues its complicated progress through the works.

'And now this Spelter . . .' I began.

'It is not yet Spelter,' they said. 'It is now Blende!'

'And what is Blende?'

'It is the desulphurized Spelter Ore mixed with a quantity of coal and salt. But you shall at last see Spelter. They will be tapping the furnaces. . . .'

The furnace-room at a Spelter works is one of the most spectacular sights in industry. I stood in a dark shed as long as an airship hangar. It was lit by thousands of delicately coloured flames.

The furnaces rose up in banks one above the other. From the white-hot glow of each one protruded two black objects like torches, flickering silently, some faintly blue, some almost mauve, some white, the flames licking the darkness in their thousands.

'No one has ever described this furnace,' I was told.

'It looks to me,' said a man with a sense of humour, 'as though members of the largest golf club in the world had put their bags in racks and had then set fire to them!'

Men with metal probes stand in the blazing heat of the furnaces, ready to tap the retorts four times a day.

It takes four tons of coal to produce one ton of Spelter.

The furnace-men approach the retorts that are ready to be tapped, break through the plugs at the end and out falls a thin stream of something that looks exactly like quicksilver.

It is Spelter at last!

The metal is at once poured into square moulds where it quickly sets into a bluish white cake of—zinc.

The process is a chemical experiment on a gigantic scale.

'What is Spelter used for? . . . It is the basis of all galvanizing processes. Sheets of iron are immersed in a bath of molten zinc so that a coating remains and protects it from the weather. Then there is zinc oxide for paint; zinc peroxide; zinc chloride; zinc sulphide; and zinc sulphate, and so on. . . .'

After a walk round Llansamlet's model Spelter works, I think that the process of burning and distillation which produces one disagreeable liquid and one very attractive metal from thin brown dust would cause an alchemist to think that the modern truth is even stranger than the ancient fiction.

§ 6

Old women, who look as though they are waiting for Rembrandt to come and paint them, sit in the Saturday market in Swansea. They wear black hats, shawls and aprons. Their gnarled hands rest on baskets full of boiled cockles.

If you wish to eat cockles the women dip into the soggy mass a little saucer that might have been lost from a doll's tea set and hand you something which may give you pleasure or pain. They accompany the cockles with a smile and a bottle of vinegar with a hole in the cork. And the price of all this is one penny.

These priestesses of the great god Indigestion are cockle-women in the summer and mussel-women in the winter. They come from a heavenly protuberance on the Welsh coast known as the Gower Peninsula and their daily search for cockles is one of the most remarkable sights in Wales.

The flat sands stretch for miles with the sea wind over them, and small salt streams, which become fordable when the tide ebbs, cutting across them. On the opposite shores rise the jet-black smoke-stacks of Llanelly's steel and tin-plate works.

This is the strange setting for a scene that might be taking place in the dawn of history.

I saw them waiting for the low tide at Penclawdd. They stood in the shelter of a stone wall by the sea. There were, perhaps, two hundred of them, mostly women, young and old. Nearly every one rode a donkey. At first sight they looked like a Bedouin tribe. They wore their shawls over their heads, bound by a band tied round the temples. So they protect themselves from the wind that sometimes tears like a mad thing over Gower, just as the Arab protects himself from the sand of the desert.

Nearly every woman and girl wore light shoes with rubber soles and black worsted stockings with the feet cut away. They stood looking out to sea, waiting for that moment when the tide would be low enough for them to go four miles to the cockle beds.

The race across the sands is a wild and amusing affair. Young and old, perched like Arabs on the hind-quarters of their patient steeds, set off at a trit-trot, splashing through the fords. I went along behind a maiden called Miriam, who sang Welsh songs in the face of the wind. Miriam was young and salted as a Bismarck herring. Her eyes were soft as a doe's, and her forearms were those of a warrior.

Oh yes, indeed, it was a hard life, said Miriam, grubbing away in the sands for a few shillings a week, and in the winter, in mussel time, with the wind tearing in from sea so that you could not breathe and your fingers frozen stiff as rope, it was even harder.

'Who are these women?'

'Miners' wives and daughters mostly. . . .'

'Cockle gathering is older than mining,' said one incredibly old woman, kicking her donkey in line with us.

And I remembered the similar cockle-women of Stiffkey in Norfolk who have been gathering cockles—'Stewkey Blues'—for untold centuries. The men, like those of Penclawdd, never, or rarely, take a hand in the work. This sea harvesting is regarded as a woman's job.

'Why did the old women hide their faces in their shawls when they saw a camera?'

'Oh, it is bad luck to have your photograph taken,' said the old lady; and, then, as if to escape from such a disaster, she dug in her heels and splashed briskly over the sands.

Half an hour's cockle gathering would be quite enough for most people. The sea deposits this india-rubber fish four or five miles away.

The women dismount, hobble their donkeys with a length of rope, and begin to scrape for cockles. The shell-fish lie an inch or so beneath the sand. Each tide deposits a fresh supply of them. The gatherers stoop down, and, using a sharp, sickle-shaped piece of iron, rapidly cut up the sand. They then scoop the cockles towards them with a scraper and pour them into sieves. Sea water is poured on them and they are washed and sifted.

It is exhausting work. It is back-aching work. But the old and experienced cockle gatherers initiate the young girls into the art of it. They show them how to economize their energy, how to cut and scrape with the minimum of effort and strain.

I suppose had they been doing the same messy, wet kind of labour for the same reward in a factory, one would have felt sorry for them, but it was impossible to feel any pity under the sky, with the gulls wheeling and the clean wind blowing and Miriam singing in a loud voice about something that happened in Wales long ago.

The cockle-women retreat before the incoming tide with heavy baskets of shell-fish. They return in the same tribal disarray but at a much slower pace.

Some sell the cockles in the shell as they are gathered; others boil them and sell them; some boil them and sell them picked from the shell. . . .

I made the mistake of buying a large quantity and persuading the wife of an innkeeper to cook them for me. She fried them in butter with chopped leeks and served them with bacon. I suppose a puppy feels the same fascination as the cockle eater as he chews a delicately flavoured rubber bath mat. The cockle is a subtle food. If they cost a shilling each they would be famous in the restaurants of the world.

But there comes a time in the eating of cockles when you begin to wonder whether it is, after all, wise. You decide to stop. Then you take one or two of the delicious little beasts and eat them, enjoying the tang of the sea in them; and so you go on. . . .

In the middle of the night the devil tiptoes to your bedside and breathes heavily on you. You try to get away from him and fall heavily through space. You awaken. It was *not* wise. . . .

§ 7

The Gower Peninsula is one of the most exquisite parts of Wales. I went there on a sunny day and found myself in a land of golden gorse, blue butterflies, and winds from the sea. This lovely peninsula is almost as remote as the wildest part of Snowdon. It has the characteristics of an island. You look across at the shore of Carmarthen and think of it as the mainland; for Gower has its own customs, its own traditions, its own speech, its own precious individuality.

Mumbles—or 'the' Mumbles as they call it—is, of course, known to every one in Swansea, and fortunately it seems to satisfy the crowds who do not penetrate into Gower. Beyond Mumbles the roads twist in the most delightful way to small, happy-looking villages, to farms, to woodland and to golden commons aflame with gorse; and always they lead to cliffs and the sea.

Two civilizations are represented by the cockle-women of Penclawdd and the tin-plate workers of Llanelly, who look at each other over two or three miles of the Llanrhidian Sands. Two distinct peoples live in Gower, as in Pembrokeshire—the English, or apparently English, and the unmistakably Welsh. The west of Gower is, like Pembrokeshire, full of English place-names: Fernhill, Knelston, Oldwalls, Reynoldstone, Cheriton, Overton, Moor Corner, Pilton Green.

'If you asked a native of Port Eynon or Middleton or Reynoldstone, for information about somebody in the eastern district, he would probably say, "I donna knaw; he lives up in the Welsheries," writes Mr. A. G. Bradley in *The Romance of Wales*. 'The vernacular of these half a dozen or so parishes of Englishmen, isolated for centuries, had for me singular interest, particularly as I knew Pembrokeshire, where the English race have no Welsh "lilt", even so much as have the West Shropshire and Herefordshire English. Here in the much smaller Gower I detected this much, though generally faint.

'Here are a few examples of Gower English I noted down during my stay, when I was fortunate in having as a frequent companion the Rector of Port Eynon himself, a native of the peninsula and a student of its lore. "To spule a great pan vule of whitepot for the sake of a doust of vlour." Now there is an unmistakable flavour of the opposite coast in the first line, but I couldn't detect any kinship to the Devonian sounds, with which I am very familiar. A Gower native does not ask you to take a seat, but to " put your weight down ", an idiom that might be taken amiss by a corpulent stranger ! He uses " clever ", too, as the old English used it, and as the Virginians still use it, for " pleasant, agreeable ". Adjectives are multiplied, as " old ancients ", " small little ". Damp is " doune ", greasy is " oakey ", gaiters are " kettlebags ", convalescence is " nepid ", humble is " cavey ". " Wimble " for a winnowing machine, is near the Devonian " wamby ", and " vitt " for handy likewise suggests the " vitt and vitty " of the opposite coast, while " I beant zorry " is any West Saxon, but miles away from Welsh. But with all this the region is too near the " Welsherie " to escape the slight Welsh " sing-song ". No doubt, however, the schoolmaster has been abroad even in Gower, attempting, at any rate, to eradicate all racy local words and idioms.'

On a little wooded cliff at Oxwich stands a church. It is so near the sea that in winter the spray must splash the old stones. I have never seen a more ghostly little church. I came to it after sunset and the tide was high in Oxwich Bay. The wind had dropped and the church stood in the shadow of the trees, surrounded by a desolate hilly little burial-ground whose tombstones leant upward from the long grass.

When I entered this haunted church I could hear the rhythm of the waves breaking below. It was a miniature church with a chancel barely three yards in length. To the right of the altar in a recess I came upon a stone man asleep in plate armour. . . .

In the dusk I came to Arthur's Stone at Llanrhidian. It is a huge cromlech about fourteen feet in height and was in the old days one of the most famous and venerated objects in South Wales. It has a queer lifelike appearance in the half light, so that you can almost believe the old story that in the night-time it moves down to the sea to drink.

If you asked me to name three of the most interesting and charming districts in Wales, I would choose Anglesey, the Lleyn Peninsula and Gower. I shall always think of Gower as a place where herds of wild-looking ponies stand among golden gorse, and where the sea whispers by day and night to little lonely bays.

CHAPTER TWELVE

I ADMIRE CARDIFF, TRAVEL THROUGH THE GLOOMY RHONDDA VALLEY, GO DOWN A MINE, TALK TO MINERS AND THEIR WIVES, HEAR A CHOIR AND, FOLLOWING THE ROAD NORTH INTO MONMOUTH, SAY GOOD-BYE TO WALES

§ 1

CARDIFF is a beautiful and dignified city. One feels on seeing it for the first time as one feels when meeting some congenial and charming person of whom one has heard nothing but slander. For Cardiff is considered by those outside Wales to be a city of smoke, chimneys, Chinese laundries, mean streets, docks and an occasional race riot.

One reason for this is that the outside world gains its impressions of Cardiff from the newspapers, because writers about Wales, almost without exception, fight shy of Cardiff and Glamorganshire as if they were plague spots, or they slur over them in an apologetic way. That is wrong. Cardiff is the most important city in Wales, and no man can pretend to have seen Wales unless he visits Cardiff and the county whose minerals have drawn into it over one million two hundred thousand human beings, or about half the total population of the Principality. Visitors from English industrial centres who go to North Wales in the summer in order to forget their own chimneys cannot, perhaps, be expected to feel any interest in Glamorganshire, but the real traveller in Wales must explore the coal valleys which stretch northward like the fingers of a hand, of which Cardiff is the palm.

Cardiff is surprising because it is the only beautiful city that has grown out of the Industrial Revolution. This is because it grew up round Cardiff Castle, which is still its centre, and because the purchase of the adjoining Cathays Park from Lord Bute gave the Corporation the opportunity of grouping its civic buildings together in the very heart of the city. Aberdeen is painfully trying to do what Cardiff was enabled to do in a moment. Liverpool and Birmingham are engaged in the same protracted process, buying up old property in an attempt to elbow a way to a dignified civic centre. Cardiff grew up as rapidly as any other industrial city of the last hundred and fifty years, but the presence of this untouched park in the centre of her streets was her salvation. All town-planning schemes of the last half century have meant pulling down; Cardiff had merely to buy Cathays Park and build up.

No wonder the people of Cardiff are proud of Cathays Park. It contains the finest group of public buildings in Great Britain. They give to Cardiff a coherence and a definite centre such as no other great provincial city possesses. London is pulled together in much the same way by Whitehall in the west and the Bank to the east. And the first thing that happens to you when you enter Cardiff is a visit to Cathays Park. The Cardiff man who insists on taking you there looks proudly at the white buildings which stand back in a leisurely way behind grass and trees, and he points to a large and still un-built-on site.

'That,' he says, 'is reserved for the Welsh House of Commons.'

And it looks like it. Cathays Park with the Red Dragon over the City Hall has the appearance of a capital.

§ 2

Cardiff is an ancient Roman fortress which has grown into one of the greatest commercial cities of our time. The tram-cars run past a high wall. Behind the wall is a green park beside the River Taff, and in the grounds of this park is Cardiff Castle, still inhabited by the Marquis of Bute.

It is a strange meeting of ancient and modern. People on top of the Cardiff tram-cars can look over this wall to lawns where peacocks walk, to a mound with its tall keep, to encircling ramparts which look like Roman walls. So a city that has grown up out of an age of steam and machinery preserves in its centre a vivid memory of an age of swords.

When Robert Fitz-Hamon, one of the Norman adventurers who was permitted to seize Welsh property, came to Cardiff in the year 1090, he saw the ruins of a Roman castrum. This was all that remained of Caer-Dŷf, the stronghold on the Taff. It was in Roman times an outpost station of the legionary base at Caerleon. When the Norman Fitz-Hamon saw it the walls were standing in a condition which made it possible to restore them. The gateways through which the Second Augustan legion marched out to police the district were still visible. The Norman dug a great moat, filled it with water from the Taff, and on the cone-shaped mound of excavated earth he built the first Cardiff Castle. To talk of Cardiff Castle is wrong : one ought to speak of it in the plural. Its wall protects a wonderful object-lesson in British history. You have the Roman camp. It was in its later days surrounded by a stone wall ten feet in thickness and thirty feet in height. You can in certain places see the red tiles and the apparently immortal cement which the Romans knew how to make. When the camp was in ruins, there came the Norman Keep. That building played its part in the stern story of Wales under the Marcher Lords. When its time had come, it fell, like the Roman camp, into decay, and the Cardiff Castle in which Lord Bute lives to-day, was built in a different part of the enclosure.

One of the most interesting features of the castle is a modern reconstruction of a Roman gateway. It is, I think, the only one of its kind in the country. It is the north gate of the Roman camp, and it has been beautifully rebuilt, complete with its sentry walk where in the dim past the eagles of Rome kept watch and ward over South Wales.

No industrial city in Great Britain lives on such intimate terms with its ancient castle. Manchester, Birmingham and Liverpool have ages ago lost touch with their hereditary landowners, but men in livery can be seen at the gates of Cardiff Castle, the representatives of the custodians who have been on duty since Norman times !

One feature of Cardiff which must impress every stranger is the University. There is no other great city whose educational enthusiasm is so obvious, except, perhaps, Edinburgh. You cannot dine out without meeting a professor ; you cannot walk anywhere without meeting the youth of Wales. And this, I think, is partly responsible for the air of vitality about Cardiff. There are moments of the day when it seems a city inhabited by young men.

A splendid building in Cathays Park is that of the National

Museum of Wales. It was founded 'to teach the world about Wales, and the Welsh people about their own fatherland'. It is a perfectly designed, and arranged, museum and art gallery.

The collection that fascinated me is the 'Bygones' Gallery. Here are assembled examples of Welsh handicrafts made before the era of mass production. There are sturdy Welsh 'dressers'; Welsh country furniture, arm-chairs, basket-work, pottery, spinning-wheels, farm implements, pack-saddles, and a hundred and one objects from a prettier and a more leisurely age.

§ 3

There is another Cardiff.

You reach it over a long, dreary and rather sinister road. The names above the shop fronts are queer and alien. Chinamen stand in doorways dreaming the apparently tragic dream of China. Lascars pad along in flimsy blue garments. Huge negroes lean against probably innocent walls. At the end of this road is a fine exciting atmosphere of ships. Here are the great docks of Cardiff. Grouped round them, in a way typical of a city with a tidy mind, are the exchanges of the commercial offices. This is the Cardiff of coal.

A hundred and fifty years ago ponies and donkeys in single file came over terrible roads to Cardiff, and each beast was laden with coal. Over the same mountain-tracks lumbered four-horse wagons piled with iron. The coal had been shovelled from surface measures and the iron had been smelted on the spot.

The labour of transporting these heavy materials was even greater than that of winning them from the earth. Then in 1798 the narrow canal between Merthyr and Cardiff was opened. Coal barges replaced the weary pack ponies. In 1841 the Taff Vale railway revolutionized coal transport, and the first coal trucks ran down to Cardiff. That was the beginning of modern Cardiff. It was the natural port of shipment for the miners of the Glamorganshire valleys.

Cardiff has to-day the largest and most modern coal transport system in the world. Her docks are a model of speed and efficiency. Coal trains converge on Cardiff from every pit that is working in South Wales. The trucks stand in their thousands in the sidings, the ships come in, are loaded and away in the space of a few hours. And these miles of quays, these high warehouses, this maze of railway lines have grown up since 1839, when the second Marquis of Bute built a dock to cope with the growing foreign trade. His dock, which is still used by the smaller ships, was the first of many. So Cardiff became the clearing house for industrial Wales.

I stood on the roof of a high warehouse which rises above the docks, and with me was a man who can screw up his eyes at a ship on the sky-line and say ;

'French—new potatoes,' or 'German—iron bars.'

Cardiff has an enormous general trade. She imports timber for the Welsh pits, live cattle, metal bars, frozen meat, flour, tin plates, oranges and sugar for the refineries at Kidderminster.

Coal is, after all, the pride of Cardiff Docks. My guide became lyrical when he described the reconstruction of the coal hoists. The old hoists lifted ten-ton wagons and emptied the coal into the bunkers of ships ; the new hoists lift a twenty-ton wagon.

'The saving in time is enormous,' he said. 'In order to encourage collieries to use the larger wagons we have made reductions in carriage charges and also in charges for weighing and tipping. There are now over 1,000 of the new twenty-ton wagons in use. . . . Come and see how quickly we can ship coal. . . .'

I was taken to one of the latest wagon tips. A line of twenty-ton wagons stood in a siding facing the dock. One after the other they ran on the platform of the tip, which is really a gigantic lift. As soon as the wagon was in position the platform rose swiftly within its steel framework, lifting the wagon perhaps sixty feet above the dockside. The platform then gently tilted. There was a noise like thunder. A great cloud of coal dust ! Twenty tons of coal had been shipped in the space of a few seconds !

'Can I go up with a wagon ?'

'Yes ; but get on the right side of the wind, or you'll come down pitch-black.'

It was a queer sensation to rise smoothly with the huge wagon. It was lifted as if it were a cardboard box. The tipper expertly knocked the pin out of the front gate of the wagon in the few seconds allowed him ; and then—crash !

For a minute ship, dock, coal-tip were obliterated in a

shower of black! The coal was still rumbling down the chute when the lift descending with the empty wagon and another twenty tons of coal took its place.

Below in the hatches of the ship work the trimmers. I think I would rather be a coal miner than a coal trimmer. Their job must be one coughing horror of dust and darkness as the tons of coal crash down on them hour after hour.

'We pride ourselves that we can ship coal quicker than any port in the world. For instance, the P.L.M. 27 arrived on the morning tide, began loading at 12.15 p.m. and finished at 4.30 a.m. on the following day. In those sixteen and a half hours 8,761 tons of coal were shipped, which gives an average shipment of 531 tons an hour. That's Cardiff for you. . . .'

When the thunder of descending coal is loudest, and when the coal dust is most dense, Cardiff is doing well. And I take my hat off to the coal trimmers and the men who tip the tons.

§ 4

The National War Memorial of Wales stands in Cathays Park.

There is, I believe, no need to apologize for looking up the record of Wales in the War, because I am certain that few people could tell you off-hand how many Welshmen served and how many fell. In spite of the large numbers of men engaged on war work in South Wales, the percentage of enlistments in England, Scotland and Wales was practically even. The following figures are supplied to me by the War Office:

	Estimated Male Population on Aug. 4, 1914	Enlistments	Percentage
England	16,681,181	4,006,158	24·02
Wales	1,268,284	272,924	21·52
Scotland	2,351,843	557,618	23·71
Ireland	2,184,193	134,202	6·14

The three regiments closely connected with Wales are the Royal Welch Fusiliers, the Welch Regiment and the South Wales Borderers. South Wales is the main recruiting ground for the Welch Regiment and North Wales for the Royal Welch Fusiliers. The idea of a special Guards regiment for Wales was carried out in 1915, when a number of men transferred from the Grenadier Guards formed the nucleus of the Welsh Guards. In the first Expeditionary Force—the 'Old Contemptibles'—were three battalions, the 1st South Wales Borderers, the 2nd Welch Regiment, and the 2nd Royal Welch Fusiliers.

In the National Museum you will find a great book in which are the names of all the Welshmen who fell in the service of their country.

§ 5

I set off from Cardiff one fine morning to explore the Rhondda Valley. In one of Cardiff's suburbs stands another of those diminutive 'cities' for which Wales is famous. While St. Asaph and St. David's are 'city' villages, Llandaff is a 'city' suburb. Its cathedral, like St. David's, goes so far back into the mists of antiquity that no certain date can be given as that of its foundation. I have called St. David's Cathedral probably the oldest cathedral in Great Britain, but I am not too sure that Llandaff may not be slightly older. The see was founded within half a century of the Roman evacuation of Britain. The present building contains some Norman work and has been well, but heavily, restored. It is the only cathedral that lacks transepts, and this produces a remarkable impression: as soon as you enter the whole church is visible. Behind the communion table is one of the finest late Norman arches I have ever seen. There is a certain Celtic richness of feeling about it. It is a provoking and disturbing arch because it suggests what an exquisite Romanesque building the first Norman cathedral must have been—something possibly like Cormac's Chapel on the hill of Cashel in Tipperary.

I had not travelled far on the road that runs north from Llandaff before I discovered the smallest spa in the kingdom. It is called, with charming simplicity, Taff's Well. Who Taff was I was unable to find out. Perhaps he was the original Taffy!

Spas, as I have so often written, interest and fascinate me. There is something comforting in the thought of being cured by water and not by Harley Street. Bath, Harrogate,

Llandrindod Wells—lying like a healing bath set in a garden—Buxton, with its exquisite blue water, and Droitwich, the potential Lido of Spadom, all minister to the aches of humanity in different ways, but with the same polite attention.

They all began with the discovery of a well or spring. Then came the first patient. Then the first cure. Then crowds of doctors! Then, no doubt, the publicity agent. If you wish to see a spa in the primitive, or healing-well, stage you must examine Taff's Well.

The village, which lies in lovely country at the foot of the Garth Mountain, has been badly hit by trade depression. Most of the surrounding mines have been closed. But the villagers put their heads together to see what could be done to brighten their prospects. An ambitious idea came to them.

Was not Taff's Well famous two hundred years ago as a healing spring? Did not the rheumaticky come from miles round to bathe in it? Did they not leave their crutches behind as a sign that they had been cured? Why not make Taff's Well into a spa?

About forty villagers put down some money. They cleaned out the old well. They built a modest covering over it, and now Taff's Well, no longer interested in solid minerals, is anxious to begin life again as a spa.

I went down to the Well House to examine what is said to be the only warm spring in South Wales. The water gushes up through the rock at the rate of from sixty to eighty gallons a minute. The temperature, which never varies, is sixty-seven degrees. The well is only a few yards from the Taff, so that the overflow runs on into the river. About ten persons could use the bath at the same time.

'No one knows how old the spring is, but there is a legend that the Romans used it as a cure for rheumatism,' said the caretaker. 'An analysis of the water shows that it is almost the same as that of Bath. Geologists have often wondered whether the fault in the earth, through which the hot springs of Bath are shot up impregnated with minerals, may not be the same as that which gives us Taff's Well. In Bath, of course, the waters are really hot: Taff's Well is only tepid. . . .'

The water, like that of Bath, is a pale pea-green colour, and its surface is broken by the rise of carbonic acid gas and nitrogen.

'In the old days,' I was told, 'the well was surrounded by crutches and sticks which patients left behind as a sign they were cured. When women used the well a bonnet was hung outside, and it was the custom to bathe naked.

'More recently, say about sixty years ago, when the few who knew of the well used to bathe in costumes, the local people were furious, and it is said even tore the costumes from their backs and ordered them to take Nature's cure in a state of nature! But we don't do that now!'

'Is there any record of cures?'

'Nothing systematic has ever been kept. The well was until now just known to local people. If anyone suffered badly from rheumatism he was told to try Taff's Well, and people used to come from all the valleys. One man in Ebbw Vale has given us a written testimony that when he came here he was so ill that he could not undress himself. After bathing for three days he could raise his arms and undo his collar, and after three weeks he went home quite well and did not suffer again. That was eighteen years ago. . . .'

'Do you believe in the future of Taff's Well?'

'Why not? We have much the same water as Bath. If we became known we could enlarge the bath. We could accommodate patients in the village at first, and afterwards —who knows?—we might even have a big hotel. . . .'

So every day the visionaries of Taff's Well go down to the riverside and gaze at the smallest spa in the world—and the cheapest—dreaming of hotels and crutches, Bath chairs and gouty colonels.

§ 6

Two hundred years ago the Rhondda Valley must have been as perfect in its beauty, and as remote, as anything in North Wales. The hills lie piled up grandly, cut across by valleys which once were glens with clear streams singing through them. Now black towns have camped out on the valleys and on the hills. It is as though Sheffield had climbed up into the Scottish Highlands. Tram-cars run the length of the valley. Railways link town to town. You see the long lines of coal-trucks, like toy trains, silhouetted against the sky as they run over a mountain-top to Cardiff Docks. There are still little isolated pockets of beauty. Every person who works in the mining towns of Glamorganshire must know some place within an hour's walk of a pit-head from which it is not possible to see a chimney.

At Pontypridd I was interested in a large factory, which looks as if it still existed in the opening phase of the Industrial Revolution. The reason it looks like this is simply because the method of forging anchor chains, iron cables, buoy bars, and mooring pendants has not altered since the eighteenth century.

Any one who has seen a battleship drop anchor must be interested in the enormous chains which slowly let the inadequate-looking irons into the sea. I have stood on the forecastle of ships like the *Rodney* during this process ; but I did not know that in South Wales I would see the forges in which these mighty chains were made.

Messrs. Brown, Lenox and Co. claim to be the oldest ship chain makers in the country. Over a century ago, when the Navy really ' sailed ', a lieutenant named Lenox had the then revolutionary idea of abolishing the old-fashioned rope cables and substituting chains of metal. He was laughed at, of course. But he had the courage of his convictions : he decided to make chains ! In those days the coal industry of South Wales was not developed. There was no Rhondda Valley. No Ebbw Vale. But there were hundreds of surface workings where men picked the coal more or less easily from the earth. Round these primitive mines grew up the iron foundries.

So in this still beautiful part of Wales (and the South must have been as beautiful as the North) the iron cable came before the iron ship.

' We made the cables for the *Mauretania,*' I was told. ' For the *Rodney*, the *Nelson*, the *Queen Elizabeth* and the *Queen Mary* and many another warship.'

' What does a liner's cable cost ? '

' Oh ; about ten thousand pounds.'

I went into a foundry which might have been untouched for more than a century. Had the lieutenant who first made iron cable so long ago seen it, he would have noticed no change. The men worked at the forges in gangs of three. They were making cable as thick as your arm. The huge chain hung from an overhead pulley. Each new link was picked red-hot from the fire and carried in tongs to the forge. It was a half-moon shape. It was added to the chain and the opening in the half-moon was closed.

This was the most interesting process. The new link was re-heated until it became incandescent. Then, while one man held it in the tongs, the other two beat the red link until the metal met and merged. The half-moon was now a complete oval; and a new link had been added to a ship's cable.

'Three men at a forge can make thirteen links a day,' I was told. 'There are eighty-five links in a fifteen-fathom length, and a big ship takes twenty-two lengths. This represents one hundred and fifty-four days' work.'

The work of chain-making is almost an hereditary occupation. Chain-makers are born and not made. The names of Pearson, Lighfield and Brooks occur with regularity on the books from the beginning of the firm until to-day.

'Tons of our chains lie at the bottom of the sea with the *Lusitania*,' I was told. 'That was a tremendous chain.'

I was introduced to Mr. Pearson, who, with his father, made half the chains of the *Mauretania* in 1905. These were in their day one of the greatest triumphs of the chain-maker's art. The whole cable with its shackles weighed one hundred and thirty tons, and the length was one thousand nine hundred feet.

Three-link samples of this chain were subjected to a testing strain of three hundred and seventy tons. They stretched six inches, but—they did not break! These tortured links are now to be seen, strangely enough, in the Scottish National Museum at Edinburgh. Another sample of the *Mauretania's* chain is in the Imperial University at Tokio, Japan.

If you think that chain-making is just a simple process of beating red-hot metal, watch the uncanny speed and skill with which the workers manufacture the smaller cables. The half-moons of metal are picked from the forge one after the other, are added to the chain, beaten into shape, and so the chain grows, the new link added to it before the one before has cooled and blackened.

'It is a matter of skill and experience,' one worker said. 'You have to learn just when to hit the metal and just how hard to hit it. An unskilled worker might hit for hours and never do it. There are tricks in all trades. . . .'

Chain-making is in hot weather one of the most exhausting occupations possible to imagine. After every link has been added the gang take a breather. They wash their hands, necks and faces. They take a step outside the factory and breathe the air. Then they return and tackle the next link.

'It's hard work,' said a link-maker, 'but there's no machinery about it, and therefore you can take a pride in it. You do it all yourself. . . .'

I went on through the black country where the pit wheels spin against the sky, where rivers and streams are black, where black men come blinking from the depths of the earth into the light of day.

§ 7

The road mounts into a high place of moor and mist. Even on clear days a stray cloud swings out of nowhere, over the head of the mountain, so that you go on for miles into a fall of thin rain that hides the distant earth. As the mist clears you drop over the crest of the mountain into Heartbreak Valley.

You see a chain of mining towns founded a little over a century ago during the Klondyke rush to the minerals of South Wales. They do not look quite at home. They have never made peace with the landscape. They exist because of something below them, something invisible that is locked away in the earth.

Ages ago, when the primeval forests fell, when the great trees rocked and rotted and sank deeper into the earth, these terraces and villas, chimneys and chapels, institutes and railway sidings were already in the mind of Time. The dead trees so far beneath the earth were to blossom again; and their fruit is Heartbreak Valley.

The towns are much alike. They have not grown up in a leisurely manner like agricultural towns. They have been hastily assembled. Chimneys point their thin fingers at the sky. Rivers, now blackened, run beneath iron bridges. Hundreds of coal-trucks stand in railway sidings. Now and then a passenger train, made up of those dirty coaches which railway companies seem to reserve for mining valleys, goes off somewhere, leaving behind it a vague sense of adventure and escape.

Heartbreak Valley lies to the north of the coal-field. The mining valleys of Wales stretch north from Cardiff like the fingers of a hand. When bad times come the hand becomes numbed from the finger-tips downward. It is the most northerly towns which first feel the pinch.

So in Heartbreak Valley you will see pits whose chimneys no longer smoke and the men who want work, and can only stand about at street corners because they were born and bred to mine coal and cannot conceive of any other employment, will tell you stories of the water rising in the mines.

Heartbreak Valley is stranded by what is called the 'post-war depression'. Town after town can only sit idly watching the pits that once gave them bread.

Beneath these towns, if you take the trouble to find it, is the beauty of pride and endurance. The beauty of North Wales is the beauty of hill lying against hill, the coming of dawn and the fall of the mists at night. But in the South you have woman struggling to keep her home together and man hoping against hope that the tide will turn.

If the thousands of people who go gaily through the mountain passes of Snowdonia and haunt the ruins of dead castles would spend only a few days in the South talking to the people, trying to understand their situation, attempting to visualize the hard facts of their lives, the nation might in time bring a little more sympathy and understanding to the problems of the Welsh coal-field. The miner is misunderstood and misrepresented. At the moment he is down and out. If he is not living on the 'dole', he lives in fear of living on it. His work is shamefully paid. Hundreds of thousands of families are existing—you cannot call it living—on marvellously fractional variations of £2 to £3 10s. And this for a week's work in a coal mine!

The Welsh miner is a proud, sensitive—I use the word with deliberation and in its true sense—gentleman. I have met him in crowds; I have met him individually. I have seen him at work; I have sat at his fireside and talked to him for hours. I would like to think, if I had entered a pit at the age of fourteen and had grown to manhood in it, that I would retain the outlook and the intellectual curiosity of the average Welsh miner.

His intellectual interests are remarkable. At a street corner in Tonypandy I heard two young miners discussing Einstein's Theory of Relativity. I know this was exceptional, but it is significant; and it is true.

It will not seem out of the way to any one who knows South Wales. It will be believed by the manager of Smith's bookshop in Cardiff, who recently delivered Murray's *Oxford*

English Dictionary, which cost £45, to the Workmen's Institute at Ton-yr-efail. This £45 was saved by miners in twopences! And they followed it up by saving £39 for the *Encyclopædia Britannica*!

I have met miners whose culture and gift of self-expression seem to me nothing short of miraculous. These men know how to think. They have a mental curiosity which leads them into all kinds of queer paths. Music is one of their passions. It does not consist in putting a record on a gramophone. In one miner's home there are four framed objects on the wall, and three of them are L.R.A.M. certificates!

I was introduced to a miner who had taught himself to play music by studying the Welsh hymn book. This has the tonic sol-fa on one page and opposite is the ordinary notation. He translated them painfully and became proficient.

How can you withhold admiration from a community in which this is not an exceptional achievement? It is going on every day.

'Hugh So-and-So,' said an ex-miner, 'was so mad on music that he could hear it in the rhythm of the wheels of the journey.'

(The 'journey' is the line of loaded coal 'trams' which travels, often for miles, from the coal seam to the pit bottom). 'The wheels make different sounds on the gradients. Hugh heard music in this, and he used to keep a bit of chalk in his pocket and write melodies on the ventilating doors. They made wonderful blackboards.'

Imagine that! Think of a man hearing music in the darkness of a pit and writing melodies by the light of a safety lamp!

'Where is Hugh now?' I asked.

'Teaching music in America.'

I asked this man to explain to me the exceptional interests of the miner.

'Every miner has a hobby,' he said. 'Some are useful; some are not. Some miners take up hobbies as amateurs; some study to escape from the pit. I did. Even now I sometimes marvel that it is possible to earn money except with my hands. Why do we do so many things? It's difficult to say. It may be a reaction from physical strain. The miner works in a dark, strange world. He comes up into light. It is a new world. It is stimulating. He wants to do something. It may be, in good times, pigeon racing, fretwork, whippet racing, carpentry, music, choral singing or reading. Think what reading means to an active mind that is locked away in the dark for hours every day! Why, in mid-Rhondda there are 40,000 books a month in circulation from four libraries. . . .'

Meanwhile, Heartbreak Valley watches the pits. Its people stand at the side of the road as if waiting for something to happen. Men wander over the immense slag heaps, which years of prosperity have vomited from the earth, wondering if salvation lies in something called by-products. Perhaps at this moment, they think, some scientist in a laboratory is bending over his test-tubes and his flames with a discovery that will once more make it possible to live decently.

But Heartbreak Valley is off the map. No visitors go there from choice. Even the long tables where the commercial travellers used to eat are half empty in the hotels.

I hope some people will take my advice. These mining valleys do not want compassion or charity. But they are worth understanding; and they are very friendly, and their beauty is not that of sun or moon, but of the human heart.

§ 8

The small, grey houses on the hill-side seem to be sliding into the valley. Behind them rises a higher hill, almost a mountain, on the summit of which is a black slag heap like some obscene boil. An iron bridge crosses the valley and over it go coal wagons on their way to Cardiff Docks. Black paths, beaten hard as ebony by the feet of generations, lead steeply from the rows of grey houses to that presiding deity of all Glamorganshire vales—the colliery.

It stands behind its high wall, its tall stack smoking, sudden jets of steam whitening the air, and its shaft wheels spinning all day, silhouetted blackly against the sky.

Men tramp down from the terraces to the pit; hours later they return to the terraces black as Satan.

The colliery is a collection of red-brick buildings dominated by the two great wheels which bring up coal and drop cages full of men into the earth. There is something sinister about those wheels spinning all day and night. Bunyan would have connected them with hell. . . .'

'So you want to go down a pit for the first time,' said a mine official. 'Hand over matches and cigarettes, and put on these.'

He gave me a suit of dungarees. When I had put them on he handed me a safety lamp that emitted an inadequate greenish glow.

'Now come along!'

The scene at the pit shaft as we waited to go down was strange and rather terrifying. As the half mile of steel wire shot down into the depths, plunging the dirty iron cages into the mine, I tried to imagine what it would be like to fall into the bowels of the earth.

I looked out over the green fields and knew that for miles in every direction men were tunnelling half a mile down in the earth. The cages shot up with a bang. A little metal truck of coal was pushed out. An empty truck took its place. The big wheels spun round, fast and faster; the steel wire shot down so swiftly that its movement was scarcely visible to the eye.

A group of miners converged on the cages. Each one held a safety lamp. They were washed and pale-faced, the afternoon shift waiting to go on duty. Among them were many young lads with the manners of grown men. They were perhaps, fifteen or sixteen years of age. They stood around with their safety lamps in their belts, waiting.

These Welsh miners are among the mildest mannered and most polite men I have encountered in industry. The visitor to any factory is fair game for the local wits, but these men, who knew that I was about to spend a few hours in a coal mine, were gravely interested. They seemed pleased that I should want to see how they worked. When I asked anything unusually silly, they smiled and put me right. I remembered the ex-miner in Caenarvon who said:

'It's a rotten job. We never say good morning to the wife like ordinary people: it's always good-bye with a miner, for we never know, you see. . . .'

There was a certain philosophic courage about the group as it waited. Then the steel wire went mad. The cage was coming up! There was an expectant movement among the new shift as they grouped themselves round the shaft.

The cage came up loaded with pitch-black devils. They had sweated and had rubbed their hands over the sweat so that streaks of grime had dried on their faces. Their white eyeballs and blood-red lips were like those of Christy Minstrels. Their chests were black with coal dust. This was the shift that went down to get coal at 6.30 a.m. For a second the cage looked like a prison full of negroes; then the gates opened and out they ran. . . .

It was curious! In all works, when a new shift goes on and meets the old one coming out, there are jokes and laughter and—'Hallo Bill, old cock, how goes it?' or 'Cheerio, Alf'; and that sort of thing, But not in a coal mine!

The old shift stampeded into the daylight, tired, dirty, without a glance at the clean men going down. One look at these men and boys told one that a miner's day of seven and a half hours is real hard work. They were thinking only of a bath and food.

Stolidly the first instalment of the new shift piled into the cage. The cage lifted an inch or two and then shot down into the mine like a stone down a well. In a few minutes it returned.

'Now we'll go down,' I was told.

The cage was encrusted with wet coal dust. It was going to drop us as swiftly as possible for half a mile. I was told that in the middle of the drop we should touch a speed of fifty miles an hour. I grasped my safety lamp and waited for the worst!

The cage moved and began to fall! I could see the walls of the shaft rushing upward. A cold, damp wind blew a gale. Then it was dark! Our safety lamps were like glow-worms. The cage fell faster and faster. It roared. It rattled. It banged. It was like being in a drunken Underground train. I felt that my feet had left the bottom of the cage and that my ears were being pulled upwards. As we shot down I had to hold on to a damp iron bar to keep my balance.

Then—just as I was wondering what would happen if something snapped—this devil's lift eased up and behaved nicely; it slowed down a bit; it became comparatively steady, and in a few seconds it dropped us very gently at the bottom of the shaft. . . .

It was an uncanny world of silence. It was cold with the chill of a vault. The weight of half a mile of rock and earth above me seemed to press on my head. A long, dark tunnel—the main roadway—lay ahead, stretching into darkness and utter silence. A few green sparks, the safety lamps of the new shift, bobbed about. There were other tunnels leading off the main roadway. A narrow track concentrated at the bottom of the shaft.

Coal from the seams more than a mile away came to this place in 'journeys' of twenty-five 'trams' coupled together. Here it was loaded in the cages and shot up into the distant daylight.

We set off in the ghastly silence to walk a mile or so to the coal. The ground underneath was a soft, fluffy grey powder, made of stone dust crushed from shales and clift, and mixed with the coal dust to minimize the danger of fire and explosive gas.

As my eyes got used to the pit I lifted my lamp and saw that here and there steel girders had been twisted and bent like matchwood by the terrible pressure of the earth above. It was rather like a conception of a geographic hell. As we stumbled on I heard a loud voice cry down a tunnel:

'Hallo, Will.'

In a few seconds an incredibly small voice, distorted like that of a ventriloquist's dummy, answered from far off with a tiny:

'Hallo-o!'

It was hardly louder than a whisper.

'Now we have a long tramp before us,' said my guide. 'The coal face is over a mile away. Come along!'

We set off, walking between narrow rails on which the coal trucks, or 'trams', come down from the distant 'faces'.

The tunnel, or 'roadway', was perhaps ten feet high in places; at others it narrowed, so that you had to bend your head. The complete silence and the utter remoteness from the world was at first uncanny and startling. It was impossible not to think of this coal mine in terms of trenches at night.

'It's just like going up the line . . .' said some one, as we plodded on. 'You expect something loud to happen at any moment. If a Very light went off we'd all be flat on our stomachs in a second!'

A green glow-worm hung in a cross-trench. It lit up the black face of a man.

'A visitor, Bill!' said my guide.

I grasped a black hand.

'First time down, is it?' said Bill. 'How do you like it?'

'I don't.'

'Oh, you'll get used to it!' said Bill, showing a set of white teeth and two milk-white eyeballs.

Then we actually heard a noise.

It was far off, a mere echo. It was like no sound you hear above on the earth. It grew louder and became a rumble; then it grew into a metallic clanking. It was as if the miners in the front line had released some dragon that was tearing towards us in the dark.

Something stealthy was swishing past my foot. I held my lamp to it and saw a steel rope moving quickly. The noise increased.

'Heavenly music!' said my guide. 'It's coal!'

At this moment a loud, hollow voice ahead of us shouted:

'Let the journey go past! Let the journey go past!'

The 'journey', I was told, is a train of twenty-five linked 'trams', full of coal, on its way from the 'face' to the pit bottom. . . .

We pressed ourselves into a bay away from the truck line and waited. We could hear the 'journey' clanking onward, spinning over the points, rumbling on. Then came a rush of air and the shadowy form of the 'journey' going past—truck after truck going by in the dark. I could have touched them. I held my light high; and I saw them go on piled with coal. . . .

Half a mile above us, I remembered, grass was growing, and there were flowers and houses and sunlight. In this remote world there was nothing but 'journeys' going past in a darkness deeper than night.

'*All clear; the journey's gone!*' shouted a voice.

So we went on 'up the line. . . .'

We met a mine inspector gathering samples of the floor dust. He was making sure that it was 50 per cent coal dust and 50 per cent stone dust. He pointed significantly to a group of steel girders that had been twisted almost double by the pressure of the earth above. Most of the dangers in a mine are due to falls of rock and the collapse of roofing and walls.

As we carried on, sweating and black—for you are always wiping the sweat out of your eyes with a coal-black hand—we left a region ventilated by compressed air and came to a stretch of stuffy tunnelling. Here I found myself suddenly face to face with a horse! He was standing in the dark, harnessed to a 'tram'. A number of green glow-worms appeared. There was a noise of shovelling. The horse moved off with his 'tram'.

In a few minutes I saw an extraordinary sight—the 'face' of the coal seam.

You who know coal only as something in a homely fire-bucket can have no conception of its appearance deep down in the earth. I looked at a shining black wall of it, perhaps seven feet high. Above it was dangerous-looking rock propped up with poles and girders. A child would realize the peril of picking at this soft black stuff, with the hard rock above always in danger of falling and crushing you to death.

The miners, each assisted by a boy, examined the coal before they struck it. They knew exactly where to strike. They were black as negroes. Their shirts, wet with sweat, clung to ebony bodies. There seemed something gallant and desperate every time a man tapped a great ledge of coal, gently felt it move until it seemed to tear like cloth, then—'Stand clear!'—and down it fell in a black rush, lumps of it big enough to break your back! All along the front line of this mine men were pushing out, advancing into the coal seam together, keeping the face of it clean and straight, pushing outward at the same pace.

When I thought of seven and a half hours in this place every day I knew why the shift going off duty in a mine never jokes with the shift going down! Seven and a half hours half a mile from light, working in a narrow chamber with a roof above that is never too safe, and in an atmosphere of a front-line trench at zero hour!

I was introduced to many of the miners. One was a musician. We talked about music. He was fond of Handel! We talked about music in this incredible limbo! Another was mad about dogs. We talked of dogs! We smiled and laughed and shook hands. It was like finding hell inhabited by angels.

We blundered back over the long road to the shaft bottom.

I was glad to go back. No one has ever pretended that mining is a nice job, but no one quite realizes that the spirit in a coal mine is exactly like that of a regiment in the firing-line. We all loathe war, but we all know that the spirit that holds men together in danger and duty is fine and splendid.

On the way back from the 'front line' I asked to be shown the 'pit ponies'.

'There are no pit ponies in Wales,' I was told. 'They are colliery horses.'

I was taken to the mine stables near the pit bottom. There were six stalls well lit by electric light. A man was whitewashing them. The horses not on duty were being groomed. I noticed that above every stall was written the name of its occupant, as in racing stables. Each pit horse is christened before it goes down a mine. No colliery horse is under 14·2 hands high. They cost between £55 and £60 each. One colliery values its horses at over £7,000.

'"Warrior" has been underground for fifteen years,' said the farrier. 'Does he look unhappy? Does he look ill-fed?'

He did not.

'How many of these horses are blind?'

'I have never met a blind pit horse,' said the farrier. 'It is true that after a number of years a horse taken above has defective sight; but they are never totally blind.

'They get the best of food, good quarters, and work which is not so strenuous as that of a London dray horse. . . .'

'What about injuries?'

'After every shift the haulier is forced to report any injury no matter how trivial. The slightest scratch must be reported. The vet then visits the horse at once and treats him if necessary. Cruelty? We never meet it. But there are very strict regulations in every colliery to guard against it. If a haulier is cruel to his horse a red mark goes down against his name. This is against him even if his action might have been accidental. Three red marks and a man is instantly sacked. There is no argument. Out he goes!'

The live-stock in a coal mine is interesting. A fat black cat was sitting in these stables on a bale of hay. All mines have cats on the ration list. They keep down the mice which get into the fodder. Colliery books contain dozens of entries like this:

'Milk . . . . 1s. 6d.

The haulier has charge also of the stable cat and its milk.

'Some of these cats are funny,' said the farrier. 'They will go to the pit bottom and wait for the cage like a man. They walk in, go up to the surface, take a look round to see if it's raining and wait for the next cage down again! Sometimes the hauliers take them home for a week-end.'

We watched the hauliers bringing their horses to stables after the shift. The pit horse has a journey of perhaps 200 yards from the coal face to the junction. He draws 28 cwt. of coal in a 'tram' on rails. He works six or eight shifts a week, but he is never allowed to work two consecutive shifts. He never works on Saturday or Sunday.

People who think that a pit horse just pulls a 'tram' have never seen these animals at work. The horse, like the haulier, knows his job. Every haulier keeps to his own horse, and would very much resent any other man working him. And the reason is that in taking coal from the seam to the junction there are various little difficulties which can only be easily avoided by a sympathy between man and beast.

When, for instance, a 'tram' runs off the line or fouls the points, a man and horse who know each other's methods of work can rail it again in a few seconds and with a minimum expenditure of energy. If you or I tried to do this we should confuse the horse and fail to get the 'tram' back. But watch a haulier and his horse. He has a special word of command. The horse knows that he has to give one sharp pull while his man puts his back to the 'tram' and guides.

The pit horse is intelligent and understanding. He knows his man. His man naturally cares for him. Even if the miner were not notoriously fond of animals; even if he were an inhuman creature he would be complicating his work by neglecting his horse or failing to establish contact with him.

Coal haulage is not one man's job; it is man plus horse. You have only to see—as you will always see in a mine—the haulier with his arm round his horse's neck, talking to him and patting him, to know that the Welsh pit horse is not a mere beast of burden.

'And,' said the farrier, 'in the morning most hauliers

take something down for their horses. It may be only a lump of sugar; but there is generally something in their pockets—even in these hard times!'

I went 'down the line' with a new idea of the miner and with the knowledge that I can never again look at a bucket of coal without remembering him, black as pitch and wet with sweat, bracing his body against the coal wall half a mile from daylight. . . .

'Well, and what do you think of it?'

A set of white teeth and two white eyeballs gleamed at me.

'You are always in the firing-line. . . .'

'We get used to it. It's got to be done! I wish a few more people would come and see us work. Cheerio! . . .'

The cage moved and shot up towards the world. It was like a resurrection. I did not mind how it banged or rattled. I knew that above was sunlight and green grass! Water began to drip into the cage. The darkness of the shaft lightened. The cage leapt up and stopped.

I had to close my eyes. Daylight was blinding. It was as if my eyes had been turned inwards. But when I opened them I saw that it was raining. But how good it looked; how clean and marvellous!

And when I walked out of the cage a friend laughed at my black hands and my black face; and I knew again why the men coming up have no time for the men going down.

§ 9

Emlyn, the miner, and I were sitting on a wall outside the village. We were smoking and talking about marriage, women, music, coal and greyhounds. Then we discussed the 'dole'.

'It's bad,' said Emlyn, 'but what can you do? It's State charity; but when the citizens of a State are thrown out of work through no fault of their own you cannot let them starve. It's bad because it makes a certain kind of man lazy. It encourages him to expect something for nothing. It's a common thing to hear a man on the "dole", who has a chance of work, thinking of his wages not as £2 a week, but as a few shillings more than he would get for doing nothing! And when wages are so low, can you blame him? Aren't we all lazy at times?

'I've been on the "dole", and I hated it,' he said. 'I'm not the only one.'

'Pride,' I said. 'I've seen pride behind white curtains in a bare room.'

'Pride?' said Emlyn, taking his pipe out of his mouth and looking over the valley. 'You're right. There's good and bad in all walks of life, but the best type of Welsh miner is proud. I could tell you . . . goodness, I could tell you. . . .'

When a Welshman says this you know that he *will* tell you, so I kept quiet and waited.

'There's a lot of very good work going on in the valley,' said Emlyn, 'in the way of feeding school-children and giving them shoes and things, but only if the father is out of work. Some of the worst cases of hardship I've known have been in homes where the father was trying to keep six children on £2 5*s*. a week and was too proud to accept help from any one. . . .

'There was Bill So-and-So. We worked together in Number Two pit. When you're on a shift you fall out for twenty minutes and eat bread and butter, or bread and cheese, which the wife puts in your food tin. Well, Bill and I used to fall out together and get away from the coal face into the stall, or heading, you see. And we'd sit on each side of the road with our feet on the tram rails and our lamps on the floor. Then we'd open our food tins and eat our food. Now, you've been down a mine. You know that when two fellows are sitting with their lamps on the floor the light only reaches to their knees. I could see Bill's knees. That was all. . . .

'One day we were sitting like this talking when Bill didn't answer. Then I saw his light go over, and he fell in the middle of the tram rails. He'd fainted. So I lifted him and carried him to the pit bottom to send him home, but before I did this I gathered up his food tin. There wasn't a crumb in it! There hadn't been a crumb in it for days! He'd been sitting there in the dark pretending to eat, pretending to me—his pal—— Now that's pride, if you like! You may think it's silly, but it's pride, isn't it?'

Emlyn knocked out his pipe on the wall and looked at me for confirmation.

'Yes; but that's surely not the end of the story,' I said. 'A man getting money, no matter how little, doesn't starve himself like that unless . . .'

'Oh, doesn't he,' said Emlyn. 'When you're on the starvation line you must keep up appearances.'

'Yes, but there was something more behind it.'

'There was. Bill has five children. The week he fainted in the pit was the week they had to have new shoes. Now I'm the only one who knows that. His wife told me. But do you think I'd ever let him know I know? Not blinking likely.'

We got up and walked back over the still countrified road to the mining village.

'If you write about that,' said Emlyn, 'you'll wrap it all up and put in different names; and you'll have a lot of letters saying you made it up! There is a feeling that the miner is a fellow who starves his family to keep greyhounds. Well, you know enough about South Wales now to see that it doesn't happen here. Mind you, I could introduce you to bad fellows—we aren't all angels—but just because we work underground and come up looking like niggers some people think we're half savages.'

'If you had a wish, Emlyn, what would it be?'

'Let's see, now. I'd like five quid a week and a pit with the coal boiling out. I'd also like to stand for Parliament. Perhaps I will some day when the good times come round.'

§ 10

The miner's wife is one of the heroines of Great Britain. For at least ten years she has been pinching and scraping. Yet you never hear her complain. The outside world knows nothing of her or of her problems. She is obsessed by three thoughts: to pay the rent, to feed and clothe her family, and to have hot water and food ready when her man comes home.

She knows perfectly well that the man who delivers coal to the cellars of London or Manchester gets more money than her husband gets for mining it. But she does not lose her temper about this. She has so often heard her husband talk about 'world-wide economic causes' that she regards living on the struggle line as a kind of disease.

In moments of optimism she will hope that some day things will be better—just as a patient passes a crisis in pneumonia. Suppose the Navy, with a generous gesture, scrapped oil and went back to coal? That would perhaps mean that one piece of meat would not have to drag its way in various disguises through the week, and that the children would not look so shabby in Sunday school.

Without such bright hopes it would be almost impossible to carry on. They may be illusions frail as rainbows, but they are necessary to the spiritual life of South Wales. One must believe in something. . . .

'Come in,' said Mrs. Jones. 'I'm not too tidy, because I've been getting Mabel ready for the Sunday school outing at Barry. They're only young once and you must make them happy. I'm sure God never intended children to go short. . . .'

On the table is a muslin dress which she had been cutting down to fit Mabel. If you look carefully at the children of South Wales you will see that almost miraculous things have been done for them with the garments of their elder brothers and sisters.

No matter how little money is coming in, appearances must be kept up. The miner and his wife during hard times are exactly like the public school man who dressed for dinner every night in the jungle in order to retain his self-respect!

The living-room is bare, but the window-curtains are snow white. You would never guess from the outside of this cottage how long and grim has been the struggle going on inside it. There is another room downstairs and three rooms above.

The house was designed about fifty years ago by some unknown woman-hater. There is nothing in it to help a woman who is always boiling water. Everything has got to be lifted up on an old-fashioned kitchen grate. The rent is ten shillings a week. . . .

'When our six girls came,' says Mrs. Jones, 'Bob was angry. He wanted sons. "I want boys," he used to say, "who can go down the pit and make good money," for his father and grandfather were colliers, and I suppose it's in the blood. But—hear him now! Girls are better than boys for South Wales now! Did you see the boys standing at the street corner on "the dole"? That's where my boys would be if I'd had sons. . . . What we should do without the girls I don't know. My three eldest are all in service in London—a place called Putney—and they're good to us when the pit's not working.

'Bob hates going on "the dole"; but what can you do? It's two shifts one week, three the next, nothing the next, and then a good week's work—up and down like that—so that I never know when I'm going to have thirty shillings or two pounds. But then it's no use grumbling. Mrs. Williams down the terrace was taken with consumption last week. And she's got seven children, the youngest only two. I might be worse off. . . .'

A black man appears in the doorway. It is Bob home from the pit. The miner is the only man who always—*always*—in good times or bad, goes straight home. He enters his house, flings a small paper packet on the table without a word and goes into the back room. Mrs. Jones takes the paper packet, and says:

'Two pounds five.'

That is Bob's wage for hewing coal last week for forty-five hours.

He comes in, having washed his arms to the elbow. He is perhaps forty-seven years of age, good-looking in the monkish way of the Welsh miner. That may seem a strange thing to say. But it is a true one. I would guarantee to go into any Welsh mining village and in ten minutes pick thirty men whose faces suggest religion and poetry.

Bob sits down at the table. Mrs. Bob puts a soup-plate on a clean newspaper, and ladles out a sort of Irish stew. He eats hungrily, and between his mouthfuls gives us the essential news of his day. Nothing much. Hugh Evans won something on a race. Young Williams hurt his foot in the pit, and had to be carried up. Then he gropes in his pocket and produces a thin strip of paper on which his 'stoppages'—the deductions from his wages—are indicated, a penny here and twopence there.

He finds a cigarette from somewhere and smokes moodily. His wife clears the table, chatting brightly all the time about Mabel's school outing at Barry. The child shall wear her Sunday shoes so that she'll be as smart as the others. She shows him Mabel's cut-down dress. Bob nods his head and looks out through the open door towards the mountain and the slag scab on the summit. He looks rather like a Trappist monk.

The woman brings in a galvanized tin bath and places it in front of the fire. One of the mysteries of South Wales is this: how do women manage to keep clean homes when every day husbands, sons or lodgers come in at different times black with coal dust and demand a bath? Even two hours in a coal mine fill your head with grit and blackens you—no matter what you are wearing—all over your body.

Bob strips and takes his bath. His wife cleans his back. He changes his clothes. He wears a blue suit, a soft collar and tie. Then, moodily, he goes to his pit clothes, gropes again in his pocket, and produces reluctantly a printed slip. It is a fortnight's notice. The pit is closing down.

'Oh, Bob . . .'

''Um . . . I'll take a walk over the hill.'

He goes out, smelling the clean air.

Mabel comes in from school, a tangle-haired child of twelve like a young Joan of Arc. She is excited. Some one has given Megan Evans two whole shillings to spend at Barry! The mother's eye turns from the retreating back of her husband to the excited child.

'Now, Mabel,' she says, 'I didn't mean to tell you till Sunday.'

She goes to a blue vase on the mantelpiece:

'Betty has sent you a shilling all the way from London so you can spend something at Barry. I'll keep it for you.'

Bob, the miner, walks up into those hills which cheer and depress the Welsh. The Welsh mind is coloured by valleys and hills: it is either down or up. When he turns he can see the colliery far below him, the stack smoking, the wheel shaft spinning blackly in the hollow . . .

Eight hours or seven and a half? Hell! . . . If only a man who is anxious to work could get work *and a fair wage*! The fresh winds come down to Bob and he begins to sing under his breath. It makes him sadder!

If only there were four or five friends with him they might be able to harmonize themselves into a brief forgetfulness.

§ II

'If I'd been able to buy a piano,' said Mrs. Williams, 'perhaps Willie might have been a musician. But he works in the pit like his father. He'll be home any time now! I'll put some water in the kettle. . . .'

The door opened. In walked a funny little man with a black face. He was perhaps sixteen years of age, but he was no bigger than a lad of fourteen. It seemed impossible that he could have had any childhood.

A broad leather belt encircled his absurd middle. His baggy old clothes only accentuated the pitiful littleness of him. Any woman, I thought, would wish to put her arms round him and protect him—an act which would have caused him to swear like a trooper!

He was a boy, yet he was a man.

This was Willie. He slouched in, pretending to be ten years older than he was, flung a curt word to a younger brother, and sat down in a chair, unable to disguise the fatigue which filled his bones.

It was difficult to believe that this little chap had done a day's work in the pit. His puny arms and his small wrists were those of a child.

More fortunate boys of his age were playing cricket at school. . . .

'Done a good day's work?" I asked him.

He grunted. It was very funny; he was copying some grown man!

'How many trams did you fill?'

'Twenty-four,' he lied sharply.

Then he hitched his belt round, spread out his legs, took a tattered cigarette stump from some inner recess of his garments, lit it, blew out the smoke from his nostrils, and sat huddled in his chair, too tired to speak. But he would not admit it. Larger and stronger men were setting the pace of his life and this gallant little child was keeping time with them.

He went out of the room and returned to eat his food. He had washed his face and his arms to the elbows. What a transformation!

As he came in from the pit he looked like some whimsical member of a nigger minstrel troupe. It was impossible to say whether he was good-looking, intelligent, stupid, or just an ordinary lout. But now, as he slouched in to eat, I saw a sensitive little fellow, pale with the mushroom pallor of all miners, frail from years of half rations, undersized, and handicapped from birth, yet behind his eyes that Cockney sharpness which, in South Wales, sometimes develops into spirituality or fanaticism. When he put his hands on the knees of his grimy trousers I remembered his mother's words :

'If I'd been able to buy a piano. . . .'

His hands, grimed with coal dust in the creases of his joints, were the hands of a musician !

Possibly he never would have made a pianist, but his tragedy—and the tragedy of thousands of boys like him in the Welsh coal-field—is that no one can afford to give him the benefit of the doubt.

The boys of South Wales are a national problem. There is no future for them in the coal-field. Their fathers cannot live on the money that coal-mining offers to an expert worker.

What is going to happen to their sons ?

You see one generation standing about the street corners, born and bred to a tradition of idleness. Another generation like Willie, is either idle or learning the dangerously precarious work of the miner.

Life in a mining valley is dominated by the pit shaft. The pit sucks all the male energy into its black depths. It appeals to all that is adventurous in a boy : the darkness, the queer, dangerous life underground, the association with older men, the spice of peril—all the exciting things which boys in these places have heard since the cradle.

There is nothing to pay for apprenticeship, and once a boy graduates he can earn the same wages as a man who has been mining for thirty years. But no one can look at the young lives which a coal pit has claimed without wondering what they might have been.

So Willie finishes his Irish stew, wipes his bread round the plate, drinks a cup of gunpowder tea, and soon emerges, washed, in his best clothes. He puts on a soft collar and a tie. The neckcloth is not for him ! He is going down to the village to gossip with his pals about football and greyhounds.

The earnest reformer will say : 'But the lad should be improving his mind. He should attend night classes ! '

I can only say that after seven and a half hours' work in a

pit at the age of sixteen few boys—especially underfed lads—have the energy or the determination to improve anything but their lungs.

You can only look at these little miners and hope that when they grow up, marry, and create the insanely large families which drag down their kind, there will be more money in the industry for them. . . .

'Ah,' say the mothers, as they watch the imitation men go down to the village, 'if only I'd been able to buy a piano! . . .'

Then they turn to snatch a child out of the fender.

'No boy of mine would go down the pit,' they explain, 'if it wasn't necessary; but, you see, when the last two children came we needed the money. . . .'

So the small wage-earners pile into the cage each day and do their bit if they are lucky enough to have a job to do. It is, of course, all wrong.

§ 12

I was passing a village hall in a mining valley on a Sunday. I heard a male voice choir trying to lift the roof from the place. The sound was so good that I opened the door and went in. Of course I could stay and listen, they said, with that instant politeness which greets the stranger in every mining town and village in South Wales.

About thirty young men in blue serge suits were grouped round an ancient but heroic piano. The pianist knew all the dead notes! The conductor stood facing his choir, waving a baton and stamping his feet with the abandon of all Welsh conductors. And the choir sang like angels in blue serge. . . .

They were miners in their Sunday clothes. Some of them had done a week's work in a pit; others were unemployed. Every one had put on a dark suit, a collar and, because it was Sunday, a dark and sombre tie.

Now, it is not often that the casual visitor to South Wales sees thirty miners together with clean faces. He sees thousands tramping home like niggers. The faces of these men would have astonished those who think of the miner as a brutalized and disaffected person. They were fine, sensitive faces; keen, intelligent, and distinguished above all, I thought, for that look of religious fanaticism which you meet in Italian art and—in South Wales!

I would have said, had I been ignorant of their calling, that they were theological students.

All over South Wales are male voice choirs recruited from the pits. English people, if they ever consider the question, think that this passion for singing has something to do with the Eisteddfod or that it has a purely financial aspect. This is not so. Most of these choirs cannot afford to sing at the Eisteddfod, and few of them make much money. They sing for the joy of singing.

The old saying that when you get two Englishmen together you get a club, two Scotsmen a Caledonian Society, and two Irishmen a riot, might be extended to Wales. When you get two Welshmen together you get a choral society.

But why ?

Because the Welsh express themselves more readily in song than in any other way. It is a national gift. They use their voices as a ladder to heaven. They are transfigured in song.

'The history of this choir is interesting,' I was told during a pause in the singing.

'When the strike was on years ago—you remember the Tonypandy riots—a number of miners went over the hill to keep out of trouble. And, of course, they began to sing! When we feel sad in Wales we sing.

'Well, they liked their singing so much that they decided to become a choir ! The members have changed with the years but the choir originated over on the hill-side there while the brickbats and the bottles were flying about below in the valley. . . .

'And now,' asked the conductor, 'would you like us to sing something in Welsh ? '

'I would ! '

The choir grouped itself. This is characteristic of Welsh choirs. The members like to face one another, and seem to be singing to one another. And they sang something ineffably sad in Welsh. At least three members looked ready for martyrdom. When the song was over the expression changed, and the singers came to earth with a smile.

'Something in English ? Right ! '

They sang a good old part-song, but there was nothing English in their rendering of it. There was no roystering village green in it, with jolly drinkers in an inn. They sang it religiously ! And I realized that singing in Wales is a spiritual interlude, something like prayer.

'Shall we sing in Italian ?'

And these miners, met so casually on a Sunday in a village hall, gathered themselves together under the conductor's baton and launched into an extremely difficult choral number in Italian !

(This is, I suppose, as unlike an English conception of a miners' Sunday afternoon as anything I could describe !)

The Welsh are a quick, temperamental and emotional race. This miners' choir was as interesting and in a way as typical of Wales as a cricket match on an English meadow is of England. These men were expressing the Welshness in them. I sensed again that foreignness which I felt at Caernarvon, where most people talk Welsh.

'If I get depressed I sing to myself,' said one man to me. 'But that only makes me worse ! If I meet three or four other men and can harmonize my voice with theirs I soon find that my mood changes. I forget my worries—for a time !'

So I left the village hall with the strange knowledge that in many a Welsh miner's throat is something that can lift him from the darkness of a mine into regions that are not far from Paradise. It is good to be able to congratulate the miner on some compensation !

. . . .

One evening I stood on a hill in Monmouthshire and looked back towards Wales. I was sorry to be leaving this friendly country, and a thousand memories, some of them in this book, others tucked away in my mind, came to me as I looked down on a river valley in which the mists of evening lay like grey smoke.

I remembered lake, mountain and valley, river bank and woodland, salt marshes of the west coast, and the high cliffs of the south where the big rollers pile in from the open sea. There were castles I remembered, and quiet towns lying under an ancient spell of ease and custom, and small villages full of quiet ways, kindly faces and soft voices. All the good and happy things a man meets on his travels return to his mind as he prepares to leave a country in which he has wandered as a stranger.

Wales is a beautiful and romantic land, owing all that is most precious within it to its own courage and initiative. Its people, like all Celts, are a queer, extreme mixture of idealism and materialism, of recklessness and caution, of vanity and humility. They are quick and sensitive, and passionate with a passion that is almost Latin. Their minds are coloured by an ancient language, because, although their tongues may speak English, their brains often think in Welsh. And there are Welsh thoughts for which there are no English words. The Welsh have, perhaps, changed less than any race in these islands. If a Roman colonial official of the second century could travel in Snowdonia he would, I have no doubt, recognize the hill-men of to-day as the tribal Britons of yesterday.

Mountains are the barriers against change. Wherever there are mountains you will find old memories, old beliefs, old habits, and unaltered ways. It is of mountains that you think when you remember Wales—mountains in sunlight, mountains in the mist of morning, mountains blotted out by rain, ominous in their very invisibility. The mystic and poetic qualities of the Welsh have been engendered, and developed, by the changing moods of mountains, for no man can live long with high places and think no thoughts of God. . . .

The twilight deepened. I could hear the quiet evening sounds of farms: the barking of dogs, the lowing of herds coming from pasture.

Night was falling over Wales, stealing down from the distant hills of Snowdonia into little mountain villages, day was fading on the wild seas round Bardsey Isle, shadows like ghosts were gathering in a hundred ruined keeps; and in the smooth depths of mountain tarns burned the first star.

Mrs. Evans was lighting the oil lamp in the little kitchen with the slate floor. Mr. Evans, at the open door, had glanced briefly towards Arenig Fawr, saying that to-morrow would be a fine day; and from the mantelpiece two Welsh soldiers were gazing down into the room for which they, in theory, died. In a different valley, Emlyn, perhaps on the night shift, was tramping the steep cinder track between grim houses towards the pit head. Perhaps he was already drawing his green glow-worm of a lamp, and standing silently among a crowd of white-faced men who smelt of coal dust as he waited for the wet cage to spring up out of the earth's dark bowels. In some stone county town lying in a hill's shadow, the archaeologist of Llanberis was, no doubt, writing with sensuous enjoyment a learned paper on druidism ; and in Caernarvon the sergeant of the castle, his uniform removed, his stick in a corner of the room, was free from his memories of the first English Prince of Wales. The fishing fleet of Milford was steaming out under the first stars ; the sky above Llanelly was orange-coloured with the glow from furnaces, and the salt water was running in before a fresh wind over the wide sands of Llanrhidian.

Good-bye.

And as I went over a bridge into Monmouth, a bridge with a defiant gateway upon it, I said to myself :

Ancient folk speaking an ancient speech
And cherishing in their bosoms all their past.

INDEX